CAMBRIDGE STUDIES IN PHILOSOPHY

The mundane matter of
the mental language

CAMBRIDGE STUDIES IN PHILOSOPHY

General editor SYDNEY SHOEMAKER

Advisory editors J. E. J. ALTHAM, SIMON BLACKBURN,
GILBERT HARMAN, MARTIN HOLLIS, FRANK JACKSON,
JONATHAN LEAR, WILLIAM LYCAN, JOHN PERRY, BARRY STROUD

The mundane matter of the mental language

J. Christopher Maloney

The University of Arizona

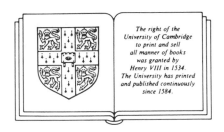

The right of the
University of Cambridge
to print and sell
all manner of books
was granted by
Henry VIII in 1534.
The University has printed
and published continuously
since 1584.

Cambridge University Press

Cambridge
New York   Port Chester   Melbourne   Sydney

Published by the Press Syndicate of the University of Cambridge
The Pitt Building, Trumpington Street, Cambridge CB2 1RP
40 West 20th Street, New York, NY 10011, USA
10 Stamford Road, Oakleigh, Melbourne 3166, Australia

First published 1989

Printed in the United States of America

Library of Congress Cataloging-in-Publication Data
Maloney, J. Christopher.
The mundane matter of the mental language.
(Cambridge studies in philosophy)
Includes index.
1. Psycholinguistics.   2. Cognitive science.
I. Title.   II. Series.
BF455.M266   1989   128'.2   88–35267

British Library Cataloguing in Publication Data
Maloney, J. Christopher
The mundane matter of the mental language. –
(Cambridge studies in philosophy)
1. Man. Mental processes
I. Title
153

ISBN 0-521-37031-0 hard covers

Para La Trucha

Verum quomodo dixit in corde quod cogitare non potuit; aut quomodo cogitare non potuit quod dixit in corde, cum idem sit dicere in corde et cogitare?

Anselm of Canterbury

Contents

Mentalistic constructs are among the central explanatory and predictive concepts deployed in folk psychology, the popular and plausible psychology of common sense. In recent years various philosophers
and psychologists have argued that these concepts are
unfit for any scientific psychology. Nevertheless, arguments in support of the conceptual basis of folk
psychology are available. We begin by assessing the
merits of the charges against mentalistic concepts, and
that requires that we first survey the presuppositions
of such concepts.

Since the notion of belief is the most fundamental of
mentalistic concepts, we focus exclusively on it. Beliefs are intentional – that is to say, representational –
states with truth-values. Any theory that counts beliefs as representations is a version of the Representational Theory of the Mind. It remains to assess the
manner in which beliefs represent. Various facts seem
to indicate that beliefs are properly modeled in terms
of what we know of the symbolic structures of spoken languages. Ascriptions of beliefs identify beliefs
by specifying their contents. The clause embedded in
an ascription of belief that specifies the content of the
ascribed belief is referentially opaque. A belief ascription is thus similar to a quotation and perhaps traces
its opacity to the presumed fact that the belief ascribed, like a sentence quoted, is itself a symbolic
structure. The fact that beliefs have truth-values may

vii

also derive from beliefs' being symbolic structures, analogous to sentences, with referential and predicative components. Beliefs typically arise in large logically related clusters. This too may devolve from the presumed symbolic properties of beliefs, much as logical relations among sentences may depend on their symbolic properties. These points collectively warrant the hypothesis of Sentientialism, that beliefs are relations to sentential structures within a language of thought, Mentalese.

1.3. Folk psychology and Representationalism 10

As an edition of the Representational Theory of the Mind, Sentientialism presupposes folk psychology and its array of mentalistic constructs. So, before further developing Sentientialism, we first attempt to refute the arguments put forth by the Churchlands and alluded to in Section 1.1 that conclude with the repudiation of folk psychology as a foundation for cognitive science.

1.4. Sentientialism 15

Behavior is typically an agent's rational response to his or her situation. The rationality of behavior is best explained by postulating that behavior is the result of an inferential process internal to the agent. Inference presupposes a language over which it is defined. This language must be Mentalese. Failure of introspection to detect Mentalese tokens does not tell against Sentientialism, since introspection is notoriously fallible and limited in its reach. The contents of mental states agree just in case the states are relations to Mentalese sentences of the same type. As mental states, decisions and beliefs certainly can agree in content. Yet ascriptions of decisions depend on content clauses that differ in verb form or mood from their associated belief ascriptions. We hypothesize that if this overt grammatical difference reflects a difference in the syntactic structure of the Mentalese sentences occurrent in the ascribed mental states, then Mentalese sentences may feature sentential or predicate modifiers.

1.5. The regress of embedded agents 22

Internal mental representations seem to entail an infinite regress of embedded cognitive agents. Appreciation of the representational powers of artificially intelligent programs serves to illustrate that internal

viii

representations do not require embedded agents. This way of avoiding embedded agents presupposes that the representations in a program are genuine representations, and this is itself a controversial assumption. Thus, to avoid basing the reply to the objection pertaining to nested agents on Artificial Intelligence, we hypothesize that the sheer intentionality of a mental state is a function of the matter of which the state is composed. This amounts to hypothesizing that mentation is materially based.

Sententialism holds that identity of mental content devolves upon syntactic identity of Mentalese representation. But it seems plausible to suppose, as Artificial Intelligence seems to demonstrate, that sameness of mental state does not require syntactic sameness of internal representations. Various replies to this objection are available. The objection trades on a questionable assumption about the identity of various mental states such as desires. The very disparity of the internal representations may be grounds for supposing that the objection's conjecture of identical mental states and behavioral agreement may be mistaken.

Sententialism denies that it is possible for an agent to have infinitely many beliefs, while allowing that, on occasion, an agent may be disposed to have any of infinitely many potential beliefs. The beliefs an agent actually has are those necessary best to explain the agent's behavior. Since Sententialism posits dynamic belief sets, it is subject to the frame problem, the task of specifying how an agent is able to modify his or her belief store consistently with changes in the agent's environment. The limited success of the theory of scripts in Artificial Intelligence indicates that the frame problem can be solved in principle. The details of its ultimate solution are properly left to empirical inquiry.

Dreyfus has raised various objections to appealing to scripts in order to solve the frame problem. These objections can be answered by noting that they depend on mistaking the current for the possible final state of the art. Our understanding of concepts comes in degree and varies across agents. A contemporary script can be viewed as a limited, artificial, and highly restricted conceptual system.

2.3. Modular cognitive systems

We take up Fodor's worry that the general processes of belief fixation may not admit of a computational solution if belief fixation is, as Fodor says, isotropic and Quinean. Four answers seem open. First, Fodor may err in taking belief fixation to be isotropic and Quinean. Belief fixation is to be modeled on the growth of science. Yet science as practiced seems not to be isotropic and Quinean. Second, the causal processes that govern belief fixation may be amenable to understanding. Third, Fodor allows that encapsulated cognitive modules are not subject to the frame problem. Yet these modules may well be nondemonstrative systems in the same sense as the central processes of belief fixation are. So, if modules are not finally subject to the frame problem, the same may be true of the processes of belief fixation generally. Fourth, it is possible that we are nothing but interactive cognitive modules bereft of any central system of belief fixation.

3. Intelligence, rationality, and behavior

3.1. Intelligent behavior and brute reaction

What distinguishes mental processes, as causal processes, from nonmental causal processes? Fodor's answer that only mental processes include representations of the rules that govern the processes is rejected on the grounds that the ability to represent such rules may surpass the actual representational powers of the agents in question. Rather, mental processes are distinguished from nonmental processes by virtue of the matter out of which mental representations are drawn. Sententialism distinguishes those effects of mental representations that are genuine bits of behavior from those that are not by adverting to the rational relations that bind the former, but not the latter, types of effects to their mental causes. Two relevant senses of rationality are proposed.

Sententialism does not maintain that all behavior is rooted in sentential processes. Instead it proposes only that behavior traced to propositional attitudes is governed by sentential processes. The Churchlands raise various objections to this thesis. Paul Churchland charges that Sententialism is too parochial ever to comprehend much of what is important to the psychology of nonverbal agents. This objecion wrongly assumes that a nonverbal agent could not instantiate an unspoken mental language as a system of cognitive representation. Patricia Smith Churchland urges against Sententialism that it incorrectly entails that concept learning is an illusion, that human language is necessarily static, and, consequently, that scientific advance is impossible. An explanation of how Sententialism allows for conceptual change is offered in reply.

Paul Churchland admonishes Sententialism for failing to account for the continuity of the psychological processes common to infants and adults. An explanation of the possibility of developmental psychology's being sententially based is provided. Also, it may, in the end, be incorrect to suppose that the psychologies of infant and adult are in fact the same. Churchland also is concerned that Sententialism imposes on the child too sophisticated a system of computation. Yet it is unclear whether proposed alternative systems are any less complex. Sententialism, Churchland finally worries, may fail to accommodate the stability of the processes that allow for belief revision. Nevertheless, this stability is ensured if the principles or laws that govern belief revision are not among the mental representations encoded with an agent. Additionally, if all accepted truths are, in principle, subject to revision, then the very principles dictating belief revision, if mentally represented, would themselves be open to disconfirmation. But this is compatible with doxastic stability if such stability requires only that epistemic principles are relatively, though not absolutely, resistant to modification and revised only rarely and over many generations.

objects that cause the occurrence of the sensory states that encompass the predicates. Those features of a sensory state that differentiate it from other states of the same type function as the referential term in the state. Sensuous Mentalese terms – subjects and predicates – are thoroughly demonstrative. They refer and attribute without describing or classifying.

Causal theories apparently entail, contrary to fact, that mental representations are infallible. Two responses are offered. First, some of the assumptions on which the charge of infallibility rest are dubious. Second, the apparent infallibility can be tolerated by Sententialism if it is restricted to demonstrative sensuous mental representations. Also raised against causal theories of representation is the complaint that although reference is supposed to be to *the* object that causes the representational state, there is in fact no unique object that stands as *the* cause of the state. This objection is parried if the referent of a sensuous mental representation is singled out as the object causally necessary only (so far as causing sensory states is considered) for the occurrence of the state encoding that representation.

Doppelgängers agree in sensuous representation, even if they do sense things of different physical kinds, so long as the causal properties of the sensed objects coincide.

The content of a nonsensuous Mentalese representation is determined by its typical causes and effects within a cognitive system. Sensuous Mentalese terms contribute to the meanings of nonsensuous Mentalese terms by contributing to the causation of the nonsensuous terms. Although the content of a Mentalese term may be fixed by its etiological relations, ascriptions of content to a Mentalese term are, at best, hypotheses as to the best explanation. Thought experiments of Putnam and Burge show not that the content of Mentalese terms of the same type depend on the contexts of their occurrence but, rather, that the content of such terms may not easily be reported in public languages.

could indeed be conscious because consciousness is a
function of sensory systems based in the proper type
of matter.

Acknowledgments

My efforts on this book began in 1985 with the forever-appreciated support of a National Endowment for the Humanities Fellowship for College Teachers. Oakland University subsequently generously advanced my work with both a Summer Research Fellowship and a sabbatical.

D. Reidel Publishing Company permitted me to draw from my "In Praise of Narrow Minds: The Frame Problem" and "The Right Stuff" for use in Chapters 2 and 5, respectively. *Philosophical Papers* allowed me to rely on my essay "Sensuous Content" in Chapter 6, and the *Australasian Journal of Philosophy* authorized me to borrow from my "About Being a Bat" for Chapter 7.

Various people assisted me along the way. Romane Clark, Stephen Stich, and George Graham graciously read and thoughtfully commented on substantial portions of the evolving manuscript. I will long and happily remain indebted to them.

Correspondence or conversation with a number of people informed much of what I have written. Here thanks are owed to Paul Churchland, Fred Dretske, Reinaldo Elugàrdo, Jerry Fodor, Terence Horgan, Lawrence Lombard, Michael McKinsey, Donald Nute, William Rapaport, Lilly-Marlene Russow, and Robert Yanal.

Various colleagues walked many hallway miles with me, discussing the manuscript. For their advice when the manuscript was first developing, I thank David Bricker, Richard Burke, John Halpin, Clark Heston, Christopher Holliday, and John Oetjens. As the manuscript took its final shape, I caught myself learning from Rob Cummins, Alvin Goldman, Mike Harnish, Keith Lehrer, John Pollock, Stephen Schiffer, and Joseph Tolliver. Although I appreciate the contributions of all of these philosophers, I do not wish to suggest that they would endorse the results or are responsible for my mistakes.

Ruth Rounds is to be applauded for her always willing and able secretarial support.

Patricia Kellner and Robert Maloney have been helpful in ways that they might not realize, and I am grateful.

Maura Nantell Maloney and Brigid Nantell Maloney edited the manuscript on several occasions when their hands reached up for me but found the delete key instead. I am afraid the text is better for their contributions.

Judy Nantell I thank last but before all others. She has persisted with me through all this and much more, sharing her keen scholarly sense, love, and life.

Introduction

Thinking comes naturally to us. Perhaps it comes artificially to machines. But regardless of how it occurs or in whom it is found, thinking is a process designed to contribute to problem solving. With this in mind, almost all philosophers who have attended to matters of the mind have characterized thought as an inferential process. Cognitive scientists have much improved on this philosophical conjecture by offering ever more detailed explanations of the computational processes that constitute cognition. Call thought inference or computation, one thing is quite clear: What we know of overt, public inferences and computations must inform any computational characterization of thought.

There are, of course, more than many different formulated and well-understood systems of logic. Mathematics and computer science abound with systems of computation. One property shared by all such systems is that they necessarily involve symbols. Inference or computation, by any name, is essentially a procedure for transforming symbols. Yet not all kinds of symbols can serve in a computational system. Only symbols under the control of a grammar could possibly serve the purposes of computation. For without a grammar sufficient to distinguish legitimate from bogus symbols, it would be all but impossible to frame a formal system of symbolic logic or computation.

So, computation requires symbols supplemented with a grammar. Once we recognize this, it is difficult to avoid seeing that computational processes take languages as their raw materials. What holds for computation generally must hold for mental computation particularly. The conclusion is apparently inescapable. There must be a mental language, a language in which the mind computes. Otherwise it would be folly to announce that thought is a matter of inference.

Well, what exactly is the mental language? It probably is not any spoken language we learn. To learn a language is to solve certain problems regarding what expressions mean and how they can combine with other symbols to form complex expressions. If this is what learning a language requires, then learning a language is a matter of thinking. Hence we must already be fluent in the mental language before we learn the languages we speak. How else could we perform the mental computations necessary for learning the target language?

Evidently, we could not learn the mental language. So, either it is innate or there is a way of acquiring it other than by learning. Nativism is indeed shocking if true. Nativists, at least the purists among them, maintain that our set of concepts is derivable from a basic, proper subset of itself, the members of which subset are endogenous. Were nativism of this sort correct, then any concept we might use would need to be decomposable into concepts drawn from our basic conceptual stock. It is not difficult to see what is untoward here. One can certainly conceive of an automobile as an aging, gas-guzzling station wagon whose resale value is a direct function of the price of petroleum pumped in Kuwait. Yet, according to the nativist scheme, in order for one so to conceive, it is necessary that the concept of an aging, gas-guzzling station wagon whose resale value is a direct function of the price of petroleum pumped in Kuwait itself be decomposable into concepts contained in the stock of concepts nature saw fit to provide originally. But is it plausible to suppose that nature could have had the foresight to supply us with just those concepts that would someday coalesce into a concept as contrived as that of an aging, gas-guzzling station wagon whose resale value is a direct function of the price of petroleum pumped in Kuwait? The point is not that it is in principle impossible for contrived concepts to be derived from innate concepts. The fear, rather, is that it is disingenuous to suppose that nature could have foreseen our conceptual practices so as to supply us with innate concepts sufficient to underwrite all the artificial, socially determined, and highly theoretical concepts we have come to use.

Locke must have been right. Somehow we must pick up, but not learn, our mental language as we lumber along. Fortunately nature did have the good sense to give us our senses. They must function in such a way as to write at least some terms in the mind's dictionary. It is probably through sensation that our mental expressions originally are encoded and first take on meaning. How they come to mean what they do is, to court inestimable understatement, hard to comprehend. Nevertheless, the causal connections between the mind and the world certainly figure in the explanation.

Settling the contribution of sensation to intelligent understanding is difficult enough. More vexing problems arise when we note that many of our mental terms could not possibly have their meanings fixed simply by way of sensation. Theoretical, moral, and aesthetic terms, we know from the history of empiricism, defy definition in terms referring exclusively to sensory experience. Much the same would appear true of our corresponding concepts, our mental terms. Yet, if some mental terms do take on meaning by virtue of their connections to sensation, perhaps these mental terms somehow, even if not definitionally, give rise to other terms still. And maybe those terms lead to others. Yes, this is speculative. But cognitive science is still young. If it is a worthy science, it will see its way to transforming philosophical speculation into scientific hypothesis formation and confirmation. What other choice is there if nativism is false?

If thought is just the computational processing of linguistically encoded information, then whatsoever processes information in this manner must think. Evidently, various kinds of inanimate devices satisfy this test. Certainly computers rival, and in some applications surpass, humans in information processing. Computers, then, must think if thinking is nothing more than the sophisticated processing of linguistically inscribed information.

Not everyone concerned with the nature of the mind needs to worry over this conclusion. But any philosopher who has ever seriously wondered with Descartes about what it is to be a thinking thing, as opposed to a brute, must pause to ask if artificial devices literally do think. Is computer cognition a revolutionary discovery of cognitive science? Should we recognize thought in computers and extend our dated, provincial, and chauvinistic conception of mentation so as to embrace artificial devices as our cognitive cousins? Or is this just the reduction to absurdity of our original supposition that thinking is just problem solving?

These questions are not easy, and it is hard to silence the idea that they may call for an answer from convention. Still, two facts – if they are facts – urge denying that computers actually do think. They *seem* not to appreciate what the information they process means, and they *seem* not to feel. Surely, when we think, our thoughts do represent things for us. Our thoughts do have content. If this is an essential feature of cognition, a feature we, but not computers, enjoy, then computers do not think. And if real thought must, on some occasions, be accompanied by conscious feeling, then, again, we can, but computers cannot, think.

Let us suppose that meaning and feeling are necessary for thought. How might this cohere with the plausible notion that thinking is fundamentally computational? If thought is computation, it involves a mental language. Given the assumption that thought must allow for meaning, the mental language must have content – its terms must be meaningful. That mental terms do have meaning must, if computers are not to be genuinely intelligent, be a function of what differentiates the naturally and (merely) artificially intelligent. Holding fast to this, we may find warrant in hypothesizing that the difference here is a material, physical difference. Cognitive agents must be made of stuff that allows their mental terms to be meaningful. Computers, as we now know them, must simply be made of the wrong stuff.

Of course we do not now have any idea what this mental matter might be. Only careful, costly, and protracted work in the laboratory could reveal what it is. Certainly it will not first be discerned in a philosopher's office. Here, then, we have a hypothesis – not a certified conclusion – to the effect that if computers are not actually intelligent, then thought must involve a mental language as encoded in a certain kind of matter. This hypothesis amounts to a hunch that mentation will, in the end, call for an analysis in physical terms. If this is correct, then just as water is really H_2O and only physical science could ascertain it to be such, so too that mental states are meaningful may be attributable to some physical fact that only physical science could be positioned to assay.

Something along the same lines may hold for the affective. It is not utterly wild to postulate that our ability to feel is somehow determined by our physical nature. Perhaps it is intimately associated with our sensory systems, systems with a certain physiology. If, then, computers cannot think because, unlike us, they cannot feel, this may be due, again, to the fact that they do not share with us the relevant physical properties.

Whether or not artificially intelligent devices really do think and feel, *we* certainly do, and so do various other sorts of creatures.

That may lead us to ask what it is like to be a thing of a given conscious kind. What separates us from other intelligent creatures besides straightforward differences in intelligence? What accounts for the apparent qualitative differences in consciousness found in different sorts of intelligent animals? What, if anything, justifies our suspicion that what it is like to be a bat is radically different from what it is like to be a human?

These too are difficult questions, questions that may puzzle philosophers if no one else. Still, if there is any truth to the idea that thought is an essentially physical process, then we might anticipate that everything we could ever want to know about the quality of consciousness found in a cognitive creature resides in a physical description of that creature. Should this be right, then there would be nothing in principle cryptic about the affective side of conscious intelligence. All there would be to such phenomena would be purely physical, and that is susceptible of scientific exposition.

Such are the themes to be pursued in the chapters that follow. Qualifications abound, and the arguments vary in their plausibility. So some signposts may help us to follow the tortuous route ahead.

Those who have traveled the path philosophical psychology has taken since the mid-1970s will recognize that this book could not have been conceived were it not for the work of others, especially Jerry Fodor, Hilary Putnam, Daniel Dennett, Paul Churchland, Patricia Smith Churchland, Stephen Stich, Fred Dretske, Romane Clark, John Searle, Thomas Nagel, Frank Jackson, and George Graham. Although I am indebted to these philosophers, none of them will agree with much, and some of them will agree with none, of what I have to say. The view from the straddled shoulders of the tall can be breathtaking, but long preserving it is difficult, perhaps finally impossible, when the big folks below are wrestling among themselves.

A scientific account of mentation ought to be based on what we already know of propositional attitudes, or so I argue along with Fodor and to the dismay of the Churchlands, Stich, and, from one perspective, Dennett as well. Taking the propositional attitudes seriously leads me to agree with Fodor and, with certain qualifications, Stich that thinking involves the use of a mental language. Dennett and the Churchlands have labored to expose the difficulties attendant on postulating a mental language. And Stich has cautioned against supposing that the mental language has any semantic properties or, minimally, any semantic features germane to the purposes of cognitive science. I try, but do not expect, to satisfy these critics.

Although I argue that cognitive theory ought to rely on a language of thought, I disagree with those, including (early) Putnam and Dennett, who think that mental states are best cast as purely functional states. I am persuaded that Paul Churchland, Searle, and Dretske are right, even if for different reasons, to worry that functionalism is excessive in its characterization of the mental.

So I suspect that the Churchlands are right in maintaining that an adequate science of the mind requires an understanding of the physical, not just the functional, properties of mental states. Still, one should not anticipate that the Churchlands will approve of my attempting to fuse a fondness for materialism with the notion of the mental language.

If the mental language is semantically ripe, it must derive its content from sensation. The empiricists knew this, and I thank Clark for teaching me that a psychology of propositional attitudes must attend first to sensation. I learned much from Dretske's enumeration of the failings characteristic of causal theories of representation, even if I persist in attempting to defend just such a view. And Dretske's analysis of the content of information-bearing states has been much on my mind, although I continue to lack the wisdom to embrace it.

A complete psychology should encompass a theory of consciousness. Nagel and Jackson despair of the possibility of an objective account of the phenomenological. Graham, on the other hand, argues that the qualia given in experience are accessible to objective knowledge because they are not themselves psychological. Against Nagel and Jackson I urge that the theory of cognition I propose admits of a scientific treatment of consciousness in part, but contra Graham, because qualia are, after all, elements in psychological states.

While this book was in press, five books appeared that I was unable to address but that certainly bear on the argument of this book. Lynne Rudder Baker's *Saving Belief* (1987), Fred Dretske's *Explaining Behavior* (1988), Jerry Fodor's *Psychosemantics* (1987), William Lycan's *Consciousness* (1987), and Stephen Schiffer's *Remnants of Meaning* (1987) each already casts a growing shadow. Anyone concerned with the philosophical foundations of the cognitive sciences had best attend to these works. I wish that I had here had the opportunity to do so.

Philosophers and cognitive scientists who come to this book with a fixed opinion on the language of thought may prefer to look first to Chapters 5–7, to see how I have exploited my idiosyncratic version of this hypothesis. They might then address the earlier chapters in their order, to learn what possibly could have induced me to reach the conclusions I do. Other readers, certainly those who wish to know what reasons support the idea that cognition relies on a mental language, will do best to begin at the beginning and continue courageously through to the end. I hope that all readers will discern the attractions of the language of thought; I am sure that the attendant difficulties will escape none.

Philosophical books often fail to establish conclusively what they promise, and what they do manage to demonstrate is typically tenuous. That seems to be one lesson from the history of philosophy. We may hope that this is a result of philosophy's continuous, even if asymptotic, approach to truth. I am willing to settle for less here. Although I have tried to say only what is true, I shall be satisfied if, at least, I have illustrated the contortions necessary for maintaining the idea that to think is to deploy a mental language encoded in just the right kind of matter.

1

The mental language

Abelard desired Héloïse. So he duped her father into agreeing that Abelard's tutorials with her should be uninterrupted private sessions. When Héloïse's brothers discovered that she was pregnant with Abelard's child, their rage drove them to storm Abelard's chambers and castrate him. Aghast and saddened, even if not sorry, Abelard and Héloïse parted and retired to separate abbeys, both taking religious vows.[1]

This is Abelard's explanation of what happened. We all understand it, and, at least in our sanguine moments, most of us accept it as true. When we attend to the story of Abelard's adversities, we draw on a host of familiar psychological concepts. Abelard's explanation adverts to desires and plans as well as to beliefs and emotions. These and related mentalistic constructs, including the so-called propositional attitudes, dominate thoroughly convincing explanations of a wide range of human behavior. Indeed, their success in this province urges their application, to varying degrees, to animals and, more recently, to selected inanimate artificial devices. Mental concepts such as these are of an ancient and uncultivated vintage. Despite their rude origins, these mentalistic notions have coalesced across time into something like a popular, even if largely unarticulated and unconfirmed, theory of behavior (Paul Churchland, 1979, 1981; Stich, 1983). Recently they have assumed special prominence in the nascent cognitive sciences (Neisser, 1966; Boden, 1977; Anderson, 1980; Pylyshyn, 1984). Nevertheless, some would say that these tired concepts beg for replacement. There remain problems in psychology that seem to defy solutions expressed in terms of our worn mentalistic constructs. A growing chorus now argues that mental notions either simply fail in their explanatory mission or are unredeemably confused and theoreti-

1 For the whole story see the autobiographical *Story of Abelard's Adversities* (1964).

1

cally empty. Convinced of this, these critics urge that our best hope for understanding intelligent activity is to purge mentalistic notions from the science of the mind. And once we have eradicated reference to the propositional attitudes in psychology, we are to proceed to eliminate them from the commonplace accounts we give of the behavior of both ourselves and others (Dennett, 1978f, g, 1982a; Rorty, 1979; Paul Churchland, 1979; Paul Churchland and Patricia Smith Churchland, 1983; Stich, 1983).

Perhaps, however, we should pause before retiring our system of mental concepts. Although these concepts may be weary and undoubtedly must make room for concepts yet to be devised by the rapidly evolving cognitive sciences, they may yet find a place in a completed psychology (Horgan and Woodward, 1985). If Abelard did not really desire Héloïse, why did he go to such lengths to finagle time alone with her? If Héloïse's brothers were not genuinely enraged by Abelard's seduction of Héloïse, why did they mutilate him? It is, after all, Abelard's seduction of Héloïse, so described, that we want explained. Given the facts of the case, it certainly seems informative to cite a general principle to the effect that agents normally do what they believe will best serve their desires. We do know that Abelard desired Héloïse and believed that the best way to satisfy his desire was to secure time alone with her. So here we have what purports to be a law linking action, belief, and desire, as well as a specification of a belief and desire from which the action to be explained is deducible. If the generalization is as well founded as it seems, and if we are not wildly misguided in attributing the relevant beliefs and desires, what could be the complaint of the critics of the mental concepts? What could prompt them to repudiate what surely must be among the most central elements of our very self-conception?

The answer is that their various arguments bear on the fault lines of the entrenched notion of the mental. So, if we want to retain the right to refer to beliefs, desires, and their siblings in explaining our actions, we had best first discern exactly what our mentalistic explanations require and then look to the complaints that can be raised against them. Otherwise, what guarantee do we have that our inherited cognitive concepts are not, like the four humors, the bequest of benighted ancestors?

Beliefs and desires apparently drive behavior and, before all other mentalistic notions, want characterization. Although both types of mental states are fundamental, in order to simplify our task we may follow the philosophical tradition and focus on belief, anticipating that what we say of it applies, with but transparent modification and qualification, to desire and other types of mental states.[2]

Certainly, beliefs are intentional structures; they truly or falsely represent, to the cognitive agent in whom they occur, objects and their states, both actual and not. The intentional or representational property of belief surely must be center stage in any account of belief. The intentionality of a state marks the state as mental, given the natural assumption that all other types of representational structures, such as languages and icons, are parasitic on mental states for their representational capacities (Loar, 1981).[3] In conveying or otherwise identifying an agent's belief, we typically favor subordinate clauses embedded in expressions predicating belief to the agent. These embedded clauses describe the content of the belief. Thus,

(1.2.1) Abelard believes that Héloïse is susceptible to charm.

The expression in the subordinate clause occurs obliquely, resisting replacement by coextensive expressions for the sake of preserving the truth-value of the containing sentence. As Frege (1892, 1918–19) knew, resistance to substitution within belief ascriptions seems to indicate something about how the agent of the ascription believes

2 More than tradition motivates directing primary attention to belief. Davidson (1982) argues that belief is the most fundamental of all propositional attitudes in that it is presupposed by all the others. For example, an agent normally does not fear that death is inevitable unless he or she has various beliefs constituting an understanding of what death is. Indeed, Davidson (1974, 1982) argues that attributing beliefs to an agent itself requires that the agent's beliefs generally be taken as true. For it is impossible to discern between rampantly false belief and extreme difference in conceptualization.

3 We have here, of course, Brentano's (1874) thesis that intentionality is the mark of the mental. Searle (1983) takes up this line, but, for the view that contentful structures are not necessarily mental at bottom, see Dretske (1981). Look to Stich (1983) for the argument that the kinds of mental states to be recognized by a sophisticated cognitive science are not essentially contentful.

or conceives. It would be wrong, however, to suppose that attributions of mental states alone do not admit of the exchange of expressions for identicals and coextensives. Quotation too disallows substitution of such expressions.[4]

Essential, then, to our conception of mental states is an idea that informs our understanding of quotation. In referring to an object by name or description, a speaker does not thereby utter every name or description designating that object. And so quotations of the speaker do not admit of replacement of uttered with coextensive terms. Analogously, even if the object x is identical to y, an agent who believes that x has some property need not thereby believe that y has that property. Ascriptions of beliefs to the agent accordingly do not admit of replacement of terms referring to x as 'x' with terms referring to the same as 'y'. Although Héloïse may happen to be the wittiest woman in Paris, (1.2.1) does not imply that Abelard believes that the wittiest woman in Paris is susceptible to charm. Similarly, although being susceptible to charm may be equivalent to being disposed to fancy Arthurian legend, neither is Abelard's believing Héloïse to be disposed to fancy Arthurian legend entailed by (1.2.1). Indeed, (1.2.1) could even be true should it have happened that Héloïse never existed at all. Abelard might be radically misinformed about Héloïse. Perhaps he has only heard of the mythic Héloïse and does not realize that she is but a figment of lonely students.[5] What accounts for this similarity between belief

4 As do expressions of probability and alethic modality, although these latter two kinds of expressions arguably follow for substitution when the relevant expressions designate necessarily identical objects or coextensive properties (Quine, 1960; Davidson, 1975, 1979).

5 Such being characteristic of a de dicto belief ascription, a statement that aims to identify a belief by conveying its content. Certainly, there are various linguistic constructions equipped for this chore, (1.2.1) being equivalent, for example, to 'Abelard believes Héloïse to be susceptible to charm'. When we are unable or unwilling to say how the agent conceives of what he or she cognitively represents, we retreat from de dicto to de re ascriptions whose truth-values survive substitution of expressions for identicals and admit of existential generalization over terms in the subordinate clause (Quine, 1956; Sosa, 1970; Burge, 1977; and Dennett, 1982a). Given, then, that Héloïse is the wittiest woman in Paris, (1.2.1) implies the awkward de re claim, 'Of the wittiest woman in Paris, Abelard believes that she is susceptible to charm', which is silent regarding how Abelard's belief refers to, or under what kind of a description it selects, Héloïse. Of course there are ways of ascribing mental states that employ simple direct-object constructions, as in 'Abelard desires Héloïse'. Such expressions presumably are elliptical for terms indicating the manner in which the intended object is conceived, as in 'Abelard desires that Héloïse meet him at dusk'. Or these expressions simply designate de re the object con-

4

ascription and quotation? Possibly, beliefs ascribed, like assertions quoted, both essentially involve symbols with particular semantic properties. These properties could then be masked if ascriptions of belief and quotations of assertions were to utilize symbols respectively alien to the beliefs and assertions.

Apparently beliefs enjoy bivalent truth-values, this devolving from the fact that they have content or somehow serve to represent the world. Identical beliefs must then have the same truth-value, which, in turn, is likely a function of how the content of the belief corresponds to the world.[6] Correspondence between belief and world, like that between sentence and world, depends, in the idealized simple case, both on what the belief refers to and on what it predicates of its referent.[7] A natural question to ask is, How, exactly, do beliefs manage to have truth-values? How is it possible that they designate objects and represent their properties? Perhaps the answer is that the assignment of truth-values to beliefs is determined much as is the assignment of truth-values to sentences.

ceived, leaving it open how the object in fact is conceived. For the most part, I attend only to de dicto ascriptions. They attribute, and thereby identify, mental states by specifying their content; de re attributions do not. None of this, by the way, should be taken to suggest that there are two kinds of belief, one de dicto, and the other de re. Rather, there are two ways of ascribing beliefs. De dicto ascriptions identify beliefs in terms of their content; de re ascriptions attribute beliefs primarily by determining to what object the belief refers. See Stich (1983, pp. 34, 111–23) for an argument that the distinction between de re and de dicto ascriptions is misconceived.

6 Accepting the idea that identity of belief entails identity of truth-value is not completely innocent. It seems natural enough to suppose, on the one hand, that if Abelard and Roscelin both say of themselves, "I believe that I am the most famous nominalist," they both believe the same of themselves. But on the other hand, how could both of their beliefs be true? So a principle that distinguishes between beliefs of (possibly) different truth-values may differentiate between such beliefs as those of Abelard and Roscelin. Compare Putnam (1975b), Fodor (1980a), Stich (1983), Maloney (1985b), and Graham and Garrett (1986). The notion of change of belief also trades on the truth-value of beliefs. Presented with a fresh apple, you might truly believe it to be fresh. Suppose, however, that, unknown to you, that particular fresh apple is replaced with a similar but frozen apple. Assume also that, confusing the frozen for the fresh apple, you insist it is fresh. Has your belief changed from true to false, or have you acquired a new but false belief? See Burge (1982) and Dennett (1982a). We will return to this matter in Chapter 4, Section 4.3.

7 I am not concerned to defend a correspondence theory of truth here, although I think some such account of truth is probably correct. Rather, the point is that mental states typically refer and predicate. Even coherentist and pragmatist renditions of truth do not deny, even if they peculiarly explicate, the reference and predication of truth-valued structures.

5

And if that is so, we should expect that beliefs, like sentences, literally contain symbols that refer, predicate, and enter into various combinations variously affecting the beliefs they form.

Beliefs normally come in semantically and logically related clusters (Davidson, 1982; Stich, 1983). Abelard believes that Héloïse is someone's daughter. This apparently implies that he also believes that she is a female, that she is not a male, and much else besides, even if we do not know exactly what. Put differently, if we were sure that Abelard did not believe Héloïse to be a female, we would be most hesitant to credit him with believing her to be someone's daughter. How could he have the concept of being someone's daughter were he not to understand that all daughters are females?

Additionally, within certain hard to specify, but severe, limits, beliefs also abide by something like selected standard logical operations. Abelard believes Héloïse's father to be a dupe *and* her brothers inclined to rage. So the odds are better than even that he also believes, simply, that her father is a dupe. Since he believes Héloïse to be *very* beautiful, he surely believes her to be beautiful. Agents then typically believe some, though never all, of the trivial and transparent consequences of their beliefs.

Beliefs thus typically exhibit certain semantic and logical relations, and this calls for explanation. Of course, sentences are just the sort of thing that admits of such relations. Sentences exhibit the logical relations they do in part by virtue of being composed of symbolic elements that can recur across different sentences. Analogously, beliefs too may submit to logical operations as a result of consisting of symbols that allow for transformations of certain sorts. 'Héloïse is very beautiful' implies 'Héloïse is beautiful'. Part of the explanation of this fact appeals to the recurrence of some of the symbols across these two sentences. Abelard's belief that Héloïse is very beautiful apparently implies his belief that Héloïse is beautiful. This too might be partially attributable to the two beliefs sharing some recurrent symbols.

Beliefs accordingly exhibit various kinds of logical relations. If the truth of one belief is guaranteed by the truth of another, then an agent who has the latter belief is likely also to have the former.[8]

---

8 This is too strong as it stands and needs to be restricted to a class of relatively trivial or straightforward implicational relations. Certainly we do not want to say that agents are logically omniscient, believing every consequence of whatever they might believe. Hence, at most what we are entitled to assert is that if the

And if the truth of one belief ensures the falsity of another, then it is relatively unlikely that an agent with the former belief will also have the latter. In order to begin to explain how beliefs might be so composed as to admit of logical relations, one might conjecture that beliefs must be symbolic structures since such structures are the paradigmatic structures over which logical relations are defined. Linguistics and symbolic logic have taught us that the logical relations among sentences in a language capitalize on grammatical relations. That is, a formal characterization of selected logical relations among sentences presupposes a grammar governing the generation and transformations of the symbols out of which sentences are constructed. Thus, to accommodate the fact that beliefs are logically related, we might venture that types of belief states are themselves types of symbolic structures, sentences. As such, the types of elements out of which these states are constructed must themselves be types of symbols, terms. These sentences and terms evidently would need to be subject to a grammar sufficient to underwrite the complex logical relations characteristic of beliefs.

Another way to state this is to acknowledge that it is often useful to exploit logical relations among mental states in order to explain and predict an agent's behavior. Abelard testifies, "Héloïse is very beautiful." We wonder whether he is inclined to assent to 'Héloïse is beautiful'. So, we attribute his testimony to his believing that Héloïse is very beautiful. This belief implies the belief that Héloïse is beautiful. Hence we conclude that Abelard probably believes that Héloïse is beautiful, and we, therefore, predict his assent. This predictive practice presupposes that an agent's system of beliefs is one of logical relations. Systems of logical relations are necessarily grammatical symbolic systems. So too, then, must be belief systems. Accordingly, beliefs themselves must be akin to sentences or symbolic compounds subject to the dictates of a grammar.

That beliefs naturally form semantic clusters is one manifestation of the inferential integration beliefs display.[9] Problem solving, both

---

truth of belief A implies the truth of belief B, then (other things being equal) an agent's having belief A contributes to the probability of the agent's having belief B.

9 Stich (1978b) and Fodor (1985), in different contexts and for different purposes, both point out the extent and importance of the inferential integration of beliefs. Dennett (1978d) and Stich (1983) have argued that the concept of belief runs into hard times when pressed on the issue of what sorts of clusters beliefs must come

theoretical and practical, appears to be the prototypical example of inferential alliances among beliefs. Discovering the solution to an equation and determining how to act on an occasion both seem to require that an agent infer new from old beliefs. If so, then, regardless of what beliefs may be, they must be related one to another as are premises and conclusions. When thinking about the apparently inferential relations among beliefs, it is hard to ignore the fact that sentences are the structures over which inferences are defined. The similarity between belief and language begins to look less and less accidental.

That beliefs tend logically to flock should direct our attention to what Fodor (1985) calls the productivity of belief. The sheer number and variety of the beliefs of which we are capable are astounding. Apparently we are capable of believing or disbelieving whatever is expressed by any, or almost any, of the infinitely many declarative sentences we can utter. How shall we explain this? Given the parallel pattern between belief and language already discerned, it would be hard indeed not to suspect that the productivity of belief, like that of language, is to be traced to the combinatory properties of symbols. The productivity of belief may then be laid to something closely akin to a grammar applied to a large but finite stock of symbols. If so, belief would again appear to require a system of symbols approaching that of a language.

The similarities between beliefs and (declarative) sentences are ignored only with peril.[10] Declarative sentences, like beliefs, are

in. We shall turn to these complaints respectively in Chapter 2, Section 2.1, and Chapter 4, Section 4.3.

10 None of this is to deny that some psychological states seem more happily modeled against nonlinguistic representations (Harman, 1973). Sensation, illusion, hallucination, dreaming, and certain kinds of memories are vividly sensuous, acquainting us with sensible properties such as colors, shapes, sounds, textures, tastes, and odors in ways that all but force a comparison with pictures such as photographs in particular, and graphic depiction in general. The portrait of Abelard on her wall may seem to Héloïse remarkably like the idea that arises in her when she recalls her introduction to her tutor. Facts such as this suggest that, perhaps, at least some of our psychological states, possibly including specific types of beliefs and desires, are best construed as if they were peculiar – mental – images. Although the whole question of imagistic thought is centrally important to any representational theory of the mind, considerations of space force its suppression here. Happily the large literature on mental imagery is instructive, even if divided. See Block's anthologies (1981a, pp. 117–96; 1981b) for representative collections. Also note Block (1983a, b), Kosslyn (1980, 1981), Kosslyn, Ball, and Reiser (1978), Shepard (1978), Shepard and Cooper (1982), Shepard and Metzler (1971), Tye (1984a, b), and Maloney (1984).

representations; they all have content. Both types are about things, actual or fictitious, and predicate properties of those things. Sentences are not alone in possessing truth-values and submitting to logical and syntactically constructive operations. And sentences when quoted, like beliefs when attributed, resist substitution of coreferential terms or representational elements. This extended analogy and the question of what sorts of things beliefs might be together prompt the answer that beliefs, like sentences, themselves essentially involve symbolic structures, symbols themselves composed of symbols. The temptation, one not to be resisted, is to think of beliefs as featuring mental sentences, sentences literally recorded in the brain in some secret yet potent neural code called, well – what else – Mentalese.[11] Any account of mentation promoting the hypothesis that mental states are representational structures is, naturally and aptly, a version of the Representational Theory of the Mind. Here we have a particular edition of that theory that favors treating mental representations as if they were sentences encoded in the central nervous system of cognitive agents. This way with Representationalism we call, following others, Sentencialism.[12]

11 Certainly Fodor (1975) is currently the most prominent spokesperson for this way with the mental. The view can be traced to Locke and Descartes and fans much of Ockham's (1349) writing too. Fodor argues that additional and familiar facts about the mind support the postulation of a mental language. Thinking apparently involves computation. In explaining, for example, deliberate action, it is reasonable to hypothesize that deliberation involves inferring what to do on the basis of what is believed and desired. But there can be no inference or computation except in a language. Hence, there must be a language of thought, Mentalese, in which the inference occurs. Further argumentation is required (and offered by Fodor) to show that Mentalese must be distinguished from all natural or learned languages. Although this raises the specter of nativism, we shall not pause to worry over it here, although much of Chapter 6 is an attempt to avoid innate mental representations. Compare Patricia Smith Churchland (1978, 1980a, b) with Chomsky (1980) and Harman (1973). Pylyshyn (1984, pp. 195–6) too endorses the idea that at least some types of mental states are actualized in sententially encoded structures. See also Stich's (1983) discussion of what he calls the Strong and Weak versions of the Representational Theory of the Mind.

12 Though no friend of Sentencialism, Dennett (1978d) has offered various conditions a system of representation must satisfy in order to be a language of thought. The system ought to abide by a generative grammar, so as to be learnable, and exhibit a salient, detectable syntax describable in terms of physical properties (presumably neural properties in humans) of the agents in which it is realized. It must be possible consistently to assign content to the system, as instantiated in any particular agent, in order to reflect at least a significant portion of the agent's manifest beliefs and desires. And finally, the system, as physical,

Before venturing deeply into Sententialism, we should pause to consider the plausibility of any psychology predicated on beliefs, desires, and propositional attitudes generally. We need to inquire whether there are compelling reasons against accepting the basic notions of that body of popular explanatory lore that has come to be called commonsense – folk – psychology. The point of the exercise is certainly not to pretend to determine the truth of the various generalizations collectively constituting folk psychology but rather to evaluate folk psychology's presupposition of propositional attitudes.

Foremost among the critics of a psychology of propositional attitudes are Patricia Smith Churchland (1978, 1980a, b) and Paul Churchland (1979, 1981).[13] The Churchlands' dissatisfaction with folk psychology (as expressed in Paul Churchland [1981]) devolves from three considerations.

(1.3.1) Although the psychology of common sense certainly does underwrite a wide variety of successful predictions of behavior, its explanatory failures cannot be dismissed. Indeed, they are so extreme as to demonstrate folk psychology's crushing limitations.

(1.3.2) As a theory, folk psychology has proved stagnant just where progress is wanting.

(1.3.3) And it is unlikely that folk psychology will be integrated into the emerging scientific picture of behavior.

The Churchlands credit this trio of problems to folk psychology's commitment to propositional attitudes as fundamental explanatory notions. Let us consider each of these three points in turn.

The mysteries of the likes of mental illness, creativity, individual differences in intelligence, and the workings of memory, the Churchlands note, illustrate some of the more striking explanatory failures of folk psychology.[14] Nonetheless, that folk psychology is

---

must be causally connected to behavior as are the mental states it embodies. Compare Fodor (1975, 1980a) and Pylyshyn (1984, p. 74).

13 See Horgan and Woodward (1985) for arguments against the Churchlands' position. Although Stich (1983, pp. 210–17) generally agrees with the Churchlands, he expresses reservations about the details of their arguments.

14 Kitcher (1984), citing the work of Miller (1956), Anderson and Bower (1973), and others, argues that this is hyperbolic. Although folk psychology understood as a loose body of unformulated lore may not have much helpful to say about, for example, memory, contemporary cognitive psychology, which is friendly

silent or misleading on these specific issues does not demonstrate the bankruptcy of folk psychology generally. Certainly its generalizations include many that are apparently *true*. That a theory, regimented and recorded or not, at present fails to explain selected phenomena is hardly reason to suppose that the theory is without promise, so long as it does enjoy some nontrivial explanatory successes. Otherwise, all of our sciences would be on the same soft sand down into which the Churchlands fear folk psychology is sinking.

Only a moment's reflection is needed to realize that much, if not most, of what we currently *know* of our own psychology is owed to folk psychology. Thus the present shortcomings of folk psychology do not seem to constitute evidence opposing the theory's dependence on propositional attitudes. Neither do the many yet-unsolved problems in psychology ensure that the propositional attitudes will, or ought to, find no place in an articulated scientific psychology. The explanatory failures the Churchlands cite might well not be attributable to the vacuity of a psychology of propositional attitudes. Rather, folk psychology's deficit in explanation might fall to the fact that, as an articulated science (as opposed to an unformulated body of common sense), psychology is yet a youngster. As it matures within the family of science, it may find ample application for the propositional attitudes, even if explanations of some apparently behavioral phenomena ultimately do not finally refer to propositional attitudes. Or scientific psychology may, in the end, turn out to be a science of propositional attitudes, but one whose domain does not include some of the mysterious phenomena we now assign it.

Absolutely none of this is to say that we may dogmatically insist that the shape that psychology will finally assume is bound to conform to the outline of the propositional attitudes. Psychology is an empirical science, and the history of the various sciences shows that we are poor at best in predicting what the basic explanatory concepts of a young science are likely to be. Who, in the halcyon days of Behaviorism, was positioned to see that its days as the dominant psychological model were numbered? Cognitivists

to the propositional attitudes, has quite a bit to say about the dynamics of memory. The point is not that cognitive psychology has totally demystified memory but rather that it seems to provide a systematic and promising procedure for investigating mnemonic phenomena.

should be sobered by the past trajectory of their discipline and allow that a psychology of propositional attitudes cannot hope to rest its case on a priori claims about mentation. Rather, the cognitivist enterprise ought to point out that a great deal of what we do seem to know about ourselves does presuppose the propositional attitudes as explanatory constructs. It is the success, albeit limited, of folk psychology to date that justifies continued pursuit of psychological explanation cast in the categories of the propositional attitudes. What remains to be seen, and what can be seen only by directing the conceptual resources of the propositional attitudes toward currently vexing problems in psychology, is whether folk psychology, in competition with alternative models of behavior, will provide sufficiently general explanations of behavioral phenomena to ensure its preservation. If an understanding of the nature of, for example, mental illness both proves central to our understanding of psychology and yet either defies elucidation in terms friendly to the categories of folk psychology or else yields more readily and comprehensively to an alternative conception of the mind, then so much the worse for folk psychology. Nevertheless, the reasons marshaled to date do not demonstrate that folk psychology is any less likely to bequeath its structure to the psychology of the golden age than any alternative picture of the mind. We may, then, be excused for promoting an account of cognitive processing that borrows its basic concepts from folk psychology.

What of the charge of stagnation? Paul Churchland claims that the psychological explanations favored in classical Greece are still in vogue. Folk psychology, then, has not evolved in anything like the way characteristic of a promising science. And this fact, when wedded to the failures charged here to folk psychology, indicates that the psychology of common sense holds little promise.

Should we so readily agree that folk psychology has stagnated? Aristotle's *De Anima* once cast a long shadow, but who now accepts unadulterated its notion of the various intellects? And do contemporary readers of Plato's *Republic* concur that the soul has exactly three parts, exactly as Socrates describes them? Not so very long ago popular wisdom attributed certain types of peculiar behavior to demonic possession, and particular patterns of bumps on the head were thought to augur a life of crime. Formerly almost all Europeans were convinced that the position of the celestial bodies on the occasion of one's birth determined one's disposition. And Shakespeare's characters are not shy about finding in the four humors the stuff of personalities. Yet current folk psychology has, for the most part, transcended these several explanatory fictions.

Moreover, whereas the Greeks had no truck with unconscious beliefs and desires, we commonly attribute behavior to propositional attitudes closed to conscious introspection. Indeed, trust in introspection itself has atrophied since its heyday with Descartes. Yes, we still maintain, as did the Greeks, that, for example, people normally say what they do because of the beliefs they have. And indeed, in league with Aristotle, we trust the practical syllogism in explicating behavior. But our continued predilection for drawing on the Aristotelian account of practical reasoning derives some warrant from the fact that, in normal circumstances, it appears readily to explain why we often act as we do. So we have retained something, though certainly not all, of Greek psychology, but what we have kept has some prima facie justification. Folk psychology is, then, hardly stagnant. And where it has not much changed since Aristotle had his way with it, that may be attributed to its continued informal confirmation. Commonsense psychology thus seems not completely becalmed, and an induction on its history does not conclusively establish that folk psychology cannot mature into a well-founded science.

So, what are the prospects for folk psychology's integration with the several eminently successful physical sciences? First, we should pause to ask whether and how, if at all, psychology is to be integrated with the physical sciences. Consider economics. It is, or at least can reasonably be claimed to be, a science even though few expect the principles of economics ever to be deducible from physics. Perhaps the same can be said for political science, anthropology, and sociology. In any event, these disciplines, since their formulation, have improved our knowledge of their respective domains. Together they constitute a lore, especially when complemented with psychology. We do anticipate that our several sciences will be integrated, but we should be alive to the possibility that the social sciences exhibit a collective harmony while resisting reduction to or derivation from the physical sciences. That is, psychology might not be reducible to any physical science. Still, it might manage to provide us with informative generalizations while sharing some of its explanatory concepts, as it does, with various other disciplines, each of which apparently contributes to our knowledge of its subject (Stich, 1983, pp. 213–14).

It is not difficult to see how explanatory concepts might resist reduction to those of the physical sciences. Suppose it should turn out to be true that married adults who both visited Disneyland as young children and regularly watched "American Band Stand" as teenagers are less likely to divorce than other married adults. Indeed, imagine that this is no accidental correlation, that one's proclivity for divorce is a direct function of the number of visits to Disneyland one enjoyed or endured as a child and the number of times one saw or suffered through "American Band Stand." If true, this might prove to be an important and useful bit of information for any number of reasons. Yet the categories of the generalization here – 'married adult', 'divorced adult', 'child visitor to Disneyland', and 'regular teenage viewer of "American Band Stand" ' – are unlikely candidates for reduction to or derivation from any cluster of concepts drawn from the physical sciences. In other words, the very categories under which agents are characterized for the purposes of psychological inquiry may, by accident, simply defy definition through or derivation from those categories current in the known laws of the various physical sciences. If such should prove to be the case, it would not be surprising if psychology were not integrated with the physical sciences in the way that chemistry is assimilated with physics.[15]

Certainly Patricia Smith Churchland (1980) is right in saying that discoveries in neurology might bear on at least some of the generalizations of folk psychology. Churchland is, for example, most probably correct when she notes (1980, pp. 191–2) that studies of

15 As Horgan and Woodward (1985) note (following Davidson [1970]), such a failure of reduction is consistent with the existence of physically realized propositional attitudes. Possibly there are not systematic bridge laws associating mental with, say, neural states. Additionally, Kitcher (1984) finds that folk psychology and transmission genetics may be parallel in their irreducibility to the fundamental physical sciences. Transmission genetics appears not to be reducible to molecular biology. But it remains a reputable discipline partly because questions raised within genetics can be answered within other sciences. Explanations within one field may, then, extend those provided in another. Thus, even if the latter science is not reducible to the former, the two may be, in a theoretically important sense, *integrated*. So, should folk psychology prove irreducible to any basic science, it might nevertheless be integrated into the family of science if, as likely, selected problems germinated by folk-psychological explanations find resolution in the hands of sibling sciences.

homonymous hemianopsia show that folk psychology cannot maintain, for example, both that (1) if one can report observationally on the perceivable world, then one has experienced it and that (2) one experiences something only if conscious of it. In other words, our concept of consciousness itself must certainly submit to alteration in the light of what we learn about the brain. Nevertheless, this hardly shows that folk psychology cannot harmonize with the various established sciences and seems rather to indicate the opposite. Certainly it may turn out that neurology falsifies selected generalizations from folk psychology. But this is something less than neurology's showing that the propositional attitudes, in terms of which the generalizations might be expressed, are themselves without any theoretical use in psychology. If a putative law of chemistry should prove inconsistent with a principle of physics, the chemical law would thereby be refuted. Still, the categories in terms of which the chemical generalization had been put would not thereby be shown unfit for use in chemistry. To demonstrate that, it would be necessary to show that the body of generalizations in which such categories figure are all false. The same evidently holds with respect to the propositional attitudes cited by the generalizations of folk psychology. Since we await argumentation showing that the physical sciences will likely falsify all of the principles of folk psychology, we may with good reason continue to suppose that the categories on which folk psychology depends may find application in explanations of behavior.[16]

I.4. SENTENTIALISM

Once we have introduced Sententialism, we can hardly pretend any longer to be exposing the mythically popular conception of mentation. Rather, we have taken the first tentative steps toward articulating a theory of mental states. So we had best offer some reasons for, and address some objections against, heading in that direction.

Anyone who entertains the plausibility of a psychology predicated on beliefs and desires had better recognize that these states are supposed to be involved in the production of overt behavior.

16 We shall return to others of the Churchlands' objections to a psychology of propositional attitudes in Chapter 4, Sections 4.1 and 4.2.

Together, beliefs and desires are presumed to cause behavior. But not only this. Holding desires constant, specific beliefs are to cause specific types of behavior. Abelard's belief that Héloïse is beautiful might, given his desires, cause him to attempt to arrange a private tutorial with her but, given the same desires, could not be what induces him to argue with William of Champeaux about the nature of universals. We expect that different beliefs potentially have some different behavioral manifestations. Beliefs, then, like any sort of efficacious structure, are physical, and, importantly, their specific effects must follow from their differentiating physical properties.[17] The state realizing Abelard's belief that Héloïse is beautiful must itself have some specific physical features enabling it to cause him to try to arrange a private tutorial with her rather than to attempt to scurry off to the university to argue with William.

However, the fact, if genuine, that beliefs are etiologically endowed physical structures does not alone secure that they are best treated as mental sentences. But when we add that behavior normally is rationally produced activity,[18] we find ourselves committed to the idea that behavior results from deliberation. Call it what you will, deliberation is nothing other than a (typically unconscious) rational procedure for generating behavior. To suppose that this procedure is rational or deliberate is to characterize it as a process of reasoning or internal inference. Once we grant that an agent's beliefs and desires cause the agent rationally to behave, we owe a down payment on an explanation of what it is about the causal

---

17 This, of course, rules out of court the various forms of dualism on the grounds that they fail to give a satisfying account of how mental states could have physical effects. If this is not a satisfactory reason for setting aside dualistic theories, then let it stand simply as an announcement that such views cannot here be given the more serious attention they deserve.

18 Although I shall comment on it, I do not have enough to say by way of a finally satisfactory analysis of rationality. Nevertheless, the literature is certainly not silent. See especially Bennett (1964), Davidson (1982), Follesdal (1982), and Heil (1985). For the most part, I shall rely on an intuitive understanding of the notion of rationality, realizing that a complete account of cognitive processes ultimately will have to settle on an explication of this notion. It is suggestive that chess-playing computer programs typically determine which moves to make by assuming that their opponents will make rational moves designed to achieve the goal of winning the game (Waltz, 1982, p. 119). The import of this is evidently that interaction with cognitive agents presupposes treating them as rational, that rationality is an essential feature of cognition. Compare Dennett (1978c), Stich (1985), Wason and Johnson-Laird (1972, 1977), and Tversky and Kahneman (1974, 1982).

16

sequence that constitutes its rational character. It will not do simply to say, even if true, that such sequences typically lead to behavior that satisfies the agent's desires.[19] We want to know *how* the beliefs and desires current in those sequences enable them to have this marvelous property. But if we hypothesize that the sequences are inferences from the contents of the relevant beliefs and desires, we thereby make our first payment toward an explanation of the rational cast to behavior.

The idea, then, is that a causal process leading from beliefs and desires to behavior is rational only if it is also an inference from the content of the beliefs and desires to the activity constituting the behavior.[20] In saying this, we neither affirm nor deny that there is no sense in which creatures that lack beliefs and desires can act rationally. There may be a weaker sense of rationality according to which a creature's activity is rational simply if it normally contributes to satisfying the conditions necessary for the creature's continued existence. This would seem to be an utterly degenerate sense of rationality. Every creature, floral and faunal, that passes evolution's test would meet this criterion of rationality. The point to characterizing as rational the deliberation carrying a cognitive agent from belief and desire to behavior is to acknowledge the contribution of the content of belief and desire to that process. What would better explain the contribution of a belief to the ra-

---

19 That is, it cannot be that the rationality of an agent's representational system resides in the fact that it is a system containing beliefs and desires that cause the satisfaction of the agent's desires. This would be the case only if the agent's beliefs were also typically true. Certainly there are cases in which the process leading to an agent's behavior is rational although that process does not satisfy the agent's desires. Such a process could be rational even if it does not lead to the satisfaction of desire if the beliefs on which it is predicated are not all true. Abelard's attempting to arrange to meet Héloïse in the garden could, apparently, be the rational product of his desiring to be alone with her and *falsely* believing that he would be alone with her were they to meet in the garden.

20 Presumably such inferences would, in the long run, need to be deductively, inductively, or abductively valid. Otherwise it is difficult to explain why an absurdly invalid inference, supposing such qualifies as an inference, is a non-rational way of generating activity. Still, it would certainly be wrong to insist that all instances of behavior must be the products of valid chains of deliberation. If it should turn out that a certain kind of cognitive agent is particularly susceptible to the gambler's fallacy but, as it happens to date, unusually lucky, should we say that those cognitive inferences in which that fallacy is called upon are non-rational? After all, is not rationality compatible with a penchant for error? And moreover, given the agent's run of good fortune, does not the fallacy appear to be inductively warranted? See Wason and Johnson-Laird (1972, 1977).

tionality of behavior than the figuring of its content in an inference from which the behavior is wrung? We may take it, then, that the rational, deliberate process that produces behavior is inference or, as is current, computation. Still, be it dubbed 'reasoning', 'inference', or 'computation', deliberation is a rational process. Insofar as it is computational, it must be defined over sentences, mental sentences. Reasoning, arguing, and computing are processes whose arguments and values, inputs and outputs are sentences. And to the extent that deliberation is rational, it must be sensitive to the contents of the sentences over which it is defined. Otherwise, we would be hard pressed to discern how an agent's beliefs could figure in explanations of the rationality of the agent's behavior.[21]

Belief fixation can also be construed as an inferential process that starts with entrenched beliefs and results in new ones. If this process is properly modeled along the lines of inference, then, since inference necessarily involves sentences, belief acquisition also apparently presupposes Mentalese. And if perception is an inferential, perhaps abductive, process culminating in perceptual judgments pertaining to the qualities and kinds of distal objects, then perception too would appear to draw upon sentential structures to advance its inferential process.[22]

21 The connection between rationality and the mental language does not preclude animals without *overt* languages of communication from qualifying as rational or cognitive. We will revisit this issue in Chapter 4, Section 4.1. For now, keep in mind that we are concerned only with the rational character of behavior. In associating the rationality of behavior with computational processes we do not thereby deny that there can be a noncomputational explanation of agental and brute activity (Lettvin et al., 1959). Rather, what is denied is that there can be an explanation of the robust rationality of behavior that does not advert to computational structures of beliefs and desires, intentional or contentful structures embodied in linguistic-like elements.

22 Perception is, obviously, a fount of new beliefs. While many, if not most, psychologists and philosophers hold that perception is an inferential process or, in any event, one that somehow depends on the perceiving agent's store of knowledge (Sellars, 1963; Gregory, 1970; Harman, 1973; Goodman, 1978), others have argued to the contrary, that perception may be a more direct form of information reception (Gibson, 1966; Clark, 1970; Fodor, 1984b; Maloney, 1984). Either analysis is quite compatible with Sentialism. Computational theories model thought against information processing and typically allow that information processing is itself an inferential process. Inferences must begin with and end in sentences. Even if perception is the direct, unmediated reception of information, the information so received must be sententially encoded upon reception or soon thereafter if it is to be computationally active. Evidently the topic of mental imagery is again relevant but demands more detailed consid-

18

Although deliberate action, belief fixation, and perceptual processing constitute evidence in favor of Mentalese, they do not presuppose that agents are conscious of all or any of their deployed Mentalese representations. Indeed, an agent is, when conscious, normally aware not of a mental sentence as such but, rather, of the content represented by that mental sentence.[23] And equally, agents are given to error in reporting exactly how certain cognitive processes unfold within themselves (Nisbett and Wilson, 1977). So it would be wrong to suppose that Sententialism is in any way committed to the view that agents must be aware of the concepts of all the Mentalese sentences they deploy, much less the Mentalese sentences themselves. These last are thoroughly theoretical structures, structures not guaranteed to be within the immediate introspective detection of the agents in whom they occur.[24] Hence, that agents do not rush to testify to the inferential or computational nature of their mental processes – much less to the prevalence of mental sentences as elements in those processes – should not be construed as compelling evidence against Sententialism.[25]

Once Sententialism construes beliefs as essentially involving mental sentences, it can advance to distinguish beliefs one from another and to differentiate between kinds of mental states generally. According to Sententialism, a cognitive agent believes by being related in a particular way to a token of a Mentalese sentence whose content is the content of the agent's belief. Different types of mental

---

eration than is possible here. Refer to footnote 10 of this chapter for references to the literature on mental imagery.

23 For instructive examples and discussion see Sternberg (1966), Patricia Smith Churchland (1983), Shepard and Metzler (1971), and Anderson (1980). Of course, if Chomsky's hypothesis about the mental representation of grammars is correct, the production and understanding of language are perhaps the paradigmatic examples of unconscious cognitive processing. Philosophical arguments about incorrigibility and the possibility of private languages are relevant here (Wittgenstein, 1953). For a reply to Wittgenstein's complaints against the possibility of a private language such as Mentalese, see Fodor (1975, p. 68) and Kripke (1982).

24 See Paul Churchland (1979) for a discussion of the susceptibility of introspective reports to the influence of accepted theory.

25 As Dennett (1978a) points out, an agent's inability correctly to describe his or her mental processes might be attributable to the simple fact that the output of certain cognitive functions is not properly configured to stand as input to the agent's speech mechanism. See especially Lackner and Garrett (1973). If psychology from Freud through Neisser has taught anything, it is that if we are ever to understand the nature of mind, we had better look to theory rather than unadulterated introspection.

19

states – beliefs, hopes, and fears – also are constituted by relations to Mentalese tokens, each distinct type of state corresponding to a particular type of relation. Thus, when Abelard finally comes to believe what he has long hoped to be true, namely, that he is to be alone with Héloïse, his belief and hope coincide in content. They thus each consist of a distinctive type of relation to tokens of Mentalese sentences of the same type, the content of which represents Abelard as alone with Héloïse. More precisely, given his belief and hope, in Abelard there are tokens of some particular Mentalese sentence, perhaps 'I am alone with Héloïse'. His belief is a relation, B, connecting him to a Mentalese token of this Mentalese sentence, and his hope is a different relation, H, relating him to another token of the same. Identity of mental states of the same type, therefore, reduces to identity of Mentalese sentences. So Abelard and Héloïse share a belief only if they are related in the same way to tokens of the same Mentalese type (Fodor, 1975, 1980a).

Now, Abelard may desire, and so decide, to meet Héloïse in the garden. Given what we so far have of Sententialism, this amounts to some Mentalese sentence's occurring within Abelard. For the moment, adopt the fiction that Mentalese is indistinguishable from English and that the Mentalese sentence internal to Abelard registering his decision is 'Abelard, meet Héloïse in the garden!' That is, assume that Abelard's decision is rendered by a Mentalese command addressed to himself. Should he carry out his decision, he will at some occasion come to believe that he is at that moment meeting Héloïse in the garden. So some mental sentence must occur to encode that belief. Imagine that this sentence is 'Abelard meets Héloïse in the garden'. We should not fail to notice that the two sentences are grammatically different (Casteñeda, 1975; Clark, 1976). The first is imperative, the second indicative. This may be problematic. There is a sense in which the content of the belief and the decision is the same. After all, by hypothesis Abelard's belief is supposed to record the fulfillment of his decision. But the preceding paragraph suggests that sameness of content of different types of mental states requires sameness of the Mentalese sentences encoded in those states. It may appear, then, that Sententialism has misconstrued identity of content across different types of mental states.

In order to circumvent this difficulty, Sententialism may travel either of two paths. One points toward construing some types of

Mentalese sentences, perhaps imperatives and interrogatives, as modalizations of indicatives. It may be that Mentalese features a pair of sentential operators, M and N, that attach to indicatives to form imperatives and interrogatives. If so, then (given the merely illustrative conflation of Mentalese and English) the Mentalese sentence recorded in Abelard's decision would not be 'Abelard, meet Héloïse in the garden!' but rather 'M (Abelard meets Héloïse in the garden)'. This modal sentence results from the application of M to 'Abelard meets Héloïse in the garden', itself a token of the very type of Mentalese sentence we assumed occurrent in Abelard's belief. Thus, Sententialism might lay it down that different types of mental states are the same in content just in case they feature either Mentalese sentences of the same type or modalizations of Mentalese sentences of the same type.

The other path begins with the admission that 'Abelard, meet Héloïse in the garden!' and 'Abelard meets Héloïse in the garden' are in fact the Mentalese sentences respectively occurrent in Abelard's decision and belief. This route proceeds to the thesis that there is some grammatical core common to these two sentences from which both are generated by different grammatical operations. We might thus hypothesize that the common grammatical core is subject to modification at the level of the predicate. Nevertheless, identity of content across different types of mental states now would be a function of the Mentalese sentences featured in those states being generated from a common grammatical element.

It matters little to Sententialism which of these two roads is to be followed. Both allow that the distinction between some different types of mental states may be secured by some grammatical differences within the Mentalese sentences registered in those states. The first path runs toward modal operators that take whole sentences within their scopes. The second ends in differences at the level of predicates. However, both explain identity of content in terms of some syntactic structure common to the generation of the Mentalese sentences in question. That is what is crucial to Sententialism. So we need not attempt to decide the issue in order to preserve the Sententialist picture. In all that follows we will abstract from considerations of grammatical mood in characterizing Mentalese. Even so, enough has been said of Sententialism to elicit serious objections.

Dennett (1978b) and Patricia Smith Churchland (1980a) have complained that Sententialism, as a version of Representationalism, is subject to the classical objection raised against any theory of thought that presupposes representations of any sort internal to cognitive agents. Representations, mental or not, are symbols, and all symbols need interpretation. Insofar as it is a trail of ink, a sentence is simply a structure devoid of content. It is only as interpreted that a sentence can be said to be contentful. Beliefs certainly have content. So, if they derive their content by way of including mental sentences, these sentences must be interpreted. It is surely the agent in whom such mental sentences occur who must do the interpreting. Interpreting a sentence is itself a thoroughly cognitive enterprise. But how, according to Sententialism, does this process unfold? Must it not itself involve the deployment and interpretation of yet another mental sentence, and this on to infinity? Put differently, every mental sentence in an agent must be interpreted. Each act of interpretation requires an embedded cognitive agent to whom the job of interpretation falls. But each interpretation itself presupposes another mental sentence to be interpreted by still another, more deeply nested agent. Here there is no final explanation of mentation. So much the worse, then, for not only Sententialism but also any other version of the Representational Theory of the Mind.

Dennett (1978e) realizes that the modest success of Artificial Intelligence points to a solution to the problem of infinitely embedded cognitive agents.[26] Programs driving artificially intelligent behavior can be construed as containing representations analogous to those presumed by Sententialism to be psychologically efficacious in naturally intelligent agents. Data structures are representations in and for computers. Our knowledge of the design and physical functioning of the computer assures us that these representations do not require interpretation by endlessly arrayed cognitive agents ensconced within the computer. Indeed, in order for a representation

26 See Boden (1977) and Haugeland (1985) for surveys of Artificial Intelligence. For particular efforts look to Simon (1969), Winograd (1971), Bobrow and Collins (1975), Schank and Abelson (1977), Bobrow and Winograd (1977), Schank (1982), and Anderson (1983). Also see Cummins (1983) for a view of the nature of intelligent understanding that draws upon Artificial Intelligence as a model for mental representation.

to function as a symbol it must be interpreted; mental sentences, if such there be, must be interpreted by the agents in whom they occur. If we may take Artificial Intelligence to model its natural counterpart, it apparently suffices for the interpretation of mental sentences that they function in a cognitive economy in ways analogous to the functioning of information-bearing structures under the control of programs operating in computers. Thus, if we are willing to suppose that studies in Artificial Intelligence reveal how representations might occur within agents, we may dismiss the objection from the regress of embedded agents, and provisionally, retain Sententialism.

This solution to the problem of embedded agents is, of course, contingent on the plausibility of Artificial Intelligence as a line of research in cognitive science. Although many, if not most, familiar with results in Artificial Intelligence may welcome this way of preserving Sententialism, room remains for misgivings. Crucial to the appeal to Artificial Intelligence is the idea that, simply by virtue of their functioning to produce apparently intelligent activity within a device, representations have content for the device. Unfortunately there are substantial reasons, which we will later examine in detail, weighing against this thesis.[27]

Perhaps, then, we are best advised not to bet too heavily on Artificial Intelligence as a straightforward solution to the problem of embedded agents. Although we would surely want to affirm that Artificial Intelligence is of unquestionable value in the study of the mind, we might wonder whether it alone furthers our understanding of how representations come to have content within cognitive agents. It is not utterly implausible to construe efforts at

27 I have in mind here Searle's (1980) well-known argument that unaided Artificial Intelligence cannot reveal what is involved in understanding or comprehension. Also see Dretske (1985), Dreyfus (1979), and Fodor (1981c), and note Boden's (1977) critique of the limitations of selected programs for artificially intelligent behavior. In Chapter 5 I shall lay out my reasons for agreeing with Searle that, strictly, artificially intelligent devices do not, for all we can tell, possess genuine understanding or intelligence. Nevertheless, I do not take this conclusion to establish the fatuity of appealing to Artificial Intelligence as a simulation of, or model for, some cognitive phenomena occurrent in naturally cognitive agents. Indeed, while I will agree that intelligent understanding cannot be simply a matter of the execution of a program of a certain sort, I do maintain that, *with certain essential provisions pertaining to the physical nature of the agent and the causal history of the representational structures*, mental representation is determined by conformity to a program of the type proposed within Artificial Intelligence.

artificially creating intelligence as producing only *simulations* of intelligence and understanding, simulations that emulate, without themselves instantiating, comprehension. Computers arguably do not understand what they are talking about. Their internal representations might not, after all, have authentic content. Or, to put this in a softer light, we may allow that *if* Artificial Intelligence should prove to provide an adequate model of mentation, *then* Sententialism can avoid the problem of embedded agents by nodding to what is known of the functioning of representations in artificially intelligent systems. But since this is consistent with the failure of Artificial Intelligence to expose the nature of the mind's intentionality, we had better canvass other solutions to the problem of ever-embedded agents.

We find infinitely embedded agents within an agent only on conceding two points: First, representations must be interpreted; second, interpretation is itself a cognitive process. Now surely an agent's mental representations, Mentalese sentences, must be interpreted by the agent. Otherwise, what sense would there be to saying that they are contentful states for the agent?[28] It is not perfectly manifest, however, that interpretation itself is *properly* taken to be a wholly cognitive process. Possibly interpretation is a process best analyzed, at least partially, in physical rather than purely functional terms. It may well be that, as a naturally arising phenomenon, the accrual of content to an agent's mental structures essentially involves physical processes or properties of a specific sort.[29]

28 One might venture that it is needlessly strong here to say that a representation must *be interpreted*. Rather, it suffices that it *have an interpretation*. Whereas the interpretation of a sentence does presuppose the interpretive activity of an agent, that a sentence simply has an interpretation does not. This line will not satisfy those who suspect that for any sentence to have an interpretation there must be *some* agent *somewhere* that *somehow* interprets that sentence. This amounts to supposing that the very notion of interpretation is a relational concept, much as is the concept of having a brother. Just as one cannot have a brother unless there is some male to whom one is related in just the right way, so too – the worry is – a sentence cannot have an interpretation unless there is some agent to whom the sentence is related in just the right way. So what we need to do here is concede that the fundamental notion is that of a representation's being interpreted by an agent. The task is to explain what it is for a representation to be so interpreted without thereby introducing an infinite regress of interpreting agents.
29 See Dretske (1981) and Paul Churchland (1986a and b and 1988) for different naturalistic theories of information processing and mental content. I am not urging here that the details of either of these accounts are correct, although they well may be. Rather, the point is that, as naturally arising states, contentful states of intelligent agents may be explicable in thoroughly naturalistic, perhaps

So, possibly, that a Mentalese structure is endowed with content for the agent in whom it occurs is determined by something unique to its physical composition or history. The incipient, tentative *hypothesis* is this: As a physical state of an agent, a Mentalese sentence may have content for the agent by way of either being composed of some sort of matter or having some physically specifiable feature. Accordingly, for mental states to have an interpretation for an agent would be for those states of the agent all to have certain physical properties. This is not to deny that the functional relations among mental representations may contribute to fixing the specific content of representations. Nor is it to reject the conjecture that the particular interpretation assigned by an agent to one of his or her states is established by the relations that the state bears to all cognitively active states of the agent.[30] The point rather is that functional role alone may be insufficient to secure the very intentionality or contentfulness of mental representations. The idea here, then, is that it is possible that intelligent understanding is a phenomenon essentially limited to creatures exhibiting certain physical properties (Patricia Smith Churchland, 1980a, b; Paul Churchland, 1982).

Already there is much to fret about. How is one to make sense of the notion that it is the physical, rather than the functional, character of a state that establishes it as intentional? After all, does not physics show that all things are made of the same stuff? If it is not earth, air, fire, and water out of which all things are composed, then it is just protons, electrons, neutrons, and, well, whatever physics discovers. The differences among different kinds of things are just functional differences in the arrangements of a matter common to all. Accordingly, any attempt to trace the intentionality of a state to its material as opposed to its functional configuration is patently wrong.

This is an important objection, but its reply can be garnered from the practice of the physical sciences. Each physical science is char-

---

physical, terms. Such an explanation would not thereby show that there really are not contentful states but rather would expose the constitution of such states.

30 In Chapter 6 I will argue for a hybrid account of mental content. There I contend that the sheer intentionality of any mental state, the fact that the state has content, is set by its physical nature. This leaves it quite open as to what the content of the state might be. So we might hypothesize that the specific content of a sensory mental state is to be determined by the state's causal connections to stimuli. And to this we could add that the particular content of a nonsensuous mental state is to be secured by its functional role.

acterized in part by a taxonomy. The categories established in a science's taxonomy constitute the natural kinds under examination. If things go well for the science and its taxonomy, then nomic relations discovered by the science will be seen to hold among objects studied by the science by virtue of those objects belonging to the categories of the taxonomy. The taxonomy of a predictive science is an enumeration of what, relative to that science, are natural kinds. To say that a particular object is made up of a certain kind of matter is to say that it is a thing that belongs to a natural kind of some physical science. Thus, to say that an intentional state owes its intentionality to its matter is to say that the state belongs to a natural kind of some physical science. Water, we all know, is a natural kind. Intentionality, according to the present hypothesis, is also a natural kind in exactly the same sense as is water. Just as water is decomposable into more basic elements still, so too may intentionality be subject to decomposition into its material constituents. The idea, then, is that whatever the philosophy of science finally takes natural kinds to be, such is precisely what intentionality will be. That then implies that just as water is best studied according to the methodology of a certain physical science, so too for intentionality.

Some kinds are not natural. They are not to be found among the taxonomies of any of the physical sciences. Such are the so-called functional kinds. Because of this, membership in a functional kind is not – for the most part – restricted by membership in a natural kind. Functional kinds are thus compositionally plastic. Wire is a functional kind. Different wires can consist primarily of various different natural kinds, copper and aluminum, for example. Water is not a functional kind and, by hypothesis, neither is intentionality. An intentional state is thus not compositionally plastic. Therefore, an intentional state is restricted in its material composition when difference in material composition is gauged in terms of the taxonomies of the several physical sciences.

Such is only and all that is to be understood by the hypothesis that intentionality is materially based, that it is a natural – as opposed to a functional – kind. This is not at all to minimize the thesis. Paramount is the notion that intentionality is materially restricted in much the same sense that water is and wire is not. If this hypothesis is correct, then we should anticipate that the methodology proper to understanding the nature of intentionality is the methodology characteristic of the physical sciences and their way with natural kinds. Equally important, if intentional states are no more compositionally plastic than is water, then we cannot hope to understand deeply the nature of intentional states by laboring under the supposition that the natural kind to which a mental state belongs is irrelevant to the representational capacity of the state.

Evidently, different things, steel and plastic gears, can be functionally identical within a certain domain while also diverging in the physical or natural kinds to which they belong. This holds despite the fact that at one level of analysis, perhaps quantum physics, the different gears can be seen to be composed of the same stuff differently arranged. Functional identity is itself a relative notion. Steel and plastic gears might be interchangeable within a clock operating under normal conditions without affecting the operations of the clock. Thus, we judge the physically different gears to be functionally the same, though we know full well that at extreme operating temperatures the functional equivalence of the steel and plastic gears will be lost.

Now it certainly seems that there could be a system that is functionally equivalent to a cognitive agent with respect to a designated realm of the agent's activity, that is, the agent's behavior. Artificially intelligent systems are supposed to exhibit just such a functional identity with natural cognitive agents. Natural cognitive agents produce their behavior by way of deploying internal intentional states, mental representations. The artificial equivalents of the natural agents generate activity indistinguishable from the agents' activity. So it seems as if the physical differences that separate the natural and artificial agents are as irrelevant to their behavior as are the physical differences that distinguish the steel- and plastic-geared clocks. The clocks both keep time. The artificial and natural cognitive agents apparently both behave. True enough. But notice that whereas it is quite plain that the gears both contribute to the operations of the clocks by *spinning*, it is not at all clear that the artificial and natural agents both produce activity by virtue of internally *representing*. Hence, if it is an understanding of intentionality that we desire, it may be necessary that we attend to the physical dynamics of the natural agent that differentiate it from its artificial peer.

Consider two clocks, one electronic, one mechanical. Both keep time, but only one does so by virtue of its electrical states. The mechanical clock is utterly empty of the kind of electrical states crucial to the operation of the electronic clock. Recall the artificial and natural cognitive agents. Both produce activity, but – by hypothesis – only the natural agent does so by virtue of having intentional states. The artificial agent is utterly empty of the kind of states, intentional states, crucial to the operation of the natural agent. Just as the electrical states of the electronic clock differ in physical kind from the states of the mechanical clock, so too, according to the hypothesis, do the intentional states of the natural agent differ from the internal states of the artificial agent. This is the sense in which artificially and naturally intelligent agents may be functionally the same with respect to behavior yet crucially diverge in the stuff that enables them to behave. It is just this difference in stuff that may be central to the question as to whether both kinds of agents enjoy intentional states. What makes a state intentional might be a matter of its physical kind. Intentional states are suited to producing behavior, much as electrical states are suited for keeping time. Nonintentional states, states materially different from intentional ones, might also be suited to producing activity indistinguishable from behavior, much as mechanical states are suited for keeping time. Mechanical clocks can keep time despite lacking electrical states, and artificial agents might behave despite lacking intentional states. So the sheer fact that possibly devices that physically diverge from natural agents themselves produce activity indistinguishable from the behavior of the natural agents does not in any way establish that the physical difference separating natural and artificial agent is irrelevant to whether both sorts of agents have intentional states.

The hypothesis on parade, then, is that a state is a mental representation by way of being a state of a selected physical kind. Should such be so, then Sententialism's response to the objection from endlessly embedded agents would be that a mental state is intentional, contentful, or representational because of its material composition. By repeated analogy, we might note that just as water is water because it is compounded of hydrogen and oxygen, so too an intentional state may be intentional because it has a certain material basis. If so, this would explain why, if true, artificial devices typically lack real comprehension and want fully intentional states. Artificially intelligent systems would fail to be genuinely intelligent for the mundane reason that they are improperly con-

28

stituted. Still, even if comprehension is restricted to agents of certain physical types, even if mental representation is peculiar to states with selected physical properties, it remains possible, consistent with the general idea of Artificial Intelligence, that the particular, *specific* content of a mental representation be set by its interaction with other representations within a cognitive system. That Abelard's Mentalese sentence 'Héloïse is charming' is contentful would thus be due to the stuff of which it is composed. That it specifically represents Héloïse as charming could be attributable to its functional role in Abelard's cognitive economy. The matter of a state may be what renders it intentional; its functional role may be at least part of what settles its content.[31]

How can one separate *particular content* from *intentionality?* An analogy may help. A newly made sheet of wax, to borrow from Locke and abuse Descartes, may have a smooth surface free of any noticeable impression. If the wax is maintained at a warm temperature, it will take on as an impression the shape of an object pressed against it. Thus, if a three-dimensional stamp on which 'Locke' is encoded in reverse is applied to the warm wax, it will leave 'Locke' impressed on the wax. The wax will then, in a metaphorical sense, represent, signify, or refer to Locke; the particular content of the wax is Locke. Prior to its being stamped, the wax is, we might say, ready to receive its particular content although it at present lacks any specific content. Working the metaphor a bit more, the unimpressed wax has intentionality without any specific content. It potentially represents without actually representing; it has the capacity to represent although it currently in fact represents nothing.

Not everything is like the wax. A quart of milk will not itself carry an inscription of 'Locke' subsequent to an application of the stamp. Only some sorts of things, then, are naturally apt to react to applications of the stamp by exhibiting inscriptions of 'Locke'. Only such kinds are, metaphor preserved, naturally intentional.

---

31 Thus, to hypothesize that material composition plays an important role in establishing the intentional character of a state is not to endorse anything like the type-type identity theory of mental states. The latter theory takes identity of mental content to be set by identity of physical type, whereas the present hypothesis of the material basis of intentionality is silent regarding type identity of mental states, proposing only that the sheer intentionality of a state, not the state's specific content, is a matter of its matter.

Prior to the impact of a stamp, such kinds have no specific content. That befalls them only if they should commune with stamps.

This is how we are to understand the hypothesis that the intentionality of a mental state devolves from its matter. Intentional states are, if the hypothesis should be true, states naturally apt to be effected by the forces of nature so as to represent in the manner of inscriptions.[32] That such representations occur as inscriptions rather than, say, pictures is independent of the thesis that intentionality accrues to a state by virtue of the material composing the state. It is rather implied by the hypothesis that mental representations are linguistic, Mentalese, representations. That such inscriptions can occur at all within the receiving system follows from the hypothesis that intentional states, mental representations, are materially based. The wax, but not the milk, is apt to encode 'Locke' on being stamped. This is determined by their physical compositions. Of course, the wax can bear inscriptions other than 'Locke'. The inscription any bit of wax happens to bear is determined by what stamp happens to impress it. So too for intentional states. They, like wax, are all made of the same stuff. Prior to exposure to the environment, intentional states are without content. In this there is nothing any more mysterious than the fact that unimpressed warm wax is amenable to impression though it be yet unimpressed. This is the only sense to be assigned to the notion that intentionality can be separated from specific content. It is simply the familiar idea of a disposition awaiting its triggering event.[33]

No doubt, when we note that wax, but not milk, is disposed to receive stamped inscriptions, we are obliged to look into the wax's physical structure for an explanation of the basis of its disposition. To say that an object has a disposition to react in a certain way is only an invitation to expose exactly what it is about the physical structure of the object that enables it to react as it does. Dispositions, then, are to be explained; reference to a disposition is not the terminus of explanation. The same is true with respect to intentional states. A state is intentional if, by virtue of its physical composition,

---

32 For the moment – but only for the moment – let us stall the temptation to say that the specific content of an intentional state is, in certain cases, the cause of the state's being inscribed as it is. In Chapter 6 we shall give in to the temptation and attempt the beginnings of a causal theory of mental content.

33 Whatever general theory of dispositions emerges from the philosophy of science and the theory of conditionals should apply here just as it must throughout scientific discourse. See Lewis (1973) and Nute (1980).

it is apt to represent. So, fully to understand the intentionality of a state requires an investigation into the physical composition of an intentional state. Such an investigation will conclude with a specification of those properties that enable an intentional state to be disposed as it is. Since the properties to be specified are, by hypothesis, those that serve to place the state into a natural kind, the specification will characterize those properties in the language of physical science. To hypothesize that intentionality is materially based is thus to hold that intentionality is to be explicated in a nonintentional idiom. It is not to maintain that the notion of intentionality is an ultimate explanatory construct. In this regard, to call a state intentional is similar to describing a liquid as water. In the latter case, we look to chemistry for an analysis of what it is for a liquid to be water. Similarly, we anticipate that mature neurology, if not some other physical science, shall someday lay bare the nature of intentionality.

What we have here is a hypothesis offered to explain why, if indeed true, artificially intelligent devices do not have intentional states and, accordingly, fail to achieve fully fledged intelligent understanding. It is not a proclamation of what is analytically implied by the very concepts of interpretation, content, or intentionality. As a hypothesis, it is an abductive attempt to say what seems necessary to save Sententialism from the problem of embedded agents while provisionally rejecting the solution from Artificial Intelligence. Evidently, much must, and will be, said in order to put meat on these bones, but certainly this much must be conveyed at the outset. If intentionality accrues to Mentalese sentences by way of their physical characteristics, then it very well may be that mentation is restricted to things of certain limited physical kinds. This hypothesis is not merely the enunciation of the bland notion that complex *animals* such as humans can think, whereas ice cubes cannot. It countenances a much more radical position. It welcomes the possibility that hard science may determine that, regardless of their functional complexity or position in the evolutionary scheme, some organisms or devices cannot have contentful or representational states simply because they are not composed of the proper material.

We can put this fancifully in order to make the point. Assume that there are silicon-based Martians who exhibit remarkable forms of activity and interaction that appear susceptible to psychological

31

explanations of the sort that apply to ourselves. Despite the apparent appropriateness of these explanations, they might fail actually to apply to the Martians because of differences distinguishing their physiology from ours. It may be that these differences establish the *natural impossibility* of these Martians' having genuinely contentful mental states. Should this be correct, the Martians could not enjoy beliefs and desires even though a psychology attributing such to them would be highly predictive. Given the material basis of mentation, a psychology of belief and desire would be literally false of the Martians even though it would predict their activity as accurately as it forecasts our behavior.[34] So, hypothesizing that intentionality submits to a physical analysis carries with it what Block (1980a) has called psychological chauvinism, implying, as it does, that mentation is not simply a matter of functional interaction of states but also requires a specified physical base. The hypothesis is not innocuous; it is at loggerheads with any general account of the mental that supports Artificial Intelligence in its claim that cognition transcends physicality.[35]

34 Well, perhaps this allows a bit too much to the predictive power of a psychology literally false of Martians. To see why, suppose that a psychology proposed for Martians were to predict that Abelard de Marte, a Martian doppelgänger of Abelard, will attempt to arrange a private tutorial with Héloïse de Marte, the Martian counterpart to Héloïse. The prediction is predicated on attributing to Abelard de Marte the desire to be alone with Héloïse de Marte and the belief that the best way to be alone with her is to make arrangements with her father for a private tutorial with her. Whether the activity in which Abelard de Marte engages actually is correctly describable as his *attempting* to arrange a private tutorial rather than, say, merely as his emitting certain vocals in the company of the father of Héloïse de Marte seems itself to be fixed by whether Abelard de Marte actually has the belief and desire attributed to him. After all, if he literally has neither the belief nor the desire assigned by the prediction, then it is at best dubious whether he is doing what the prediction attributes to him, namely, attempting to arrange the tutorial. Certainly some events occur when he vocalizes in the presence of the father. But the fundamental question is how best to describe these events. Are they behavioral episodes or not? If Abelard de Marte fails to have the mental states the prediction assigns to him, then his vocalizing in the presence of Héloïse's father appears not to be a bit of behavior. It must be some other *kind* of event. Thus, once it is conceded that Abelard de Marte lacks beliefs and desires, it would seem as if the prediction the psychology makes of him actually is itself false. We shall see more of this issue in Chapter 3, Section 3.1.

35 Functionalism is, of course, at issue here. See Block (1980d) for an explanation of the types of, and theses central to, functionalism. The theme characteristic of functionalism is that mental states are type identified solely by their relations to other mental states and the inputs and outputs of cognitive systems. Thus, for functionalism, the belief that P is whatever typically results from certain input

Here is not the place further to develop the hypothesis that psychological states owe, even if only partially, their content to their physicality. The point to be emphasized at present is that Sententialism enjoys at least two ways in which it might keep at bay the objection from endlessly embedded agents. On the one hand, if Artificial Intelligence approximates a true science of the mind, then Sententialism may call on the manner in which programs deploy representations in order to explain how naturally intelligent agents use contentful Mentalese sentences without succumbing to a regress of ever more internal interpretive agents. On the other hand, if unsupplemented Artificial Intelligence should fail for want of recognizing the essentially physical nature of intelligence, then Sententialism may depend on natural science, perhaps buttressed with Artificial Intelligence, to explain the intentionality of an agent's mental states. So, although later we will look to reasons supporting the latter alternative, for now we happily allow that, one way or the other, it seems that Sententialism is free from the fear of embedded agents.

1.6. NOTATION AND CONTENT

We just saw that one way of avoiding the regress of embedded agents is to endorse Artificial Intelligence as a model of the mind. On that score, mental representations within an agent do not require an embedded agent to interpret them. Representations, according to Artificial Intelligence, represent simply by virtue of their coordinated, functional roles in producing behavior. Although the model from Artificial Intelligence may neatly put to rest Sententialism's difficulty with embedded agents, it in turn itself creates another problem for Sententialism. Beliefs, Sententialism would have it, are realized in Mentalese sentences literally tokened with cognitive agents. Thus, if Sententialism is correct, for every true ascription of a belief to an agent, there must be within the agent a Mentalese token whose content corresponds to the attributed belief. So, if Abelard believes that he should begin each lecture to Héloïse by referring to Plato's *Symposium*, there should be in Abelard a Mentalese inscription to that effect.

and, in turn, produces certain output. Look to Block (1980c) for a selection of essays examining the tenets of functionalism. For reservations note Block and Fodor (1972), Block (1980a), Davis (1982), Owens (1983), and Stich (1983).

To test this, imagine that someday in the distant future a clever programmer were to write a program, ABELARD PRIMUS, that simulates Abelard's romance with Héloïse. This PRIMUS enables devices in which it is instantiated to behave in the presence of Héloïse exactly as would Abelard. Yet, it is quite possible that there is in PRIMUS no statement most plausibly construed as an inscription of 'I should begin each lecture to Héloïse by referring to Plato's *Symposium*'. After all, PRIMUS might itself be artificially simulated by a *notationally distinct* program, ABELARD SECUNDUS.[36] Simulation being transitive, SECUNDUS would also simulate Abelard. Therefore, like both Abelard and PRIMUS, SECUNDUS should also believe that it should begin each of its lectures to Héloïse by referring to Plato's *Symposium*.[37]

Once buttressed with a model of the mind from Artificial Intelligence, Sententialism assigns PRIMUS and SECUNDUS the same beliefs as it does to Abelard. The reason is that, by assumption, they all agree in behavior. Still, in either PRIMUS or SECUNDUS there is no inscription of 'I should begin each lecture to Héloïse by referring to Plato's *Symposium*'. Hence, either at least one of PRIMUS or SECUNDUS is not, after all, a doxastic clone of Abelard or Sententialism is fundamentally wrong in postulating Mentalese sentences to realize the content of beliefs. The first of these alternatives is at odds with versions of Sententialism that accept Artificial Intelligence as a model of the mind, and the second eviscerates any edition of Sententialism worthy of the name.

The objection comes to this: Agents guaranteed to behave the same in all the same circumstances share the same beliefs. Sententialism trades in syntactic coin and wagers that beliefs are the same only if they are tokens of the same syntactic or notational types.[38]

---

36 Then SECUNDUS is just a program that does whatever PRIMUS does, but the code constituting SECUNDUS is not identical with the code that is PRIMUS. This is a common feature of programming and is typically exhibited within any class of students who have successfully completed a programming assignment. The programs that pass muster will all produce the same relevant output given the same specified input despite the fact that the students' programs will often differ in how they achieve their results.

37 For a discussion of the sense in which notationally distinct programs can be functionally equivalent see Haugeland's (1981a) introduction to his *Mind Design*.

38 The reason is that beliefs that are the same should cause the same behavior. The only way it would seem that beliefs can cause behavior is by virtue of their physical properties. So beliefs that are to have all the same behavioral effects likely will be similarly encoded. They will, then, need to be beliefs with the

But Artificial Intelligence maintains that devices running notationally distinct programs can nevertheless behave the same. Such devices would, given the behavioral criterion for identity of belief, believe the same. And that contradicts Sententialism's notational criterion of belief identity.[39]

Perhaps the first thing to say here on Sententialism's behalf is that in order to enable the objection to get off the ground we must suppose that taking agents to be in the same circumstances includes assigning to the agents the same desires. Otherwise, sameness of behavior would be compatible with difference in belief. If you believe that snow is white and desire to tell the truth, you will say, "Snow is white." If I believe that snow is not white and desire to lie, I will say the same. When we know of agents *only* that they behave the same, we might choose to attribute to them identical desires in order to simplify our ascriptions of belief to them. Such a choice is not without peril. Although we normally take behavior to be criterial for belief, this practice, we should remind ourselves, is predicated on our ignorance of the behavioral dynamics specific to agents. So let us keep in mind that the objection under consideration rests on the unargued presumption that agents possessed of notationally distinct Mentalese inscriptions possibly coincide in all their desires.

Additionally, once we discover that the agents' patterns of behavior are controlled by the kinds of physically different structures necessary to assure fundamental notational differences in the notations in which the programs guiding the agents' behavior are written, our confidence in attributing sameness of belief to the agents should wane. Offered this additional information about the dynamics of the agents' behavior, we should be alive to the possibility that the congruent behavior emanates from different causes. We ought seriously to entertain the idea that the extraordinarily different physical systems giving rise to the behavior encode coordinated but divergent beliefs and desires. Certainly, granted the objection's hypothesis of the notational differences among the three

same syntax. Thus, sameness of belief evidently requires that the Mentalese inscriptions encoding the beliefs be syntactically the same. This is not to deny that beliefs that are the same will have the same semantic conditions (though consideration of indexicals raises certain problems). Rather, it amounts to supposing that central semantic differences among beliefs will be reflected by syntactic differences. See Fodor (1980a) and Stich (1983).

39 A similar argument was originally advanced by Dennett (1978b).

Abelards, it is a real possibility that their indistinguishable behavior is the consequence not of indistinguishable beliefs but rather of dramatically different beliefs in the contexts of varying desires. If this is a genuine possibility, and it seems to be, then the objection does not conclusively demonstrate an error in Sententialism.

It is also worth noting that the objection ignores certain complexities in supposing that the notational distinction between the representations of PRIMUS and SECUNDUS entails that at least one of them lacks a token of a certain inscription. Notational distinctness takes two forms. Notations may differ either as notations in different languages or as different notations within a single language. So, taking each type of notational difference in turn, suppose first that PRIMUS and SECUNDUS use different languages. Under this assumption the objection poses no difficulty for Sententialism. Although Sententialism is typically described in terms of a single language of mentation, it is by no means fundamental to the Sententialist program that mentation be instantiated in a single mental language common to all types of cognitive agents. Indeed, if Sententialism is correct, it is most reasonable to suppose that cognitive agents of different natural kinds deploy different mental languages (Maloney, 1985a). Thus the Sententialist thesis that sameness of belief requires sameness of notation is to be read as relativized to mental languages. It is, therefore, quite consistent with Sententialism that agents utilizing different mental languages realize the same belief in different notation. Thus, if PRIMUS and SECUNDUS are written in different languages, then, contrary to what the objection would have, their notational differences do not compromise their doxastic coincidence.

Most likely, differences in mental inscriptions across naturally intelligent agents that suffice to distinguish their mental languages constitute differences enough to distinguish the agents according to cognitive kind. The reason for this is that cognitive kinds apparently supervene on natural kinds. Cats and humans are different kinds of cognitive agents, the difference arising from the fact that certain basic differences in their physical natures place them into different natural kinds. Cats, no doubt like humans, exploit some features of their physical configuration to support their intelligence. When different natural kinds draw on distinctive physical features to produce their characteristic intelligence, the type or level of intelligence they possess may be peculiar to themselves. Such, presumably, is part of the explanation of the difference in the intelligence manifested by cats and humans. On the Sentientialist scheme, this amounts to saying that across different cognitive kinds, physically distinctive contributions to intelligence support different mental languages, languages dependent for their idiosyncratic notations on the different physical features of which they are composed.

Sentientialism's allowance for notationally, and hence physically, different mental languages may be thought to be problematic. This is because Sentientialism advocates – as must any nondualistic version of the Representational Theory of the Mind – that (1) beliefs cause actions, (2) the same belief in different agents should, other things being equal, cause the same actions, and (3) beliefs are enabled to cause the actions they do by virtue of the physical structure of the states realizing the beliefs. If PRIMUS and SECUNDUS use different mental languages while they both believe the same, then how is it possible that their same beliefs have all the same behavioral effects? The causes of their respective behavior are, as sentences in notationally different languages, physically different structures, and these physical differences should produce some different – even if esoteric – effects. But if there is some detectable difference in behavior, then what permits Sentientialism, insofar as it ascribes to Artificial Intelligence as a model of mentation, to attribute the same beliefs to PRIMUS and SECUNDUS?

If their use of notationally different mental languages secures membership in different cognitive kinds for PRIMUS and SECUNDUS, then they very well might exhibit some behavioral differences resulting from the notationally different structures presumed by Sentientialism to encode the same beliefs. But this would not obstruct the Sentientialist program. The thesis that sameness of belief entails sameness of behavior is certainly relative to kinds of cognitive agents. So much had better be respected by any theory of belief. Abelard and Brunelus, for example, are, according to our intuitive (and perhaps self-serving) fashion for distinguishing cognitive kinds, different kinds of cognitive agents, man and jackass. Apparently they might agree in some of their mental states. So suppose that they are both hungry, desire food, and believe of the carrot at the end of the stick that it is food. Abelard's belief might cause him to attempt to reach the carrot with his hands, Brunelus's belief might induce him to extend his neck. No one would take these differences to betray any cognitive difference. Hence, the simple fact that similarly situated agents of different cognitive kinds display some behavioral differences does not establish, on any adequate theory of the mind, that the agents must therefore have different beliefs. And this is quite independent of Sententialism. Thus the objection's dissatisfaction with Sententialism seems unfounded. Even if, by virtue of realizing different mental languages, cognitive agents (of different cognitive kinds) should act differently, it would remain for the objection to establish against Sententialism that this specific difference in activity entails a relevant difference in belief.

Besides, the differences between the activities of Abelard and Brunelus may be irrelevant to determining their behavior. While each moves in different ways to reach the carrot, they both do *try to reach the carrot.* The Sententialist can, in this case, say that in fact Abelard and Brunelus are *behaving* the same even though they are *moving* differently. The Sententialist's point, then, is that notationally, and hence physically, different mental sentences in different mental languages may, by the grace of their physically different notational structures, cause the agents in whom they are encoded to move differently. Nevertheless the difference in movement may not suffice for a difference in behavior. And it is difference in behavior that, for the moment, is at issue.

The objection can be put another way: PRIMUS and SECUNDUS, it is granted, rely on notationally different mental languages. That, according to Sententialism, implies that the structures that cause their behavior are fundamentally different. If so, this entails that PRIMUS and SECUNDUS must differ, at least potentially, in some of their behavior, not simply in some of their movements. It is here, the objection claims, that Sententialism founders. By allowing that PRIMUS and SECUNDUS are perfect simulations of one another, Sententialism is said to be unwittingly committed to the idea that notationally different agents need not differ behaviorally. The objection's contention thus is that Sententialism is locked into the inconsistency of supposing both that agents with differently notated mental languages can simulate one another perfectly and that notational divergence suffices for behavioral difference. From this it follows that Sententialism can hold that behavior is caused by the notational or physical character of states realizing mental representations only by undermining the cornerstone of Artificial Intelligence and denying that differently notated programs can simulate one another.

The Sententialist reply should be apparent. In agents of different cognitive kinds there will be physical aspects of the agents not included among those elements defining the notation of their mental languages. Brunelus, but not Abelard, has a tail; Abelard, but not Brunelus, is bipedal. That Brunelus has a tail and Abelard is bipedal is irrelevant to the structure of their mental notations. But, for all this, it remains possible that Brunelus's having a tail and Abelard's being bipedal respectively contribute to the production of their behavior. Both Abelard and Brunelus believe of the carrot that it is food. By hypothesis, their common belief is encoded in them in differently notated mental languages. How could this differently configured belief possibly result in the same behavior? It may well be that when notated as it is in a cognitive agent with a tail, it causes action A. And possibly, when notated as it is in a bipedal cognitive agent, it also causes action A. That is, although the belief is differently configured in different kinds of cognitive agents, it may have the same behavioral results because of its being encoded in physically different kinds of agents.

Put schematically, in Brunelus the belief may have physical structure F, in Abelard, physical structure $F^\star$. Brunelus's noncognitive elements constitute physical structure G. Abelard's noncognitive features are $G^\star$. Sententialism is consistent with both F, in the context of G, causing A and $F^\star$, in the context of $G^\star$, causing the same. If this is correct, then Sententialism can consistently maintain that agents equipped with differently notated mental languages can simulate the behavior of one another. Sententialism's notion of notation is not, as the objection would have it, inconsistent with the research program of Artificial Intelligence.

Of course, PRIMUS and SECUNDUS, as artificially intelligent agents, presumably can be realized in the same kind of device, if not the very same device. And so it may appear that reference to different mental languages instantiated in different natural kinds of cognitive agents is irrelevant to the objection's example of artificially intelligent agents possibly realized in the same, or same kind of, device.

Not so. Given the objection's assumption that PRIMUS and SECUNDUS represent in dramatically different notations within the same, or same kind of, device, we must ask how these different

39

notations function when realized. If PRIMUS and SECUNDUS are programs written in different programming languages ultimately compiled in the same machine language, then the objection's assumption that the notations of PRIMUS and SECUNDUS occur in different languages is violated. For the notation in which the representations properly occur can be taken as the same machine language.

Alternatively, if PRIMUS and SECUNDUS use programming languages that are, *somehow*, differently compiled so that PRIMUS and SECUNDUS are best construed as operating in ultimately different machine languages, then the assumption that these agents are realized in the same, or same kind of cognitive device, is falsified. Such devices can reasonably be classified according to machine language of use. And this language determines what physical states of the device count as essential to its operation. Should this be the case, then PRIMUS and SECUNDUS can be considered to be different kinds of cognitive agents employing different mental languages. They would then conform to the previous remarks about how Sententialism can acknowledge notational disparity among different kinds of cognitive agents. The same obviously can be said if the proprietary languages of PRIMUS and SECUNDUS should be taken to be the high-level programming languages in which they may be written. For, if proprietary, these languages too can serve to distinguish kinds of artificially intelligent agents.

These remarks might suggest that since selected cognitive agents may, for certain reasons, deploy different mental languages and, a fortiori, different notations with different causal powers, it is possible that representations agreeing in content produce in those agents markedly different types of behavior. If Martians and humans display different mental notations, they seemingly may behave quite differently even when the contents of their representations are identical. Indexical considerations aside, a representation in human mental notation meaning the same as 'This planet is my home' may, in specified circumstances, cause a human to try to franchise Earth. A presentation with the same meaning in Martian mental notation may, in the same circumstances, induce a Martian either to become an environmental activist or, bizarrely perhaps, to tap dance to a bagpipe rendition of "Smoke Gets in Your Eyes."

Taking this putative possibility seriously presupposes that in any given mental language any structure sufficient to cause behavior could carry any content. This, however, is simply not correct, at least if Sentientialism is right in assuming as a condition of belief ascription that the content of a physical structure is constrained by the behavior that structure is capable of producing. If, under certain specified conditions, a specific efficacious structure in a Martian's cognitive economy is capable of causing a Martian to tap dance to a bagpipe rendition of "Smoke Gets in Your Eyes," then it simply could not agree in content with 'This planet is my home'. In order for the mental structure to have that content, the Martian's tap dancing, so described, would need to be deducible, which it presumably is not, from the set of the Martian's current mental states taken as mental sentences one of which means the same as 'This planet is my home'. By Sentientialism's lights, the chain of events causing an agent's action, must, if the action is to qualify as intelligent behavior, conform to a rational inference of the action from a specification of the content of the structures in its causal chain. Here the counterexample falls down. The Martian's chain of mental states that cause the dancing cannot be construed as a rational inference.[40]

Evidently ascriptions of content to cognitive states are underdetermined by the evidence on which they are abductively based. Equally, assignments of mental content are typically (but not necessarily) holistic (as we will see in Chapter 4, Section 3) (Churchland, 1979; Stich, 1983). Normally content cannot be attributed to the structure causing the Martian to tap dance independent of content assignments to all cognitive states implicated in the causal sequence concluding with the tap dancing. As Quine (1960) has shown, there is no unique assignment of content to cognitive structures that satisfies the conditions on belief ascription laid down by Sentientialism. But that no more shows that cognitive structures do not have content or that it is unreasonable to attribute specific content to specific states than it indicates the same regarding overt natural languages (Chomsky, 1968, 1980; Stabler, 1985). Specification of content to any structures, internal or external to cognitive agents, is fraught with the problems typical of abductive inference. And although this is a problem Sentientialism must face, it is a

---

40 We shall look more closely at the character of the inferential chains leading from beliefs and desires to behavior in the first two sections of Chapter 3.

problem of a kind common to all theoretical endeavors in which explanation is not completely determined by the phenomena to be explained.

Let us return to the objection regarding PRIMUS and SECUNDUS. At the outset we assumed that they operated in different mental languages. Here we exchange that assumption and suppose that they employ the same mental language in simulating Abelard's wooing of Héloïse. Under this assumption it is not at all evident, contrary to what the objection would have, that they in fact do notationally diverge while enjoying the same beliefs and behavior. Within the same overt natural language, tokens exhibiting marked physical differences can count as tokens of the same type. There are countless ways of writing, printing, or uttering any given term, each token of which may exhibit striking physical differences to other tokens of its kind. So the sheer fact that PRIMUS and SECUNDUS deploy terms displaying certain physical differences does not of itself ensure that they use different notations in the same language. And should we endorse what the objection concedes, that PRIMUS and SECUNDUS do have the same beliefs, it is no longer evident that their notations could differ. If they do believe the same, there is prima facie evidence that the physical differences their terms display are irrelevant to determining the terms' assignments to notational types. Roughly, since their notations are to instantiate the same beliefs, there is every reason to consider the physical differences among their notations as irrelevant to their notational types.[41]

Nevertheless, suppose that we concede the notational divergence of PRIMUS and SECUNDUS, granting that one, but not the other, contains an inscription of 'I should begin each lecture to Héloïse by referring to Plato's *Symposium*'. Certainly, under the assumption that PRIMUS and SECUNDUS notationally diverge while sharing the same mental language, Sententialism will be unimpressed by the objection's claim that the three Abelards agree in belief. Attributions of belief to the Abelards, like such attributions generally, rely on behavioral evidence. Here the behavior of each of the Abelards is

---

41 Thus, Sententialism abjures strict synonymy in Mentalese. It insists that within a mental language every *notational* difference amounts to a semantic difference. Compare Fodor (1980a) and Maloney (1985b). Mentalese is not necessarily unique in lacking synonymy. Goodman (1949, 1972), for example, has argued that, contrary to appearance, natural languages are necessarily free of synonymy.

presumed to be indistinguishable, this supporting the ascription of the same mental states to each of the Abelards.

Once the situation is so described, however, a circumspect Sententialist can be excused for asking whether the description is consistent. According to the Sententialist scheme of things, beliefs cause behavior. Beliefs with different content cause, in at least some circumstances, different types of behavior. Moreover, Sententialism offers an explanation of both *how*, generally, beliefs could cause behavior and *how* beliefs with different content could produce different behavior. That is, Sententialism recounts *how* behavior could be appropriate to belief. Beliefs can generate behavior because they are physically realized as are sentences. As such, they have physical properties, some of which constitute their notational or syntactic properties. These properties reflect mental content, with difference in content being reflected by difference in notation.[42] It is the notational, qua physical, properties of mental sentences that directly cause behavioral events.[43] So, content varies with notation within

42 See Pylyshyn (1984, p. 74) for a similar account of Sententialism.
43 Yes, it would be wonderful to have an independent way of describing exactly which properties of a mental state are notational other than saying that such are the properties that enable the state to cause behavior. But such descriptions are surely the province of empirical enquiry, presumably including the intersection of neuroscience and linguistics. To appreciate the importance of fixing the notational or syntactic properties of Mentalese inscriptions, consider the case of a coffee machine designed to respond to quarters by producing cups of coffee. This machine cannot distinguish quarters from slugs of the same size and will produce cups of coffee when slugs are inserted. Slugs are physically distinguished from quarters in various ways that ensure that slugs and quarters will have different effects in some circumstances. Within the context of the coffee machine, however, these causal differences are latent. So there is a clear sense in which physically different objects can result in all and only the same behavior within the coffee machine. But – and still within the context of the coffee machine – quarters and slugs are evidently both tokens of the same physical type, namely, quarter-size, metallic disks. It is the size, weight, and shape of an inserted object to which the machine is designed to be sensitive. Only these properties are germane to establishing the notational or syntactic properties of tokens on which the machine operates. Under normal circumstances, these properties alone elicit behavior from the coffee machine. It is variation in these properties that results in variation in the machine's behavior. Perhaps to a dime or a similarly sized slug the machine responds with less coffee than if it had been fed a quarter or slug of the same dimensions. Importantly, once the parameters relevant for determining the notational properties of the machine's tokens are fixed, variation in those parameters produces variation in behavior.
  The case is presumably similar for PRIMUS and SECUNDUS. If, as by current assumption, they share the same programming language, then under some cir-

a mental language. Otherwise, there is no telling why or how beliefs with different content can produce different behavior.[44] Thus, all other types of mental states held constant, beliefs can cause behavior in such a way that differences in the contents of beliefs are manifested in differences in the types of behavior the beliefs produce. Conversely and other things being equal, perfect congruence in behavior of agents operating within the same mental language entails perfect congruence of belief. If the behavior of various agents within a cognitive kind, each of whom has the same mental language, is absolutely the same in all *possible* circumstances, then, desires fixed, the beliefs causing the behavior must also be the same.

This is not sheer, simpleminded verificationism applied to the mental language. The claim is not that, individually, each belief produces a unique bit of behavior. Rather, the idea is that each distinctive belief, in concert with who knows what other mental states, can make some difference, somewhere, to behavior broadly construed. After all, beliefs, at least for Sententialism, are theoretical posits functioning to explain behavior. Thus a difference in belief that has no conceivable bearing on behavior is no difference at all.

Now recall the objection's present assumption that the three Abelards are notationally different despite using the same mental language and concurring in all relevant behavior. This assumption is tantamount to saying that those properties of the Abelards' mental states that are implicated in the causation of their behavior are

cumstances there should be some variation in behavior resulting from notational variation in their functioning instructions. Otherwise, the physical differences separating their instructions would not count as notational. And this is just as certain differences between coins and slugs are not germane to the notational properties of inputs to the coffee machine.

44 We want two things here. First, within agents of a kind, difference in mental content implies difference in Mentalese notation. Second, still within agents of a kind, difference in Mentalese notation brings difference in content in its train. That difference in mental content entails difference in Mentalese notation follows from the fact that beliefs with different content can, under at least some identical circumstances, bring about different behavior. Beliefs cause behavior by way of their syntactic or notational properties. Thus, difference in content implies difference in behavior, which in turn implies difference in notation. That difference in Mentalese notation ensures difference in content is established since notational difference causes behavioral difference. Beliefs with the same content could not then be notationally different without thereby having different behavioral consequences. Circumstances held constant, however, beliefs with the same content are supposed to coincide in their resulting behavior. Otherwise, what sense is there to assigning the beliefs the same content? Hence, notational difference entails difference in content.

themselves different. If these etiologically empowered properties are different, then they must, as structures with different causal powers, potentially result in *some* different effects. By hypothesis the effects of these properties are instances of behavior and not just brute movements. Therefore, it could not be, as the objection blithely supposes, that the Abelards engage in all the same possible behavior. Or, to make much the same point in another way, if the Abelards notationally diverge while sharing a common mental language, then they could not perfectly concur in *both* belief and behavior. Otherwise there would be no general explanation whatsoever as to how differences in the contents of beliefs could contribute to differences in the overt behavior of cognitive agents. As a *methodological* matter, we should treasure explanation, as tentative and as incomplete as it may be, over fancifully proposed counterexamples. Accordingly Sententialism urges that the objection from the three Abelards is misconceived and thereby offers the beginning of an explanation of how belief might cause behavior.

Sententialism denies then that PRIMUS and SECUNDUS coincide in mental content *if* they diverge in mental notation within the same mental language. So Sententialism does not illumine what, exactly, either PRIMUS or SECUNDUS actually believes. But it never promised to provide a general criterion for correct belief ascription. Sententialism modestly attempts only to explain what beliefs generally are. It does not of itself pretend to determine precisely what any given agent may or must believe. In order best to ascertain the content of the beliefs of PRIMUS and SECUNDUS it may be necessary to look at *all* (or if that is impossible, then to an adequate sample) of the supposed behavioral consequences of their beliefs. We must note differences as they arise and, on that basis, postulate the content of states sufficient to explain these behavioral differences. We can do no better if we, with our feet firmly planted in folk psychology, insist that contentful mental states cause behavior. Nevertheless, this practice is obviously subject to the sort of fallibility typical of abductive inferences generally. We cannot escape the fact that conclusions concerning the content of mental states are normally not conclusively established by the data constituting their premises.

The Sententialist advocates, then, that, despite the statement of the objection, the three Abelards must have different beliefs if their beliefs are realized in different notations within the same language. Naturally the objector might ask why, in that case, do the Abelards exhibit the same behavior? Are not beliefs with different content supposed to result in different behavior? Well, yes. But the sheer statement of the example of the three Abelards is no proof that they could behave the same in all possible circumstances if the structures responsible for their behavior themselves are differently constituted. For, so constituted, these structures should, in some situations, lead to behavioral differences. Otherwise the notations would not be different. Difference in notation within a mental language is sufficient for difference in the effects of the notation since notational difference is, on the face of it, causal difference. The Sententialist, therefore, is not satisfied that the objection is itself coherent. After all, how could mental structures causing behavior both differ in their very causal properties and yet result in all the same possible behavioral effects? They could not. And that underwrites Sententialism's rejection of the objection's claim that PRIMUS and SECUNDUS coincide in all beliefs.

One way of illustrating this point is to note that the behavioral differences latent in the operations of PRIMUS and SECUNDUS can be elicited if a tracer should be appended to these programs. This tracer is simply a subroutine that makes PRIMUS and SECUNDUS print out each line of their respective programs as executed. Since PRIMUS and SECUNDUS notationally differ, they will in fact behave differently when they report their internal states. Let 'A' and 'B' be notationally different statements in the language in which PRIMUS and SECUNDUS are written. On some occasion, PRIMUS will report itself to be implementing 'A', and SECUNDUS will describe itself as executing 'B'. Their introspective reports will then mimic their notational differences. Thus the notational differences distinguishing PRIMUS and SECUNDUS ensure that some of their verbal behavior will indeed diverge. Hence, if we can attribute beliefs at all to PRIMUS and SECUNDUS, it is necessary minimally to concede that they have different introspective beliefs.[45]

45 One might insist that the objection is underwritten by an instrumentalist interpretation of belief ascriptions, an interpretation according to which references to beliefs as the causes of behavior fail to refer to actual efficacious structures internal to the agent. Rather, such ascriptions are, at best, promissory notes issued in ignorance of how behavior is actually produced. Although instrumentalism with respect to the mental may finally be correct, it is not ensured simply by the example of the three Abelards. Such instrumentalism and the fiscal metaphor used to convey it are, of course, Dennett's (1978c). See Stich (1983, pp. 242–6) for objections.

2

The frame problem and scripts

2.1. COMBINATORIAL EXPLOSION

Even if notational problems do not undermine Sententialism, other considerations may. No doubt we all can be said to have many unexpressed beliefs. It would seem that you believe, even if it has never occurred to you, that logicians do not live at the center of the sun, that you yourself are not now being swallowed by a vacuum cleaner, and who knows what else besides. Indeed, we each apparently have a massive, if not literally infinite, number of beliefs.[1] Were Sententialism correct, each of these beliefs would need to be encoded in each of us. Yet it hardly seems possible that we could contain so many Mentalese inscriptions, each of which would consume some space in our finite brains. Even if we have only a finite number of beliefs, they seem too many to fit within the limited space the brain affords. So, since Sententialism is deficient in the face of this simple fact about belief, it cannot long pose as a true theory of mentation.

The obvious response is that although there may be an infinite number of beliefs each of which we are, under certain circumstances, disposed to have, at no particular time do we actually have

---

1 The point belongs to Dennett (1978d). Although it may be easy to show that, on any given occasion, we possess abundant beliefs, it is somewhat more difficult to show that we can, and indeed do, have an infinite number of beliefs at any one time. If you are familiar with the natural numbers, you believe that the number 1 is not a cup of coffee, that the number 2 is not a cup of coffee, and *apparently* so on for each number. But this may be *only* apparent. As the numbers grow larger, you may find yourself saying, "Well, yes, I do believe that that very number is not a cup of coffee, but, to tell the truth, I never really thought of it before." And similarly, if presented with a drawing of a short straight line, you may be inclined to report that you believe of the (more than) infinite number of points on that line that none has a unique successor. Does that mean that, of each of those points in particular, you believe that it has no unique successor? Perhaps. Yet, if enough points are ostended you might find yourself saying, "Now that you draw my attention to it, I do believe of that very point that it has no unique successor. But I'm not so sure I had it in mind before you designated it."

infinitely many beliefs. Rather than actually having believed before it was suggested to you that logicians do not live at the center of the sun, you were merely disposed so to believe. When the suggestion arose, you came to believe as disposed. This new belief was implanted in accordance with the computational processes governing your doxastic system as it applied to your then-current store of beliefs. Given what you believed and heard, you calculated, and so came to believe, that logicians do not live at the center of the sun. The example, then, simply fails to show that on any occasion we must actually possess too many beliefs to be sententially encoded within our brains. Thus we need not fear that the objection has shown Sententialism's realistic characterization of belief to be fatuous.[2]

Nevertheless, the objection might take another tack, proposing that behavioral evidence suggests that our beliefs are more plentiful than Sententialism can plausibly allow. Beliefs are presumably among the causes of behavior and thus figure in the explanation of any given bit of behavior. Differences in behavior are, at least partially, to be traced to differences in belief. Now, given only changes in a person's external, nonmental circumstances, the person typically will engage in different and even new behavior. The range of coordinated circumstantial and behavioral variation seems nearly limitless. For example, Abelard may transport himself from the university to the cathedral and alter his behavior to suit his location without changing many, if any, of his beliefs. Surely, the objection continues, this adaptivity to varying circumstances is attributable to the fact that Abelard must have all the beliefs necessary to accommodate his corresponding behavior. And the number of beliefs required is certainly too immense to admit of encoding in Abelard's brain. So the beliefs Abelard *has* are not restricted to those he *encodes*. Yet it is the beliefs that Abelard has that enter into the explanations of his behavior. The only way to allow for all this is to suppose, contrary to Sententialism, that beliefs are nothing other than dis-

---

2 Cognitive psychologists have distinguished between short- and long-term memory, noting that the contents of short-term memory persist only briefly and typically do not survive for storage in long-term memory (Brown, 1958; Peterson and Peterson, 1959; Neisser, 1966; Anderson, 1980). This is a happy fact for Sententialism. Otherwise the constant barrage of perceptual information would overwhelm our storage facilities.

positions to behave, that beliefs are not explicitly encoded sentences looking for *lebensraum* in an agent's head.

First, it is not clear that the objection is coherent. Abelard's behavior is supposed to accommodate his changing locations without requiring variation in his belief store. His behavior is certainly contingent, however, on his perceiving the changes in his surroundings. And this perceptual evidence constitutes an alteration in Abelard's beliefs, even if the emendation is of only brief duration. Thus Sententialism does not require quite the stock of beliefs that the objection supposes.

Second, the objection trades on the worry that a finite agent could not store all the beliefs requisite to explain his or her behavior. It would rather exchange the Sententialist's too numerous Mentalese sentences with just the appropriate number and variety of dispositions to behave. Sententialism will not be much impressed by the objection. Just how many dispositions are necessary to enable an agent to act as able? Lots. Now, dispositions require physical bases. If Abelard is disposed, under some circumstances, to sing the blues and, under other circumstances, to sing vespers, some physical feature of Abelard enables the first disposition and – presumably – another physical feature the second. And how many such features of Abelard must there be if he is to act as disposed? Exactly as many as the beliefs Abelard is conceded to have since, according to the objection, beliefs and dispositions to behave come to the same thing. This is exactly as many as the encoded sentences the Sententialist seems forced to postulate. So the Sententialist might reasonably ask whether the objection can consistently deny that Abelard could encode as many beliefs as necessary to behave as he is disposed while also affirming that Abelard is stocked with as many physical bases of dispositions as necessary to behave as he might. If there is room enough in an agent to accommodate a dispositional analysis of belief, there is space sufficient to satisfy Sententialism, if dispositions to behave, like mental sentences, are rooted in physical structures internal to agents.

On behalf of the objection, one might conjecture that various of Abelard's behavioral dispositions might be rooted in a single physical structure. Salt is disposed to dissolve in both water and beer. Both dispositions are set in the same chemical configuration. So, by analogous reasoning, one might suppose that Abelard's many dispositions to behave arise from a stock of internal physical structures small enough in number to be accommodated by Abelard's central nervous system.

If this should suffice to preserve the objection, then much the same can be said for Sententialism. The Sententialist is equally free to hypothesize that a wide range of Abelard's behavior is the result of the interaction of a manageably finite set of sententially encoded beliefs. As Abelard's circumstances vary, different subsets of his set of beliefs may be called on to produce variation in his behavior. Thus it would seem that Sententialism and the present objection are on all fours together.

Besides, a Sententialist is free to construe some belief ascriptions as veiled attributions of dispositions to believe. Yet this does not force the Sententialist to endorse a dispositional analysis of belief according to which a belief is *nothing other* than a disposition to act in prescribed ways under certain circumstances. This is not altered by the fact that, ideally, beliefs do produce in agents dispositions to act in ways typically coordinate with the agent's desires. Rather than ascribe to a dispositional analysis of belief, in particular, and mentation, in general, the Sententialist supposes that *some* of our casual attributions of belief are literally false. Prior to its suggestion, you did not actually believe, although – given what you did believe – you were disposed to believe, that logicians do not live at the center of the sun. The ascription to you of this belief before it was suggested to you is, if true in any way, best construed as attributing to you what you would be inclined to believe should you but consider it. The only way to have a belief, if Sententialism is correct, is to have an internal sentential representation whose content is characteristic of the belief. Agents, then, can be disposed to believe and have dispositions to act by virtue of actually believing what they do believe, although actually to believe is sententially to represent, not simply to be disposed to act.[3]

It is one of the special virtues of Sententialism that it does not propose that beliefs are analyzable as dispositions. It maintains that,

---

3 Also, as is well known (Bennett, 1964, pp. 60–4), dispositional analyses of mental states are typically and debilitatingly circular. Dispositional accounts suppose beliefs to be dispositions to act in certain ways, given certain desires. But desires are rendered as dispositions to act in certain ways, given certain beliefs. Evidently, then, dispositional analyses of intentional states are doomed if the analyses eschew intentional idioms.

relative to prevailing circumstances, including desires, agents are usually inclined to act as they do as a result of believing what they actually do. Dispositions are rooted in physical bases or structures, and reference to a disposition always carries with it the obligation ultimately to explain how the disposition arises from its instantiating structure.[4] Sententialism is a schema for an explanation of how dispositions to behave arise out of beliefs. Beliefs, for Sententialism, are physically encoded sentences internal to cognitive agents that cause behavior through their syntactic or notational properties. The semantic properties of the same representations reveal that the causal chains in which the representations occur also are themselves derivations of, or inferences to, the resultant behavior from its mental causes. The attraction of Sententialism, then, is that it not only accommodates the undeniable fact that, always relative to context, cognitive agents are disposed to act in accordance with their beliefs but also indicates how these dispositions are set. That these dispositions are thus secured ensures that the overt activity emanating from the dispositions can be intentionally characterized. A bit of behavior, say an act of tap dancing, is properly described as tap dancing, rather than simply as the sequence of bodily movements it happens to be, since it is only as described as tap dancing that the behavior is semantically related to, or otherwise derivable from, its cognitive causes, causes themselves construed as contentful mental representations. But let us set this aside until Chapter 3, Section 3.1.

Sententialism proposes, then, that some belief ascriptions should be taken not as predicating beliefs to agents but rather as saying what the agents are inclined to come to believe on the basis of what they currently do believe. This doctrine does not, as we have already noted, thereby embrace the idea that an agent's current beliefs must all be conscious to the agent or that the agent must be able to testify to the occurrence of derivations of new beliefs as they arise from old. It would be futile, not to say stupid, to ignore the impressive

---

4 Functional characterizations of mental states and processes, including programs and models spawned by Artificial Intelligence, may analyze a particular mental state as the typical effect of certain states and typical cause of others. Such explanations must finally be underwritten by descriptions of how these states could enter into these causal relations. These latter descriptions may advert to the structure of programming and machine languages, though at last there must be reference to the engineering making all this possible (Dennett, 1978c; Paul Churchland, 1982).

results of cognitive psychology establishing the occurrence of un-conscious mental processing (Lackner and Garrett, 1973; Nisbett and Wilson, 1977). Sentientialism is quite content to maintain that an agent's occurrent encoded beliefs can be largely unconscious and that the processes in which these beliefs figure may themselves go undetected, and perhaps be undetectable, by the agent. If this is so, then we must ask exactly which belief ascriptions, according to Sentientialism, pick out current beliefs and which ascriptions, though literally false, designate beliefs an agent currently lacks but is inclined to adopt.

Ascriptions of beliefs are, in the first place, hypotheses advanced to explain an agent's behavior (Sellars, 1963). As such, they should conform to principles of parsimony common to scientific expla-nation. Sentientialism proposes that only those beliefs necessary to explain an agent's behavior over a specified range of time and cir-cumstances are properly attributed as currently lodged in memory, short and long term. It is for successful cognitive psychology to determine the principles of perception and memory that determine belief acquisition, retention, and decay. And, equally evident, the principles of computation – the system of (presumably rational) belief transformation and generation – on which cognitive science settles will also influence which beliefs are properly attributed to an agent. Fixing these principles is just as clearly the task of em-pirical inquiry as is establishing the laws of biology. Thus, although Sentientialism can lay down the most general tenets dictating the conditions under which belief ascriptions are literally true of an agent, it is finally up to cognitive science to ascertain what any given agent actually believes. Cognitive agents themselves may, of course, advance hypotheses as to what they themselves believe, and these hypotheses will normally command respect. But such avowals of cognitive agents, even if predicated on privileged information, must in the end meet the same canons of confirmation as the belief ascriptions advanced by the cognitive scientist.

As Dennett (1978d, e) rightly notes, avoiding an infinitely large store of internally encoded beliefs by appealing to a limited store of current beliefs and a (perceptual) system or process for generating new from old beliefs imposes on Sentientialism the burden of re-solving the so-called *frame problem* (McCarthy and Hayes, 1969, pp. 487–90, 499; Raphael, 1971; Boden, 1977, p. 386; Fodor, 1983 and Haugeland, 1985). The problem is to explain how, especially in the context of belief-directed action, an agent's potential beliefs are extracted or computed from those the agent actually has. This is no simple matter. Given an occasion on which it is appropriate for an agent to revise his or her beliefs in a specific way, the task, from the Sententialist perspective, is to explain how the agent's cognitive system is able exactly to identify antecedently stored mental representations, including both specific representations of fact and applicable general rules of deliberation or inference, which collectively deliver appropriate modifications of the agent's belief store. When Abelard realizes that he will be separated from Héloïse and forced to retire to a monastery, many of his former beliefs require revision. Which ones and in which ways? Must Abelard's cognitive system undertake to examine each of his beliefs and each of its consequences in order to estimate whether they are consistent with his newly acquired beliefs? If so, it would appear that, given realistic limitations on computing time and space, his cognitive system could never hope to pursue and check the more than myriad representations necessary to complete the process of revision.

In order to settle on the appropriate representations for revision in his or her belief store an agent must effectively determine which are germane. How, precisely, is this done short of a combinatorily explosive search through all the agent's representations and their consequences? No ingenious little person inside the agent's head monitors the situation, calling up just those of the agent's mental representations that apply. Equally evident, the process cannot involve a mechanism that computes new beliefs by selecting from a store of actually encoded beliefs those relevant for inferring the new beliefs if the mechanism must first *infer* which of its own private stock of encoded principles of selection and inference apply in the given case. That would circularly presuppose the very process to be explained, namely, how a cognitive agent derives new from old beliefs.

Sententialism's difficulty here is to expose, without a circular or otherwise illicit appeal to intentionally characterized processes, how a cognitive agent, when presented with either novel data or the necessity of generating new from antecedently stored information, is able to select, modify, and extend current representations. In this regard, Sententialism may appeal to the limited success of Artificial Intelligence with the frame problem. Chess-playing programs, for example, vary in their success in balancing their need exhaustively to search through the consequences of all possible moves in a situation with constraints imposed by time and computational resources (Waltz, 1982). The more successful programs engage in modestly deep searches inspired by ingenious heuristic strategies for determining which possible moves merit serious consideration and which should be ignored. The price such programs pay is that they occasionally ignore some of the better, if not also the best, moves. What, if anything, is to be learned from this is that, probably, cognitive agents generally also rely on heuristics that are compromises between the ideal of complete and consistent belief modification and the limitations of time, space, and energy available to the agent's brain or computational center. In other words, if cognitive agents are able adequately to modify their belief stores, they will suffer some mistakes. But that is not news, is it?

Schank and Abelson (1977) and Schank (1982) have had some promising results in composing programs able to answer questions about certain limited types of stories, and their work can be construed, consistent with Sententialism, as approximating the kind of data-handling abilities someday to be found in cognitive agents.[5] Schank and Abelson adopt the hypothesis that the mind contains large, topic-specific structures of representations – scripts – designed so as to facilitate and constrain searches through and modifications of the structures.

Abelard, on their scheme, would have a script pertaining to his relationship with Héloïse, which script would be activated by receipt of representations whose syntactic properties reflect their semantic property of being about Héloïse.[6] Once activated, the script

5 Minsky's (1975) work on frames is also relevant here, although we need not distinguish between frames and scripts. See also Winograd (1971) and Bobrow and Winograd (1977). Compare Fodor (1983) and Chomsky (1980) for discussions of evidence supporting the idea that some of the operations of the mind are modular, that some mental faculties are naturally structured in domain-specific ways to facilitate their information processing. See Anderson (1983) for arguments to the contrary. Brand (1984, p. 232) argues that Schank and Abelson's work is a significant contribution to the solution of the frame problem as it bears on action theory. Fodor (1983, pp. 112 and 128) worries that the frame problem may stymie any attempt to provide a computational model of those mental processes that govern general belief fixation.

6 It may be that not all of Abelard's beliefs about Héloïse come into play. Abelard, in some sense, can be said to believe that the mole on Roscelin's nose is not Héloïse's maternal grandmother. Apparently this belief very well may not enter into Abelard's normal ruminations about Héloïse. So we await an explanation of why only some of Abelard's beliefs about Héloïse are relevant to his reflecting

would admit of only certain, limited searches and modifications. Although these might not be epistemologically ideal, in that they might preclude Abelard from registering important new – or erasing wasteful old – information, they nevertheless could be tailored to enable him to log new information while modifying some of what he already possesses. In any event, there is no reason to believe that cognitive agents actually do abide by epistemologically ideal doxastic procedures (Tversky and Kahneman, 1974). What Sententialism wants is some sort of start on an explanation of how cognitive agents might handle the frame problem, and scriptlike structures may be the first step. Still, Artificial Intelligence is an immature science, and it is too early to tell with much assurance whether or to what extent, compatible with Sententialism, it can lay open the processes of cognition. Nonetheless the prospects are not without hope. What is centrally important is that advances in Artificial Intelligence strongly suggest that it is an empirical question as to how, consistent with Sententialism, the mind generates and modifies its beliefs. Certainly nothing known to date entails that the problem is in principle beyond solution because based on a false Sententialist presupposition. One thing is evident: Naturally intelligent agents are solutions to the frame problem. What remains to be demonstrated against Sententialism is that the solution to the frame problem is incompatible with cognitive agents processing information as if the information were encoded as sentences. Pending that proof, there is no more reason to forswear Sententialism than there is to abjure any plausible theory in any yet to be completed area of research. That a theory awaits extension to solve all problems in its domain is not a certain sign of its inadequacy and instead may be an invitation to attempt its extension. Thus the frame problem's call for solution is not itself a refutation of Sententialism although it certainly illustrates that Sententialism, as a

about his relationship with her. The point to adverting to Artificial Intelligence here is that the relevance in question is to be empirically determined. Notice, by comparison, that not every fact about lung cancer is germane to the study of the disease's etiology. That the cancer in Roscelin's lung is not Héloïse's maternal grandmother is a fact about lung cancer that nobody expects to contribute to the understanding of the affliction. This certainly is an empirical fact. The point is that just as cancer research must delineate the relevant from the nonrelevant, so too must Artificial Intelligence. And just as this does not in principle preclude a science of cancer, neither does it in principle render hopeless a science of intelligence, artificial or not.

general account of mentation, is subject to, though not yet a casualty of, empirical disconfirmation.

Dreyfus (1979, 1981) is perhaps the most outspoken skeptic regarding the prospects for a solution to the frame problem arising from Artificial Intelligence.[7] Although his arguments are varied and typically directed at specific research programs, two themes pervade his writing. First, understanding a concept typically involves knowing, among other things, an utterly enormous number of facts. To appreciate, for example, what a chair is, one needs to be able to recognize a wide variety of types of chairs. That apparently requires knowing, among other things, about the construction, purpose, and use of chairs. In understanding the notion of a chair, one seemingly must realize how the functional roles of chairs cohere with those of other artifacts. Indeed, to comprehend fully what it is to be a chair involves knowing a fair amount about human beings, including what makes for their comfort and the etiquette they follow when using and providing chairs. The list of what one must know in order to understand completely the notion of a chair is so surprisingly extensive and varied that compiling representations constituting the common knowledge of chairs would be a herculean chore (Putnam, 1983; Stich, 1983). Yet surely it is necessary to understand what a chair is in order to understand a story, say about a visit to a restaurant, in which chairs may figure. The same evidently can be said regarding all the various artifacts, foods, practices, and roles normally encountered in restaurants. Representing the knowledge of all such things and how they interact – and it is a massive amount of knowledge, especially when measured in terms of the sentences it would take to represent it – is what is required of any frame or script that can plausibly claim to represent what is

---

7 Dreyfus considers Artificial Intelligence to be a failed research program on almost all counts. Although I shall urge in Chapter 5 that, under one interpretation, unaided Artificial Intelligence will probably not provide the sort of full understanding of intelligence it promises, I do not endorse Dreyfus's general critique of Artificial Intelligence. See Dretske (1985) for remarks to the effect that one can concede that Artificial Intelligence might, in its golden age, be an adequate model or simulation of natural intelligence while also denying that artificially intelligent systems genuinely understand anything. Here I am concerned only with Dreyfus's remarks on the ability of Artificial Intelligence to meet the frame problem.

cognitively presupposed in fully understanding a tale about a restaurant. Nonetheless, Dreyfus adds, no fabricated frames or scripts now begin to approximate such systems of representation, and, more important, it is unlikely that anyone could assemble scripts adequate to mimic the understanding displayed by natural agents in their intelligent commerce with the nearly innumerable different types of situations they regularly encounter.

To all this the natural reply is yes, *fully* understanding any given concept is holistic and requires knowing how that concept fits in with other concepts we may have. But that should not blind us to the fact that understanding a concept is a matter of degree. Young children certainly know less about the place of chairs in human culture than do furniture designers, but surely children can and, indeed, do have – to some degree – the concept of a chair. It is also obvious that adults within a given culture can diverge in their knowledge of chairs and still be said to understand what a chair is.[8] Once it is recognized that concepts typically admit of acquisition by degree, there should be less reservation in accepting scripts. They are representations of systems of concepts, and if the concepts they represent come in degrees, then so too for the representational adequacy of scripts themselves. Different scripts on a common theme may vary in their conceptual sophistication just as do people. Although artificially composed scripts cannot hope to approach the comprehension enjoyed by a functioning adult human, they may still model genuine, even if truncated, knowledge structures. Indeed, in fields that are well defined, such as medical diagnosis and projectile guidance, there is reason to believe that artificially intelligent expert systems are as knowledgeable as necessary to simulate a high, albeit narrow, degree of intelligence. Besides, it takes a naturally intelligent human agent years to lay down the information that guides his or her behavior. People are information sponges, continually soaking up behavior-modifying information. It is thus no surprise that constructing adequate artificial

8 And, as Putnam (1975b) urges, one's understanding of a concept may not necessitate one's knowing very much about the concept, so long as there are experts within one's community who are fully informed about the concept. A layperson who is passably conversant, but not particularly knowledgeable, about elms and electrons can be said to have the concepts of them, even if he or she does not know much of either, in part because botanists and physicists in the general linguistic community do. Were this not so, then none of us could, as we surely do, have many of the concepts intuitively attributable to us.

scripts is so arduous and subject to so many limitations. Simply discovering what knowledge is normally deployed by a naturally intelligent agent in understanding a familiar type of situation is itself a difficult enterprise. We are not at all good at explaining what we ourselves understand by a particular concept. This contributes to the difficulty of constructing scripts. What is understood in a concept cannot simply be what people say they understand by a concept.

Dreyfus seems to maintain that the limitations on the information a frame or script records as characteristic of a type of situation shows not only that naturally intelligent agents do not employ similar data structures in understanding but also, and paramountly, that natural agents do not utilize representations of the sort found in artificially intelligent devices. If this last were so, then Dreyfus's complaint against Artificial Intelligence would cut deeply into Sententialism itself. For Sententialism concurs with Artificial Intelligence in supposing that mental representations are (sentential) structures whose syntactic properties centrally figure in the production of behavior. Nevertheless, once we recognize that understanding a concept admits of degrees, we can see that Dreyfus's indictment of scripts does not dislodge the Sententialist thesis that mental representations are sentential structures. Dreyfus simply fails to show that scripts do not underwrite or otherwise model intelligent, even if limited, comprehension of concepts. A script-driven, artificially intelligent agent may not perfectly simulate our understanding of chairs, but from this alone it does not follow that it simulates our understanding not at all. Failing that, it remains, consistent with Sententialism, possible that intelligent agents deploy sentential representations in understanding concepts. Thus, insofar as scripts enable Artificial Intelligence to address the frame problem, Sententialism may continue to hope that it can look to Artificial Intelligence for an explanation of how naturally intelligent agents defuse the threat of combinatorial explosion.

There remains to be considered the second of Dreyfus's themes on what he takes to be the illicit appeal of Artificial Intelligence to scripts in order to resolve the frame problem. The context of an agent is crucial to determining exactly how his or her mental states change in response to new situations. By an agent's context we are to understand the social and cultural practices germane to the agent's situation.[9] Also included are the prevailing physical array and the agent's relevant skills and states, both cognitive and not. These context-determining elements are to be culled from an indefinitely large range of states, practices, skills, and physical facts that are, on any particular occasion, generally irrelevant to the current course of the agent's mental life. For example, if you are deeply depressed about your recent divorce, famished, and a gifted athlete, your reaction to a story about a couple's visit to a romantic restaurant before attending the seventh game of the World Series might differ radically from the reaction of a recently fed, athletically inept newlywed. If frames or scripts guide an agent's reaction to or interpretation of a story or situation, then – according to Dreyfus – the difference between your and the newlywed's reactions should be attributable to differences in the scripts you two deployed. And this difference apparently is to be traced to differences, among other things, in your moods, physical states, and abilities, differences that seem to be noncognitive.[10]

Proposals from within Artificial Intelligence for resolving the frame problem typically require representations of those elements that, in fact, fix the context that determines the selection of frame or script. Yet, Dreyfus argues, there is simply no way for these representations reliably to be generated once the artificially intelligent agent is not assured of meeting situations and contexts contrived to conform to the scripts it is prepared to utilize. That would first require the agent to detect cognitively which of all possibly relevant contextual factors are actually relevant. And that, in turn, would presuppose what is to be explained, namely, how new mental representations are generated from old. Or to put the same differently, calling up a frame or script of mental representations to serve in the processing of new information is itself a process requiring explanation. Why call up this frame or script rather than another? Thus it is

9 Compare Burge (1979) for an argument that linguistic practice partially determines the content of mental states.
10 Haugeland (1981b) too fears that moods and skills are beyond the explanatory reach of cognitive science and Artificial Intelligence. Compare Pylyshyn's (1984, pp. 263–72) and Fodor's (1975, pp. 197–205) remarks to the effect that it may be an unwarranted a priori assumption to suppose that the domain of a mature cognitive science must include all of the phenomena bequeathed to scientific psychology by popular wisdom.

of no avail to refer to a process that would, as Artificial Intelligence apparently requires, itself circularly involve the deployment of a frame.[11]

The only way out, according to Dreyfus, is to recognize that genuinely intelligent agents either are in, and (cognitively) influenced by, contexts without mentally representing the elements in those contexts or else use "informal" representations of their contexts, representations of the sort anathema to Artificial Intelligence and the formal operations it presupposes. More simply, Dreyfus would have it that our ability to call up cognitive scripts, if such there be, is itself a noncognitive ability, an instance of *knowing how* rather than *knowing that*. Calling on a script is not, if Dreyfus is right, adequately explained solely by reference to what an agent either explicitly or implicitly believes. The ability to deploy a script is, for Dreyfus, noncognitive in a sense analogous to that in which the ability to breathe is noncognitive. Knowing how to breathe presumably enables one to breathe without the intervention of cognitive processes. Similarly, the ability to call up a frame enables one to draw on a frame without the drawing itself depending on cognitive processing. Thus, insofar as the study of Artificial Intelligence is restricted to the arena of mental representations and computational cognitive processes, it alone cannot hope to provide a solution to the frame problem.

The Sententialist response is that certainly the cognitive processes that arise within us are partially a function of the situations or contexts in which we find ourselves. And yes, these contexts may involve noncognitive elements, perhaps including moods, abilities, and who knows what else besides. It would be unreasonable for anyone to deny that. But presumably the interaction of context and

11 Pylyshyn (1984, pp. 220–3) also worries that state-of-the-art frames and scripts fail to show how the mind modifies its belief store since it remains an open question how it selects frames or scripts for application in any given situation. Pylyshyn (pp. 220–1) puts it this way: "Among the proposals for dealing with this combinatorial problem are such large-scale data structures as 'frames' (Minsky, 1975) and 'scripts' (Schank and Abelson, 1977). Even if there is something like these structures, however, they are relatively easy for people to override, given the motivation (that is, they are cognitively penetrable). In other words, people can still use arbitrary knowledge of the world to understand sentences and scenes; you cannot exclude any part of the knowledge base in advance, using some general prestructuring of that knowledge. Therefore, the content of such structures as frames and scripts must themselves be both analyzable and subject to reasoning by their users, which puts us back *almost* where we started."

60

cognition is a lawful process, even if the laws are poorly understood. However, there is, for all that Dreyfus says, simply no reason to suppose that such laws could not in fact bind artificial cognitive scripts to their contexts, whatever they might be. Such laws could well ensure that contexts simply cause scripts to be deployed without the laws themselves being represented.[12] For all we know, contexts of the sort Dreyfus has in mind are themselves relative to the type of cognitive agent in question. Certain factors relevant to specifying the context of a human agent may be irrelevant to setting the context for a Martian. This might be so if either the physiologies or cultures of humans and Martians are worlds apart. Similarly, what is characteristic of the context of an artificial device possessed of real intelligence (supposing for the moment that there are such devices) need not be at all similar to what sets the context of a naturally intelligent agent. So, while our culture may contribute to our context, it may not figure in that of a programmable silicon device. Its contextual factors may be utterly alien to us, thereby blinding us to their interaction with the internal processes of the device. Whereas art and politics may matter to our cognitive contexts, current and temperature may set the context for the silicon device.

Once we allow that subsequent generations of artificially intelligent devices may be contextually dependent for their cognitive processing, Dreyfus's complaint against the possibility of their standing as solutions to the frame problem withers. For a device equipped with a sufficiently wide array of scripts called according to certain lawful, albeit noncognitive, relations obtaining between the device and its proper contexts would have a claim to having

---

12 How could a causal activation of a script be noncognitive? How could a noncognitive call to a script not involve perception, a thoroughly cognitive phenomenon? Mathematics is, for most, a difficult subject to think about. Some of those who find mathematics tiresome enjoy daydreaming of baseball. No one knows why this is so but it is conceivable – even if the details are certainly fictitious – that thought about mathematics literally demands more energy than does thought about baseball. It is conceivable that when one's energy level hits a certain pitch, the mind is thereby caused to turn to mathematics, and when energy drops below a certain critical level thoughts of baseball inevitably arise. If something *remotely* like this is the case, if mental functioning is a partial function of environmental changes that affect, but are not sensed by, the mind, then whether a script is deployed could be a partial function of selected noncognitive states of an agent. These states would themselves be the effects of environmental conditions constituting an agent's prevailing context.

61

solved the frame problem. Obviously no one now knows the details of such an artificial device, the data structures it would require, or the contexts to which it would be subject and sensitive. But neither, according to Dreyfus (1981, pp. 181–2), can anyone precisely say what constitutes the context of any particular natural exercise of cognition.[13] So just as our present inability to formulate the contexts of natural cognition does not preclude natural, even if not yet understood, solutions to the frame problem, so too our ignorance of what might constitute artificial cognitive contexts does not prevent the possibility of there being artificial solutions to the frame problem. Admittedly such solutions may not much resemble current ones that ignore context. But that is primarily due to the fact that current research reasonably takes the path of idealization, ignoring for now the issue of context by taking it as given and focusing on the data structures required of rudimentary scripts.

Suppose then that Dreyfus is right in maintaining that noncognitive elements play an essential role in determining an agent's cognitive reaction to a situation. Assume additionally that we come to understand better what constitutes the noncognitive context of a cognitive episode. Artificial Intelligence would then be positioned to devise programs to be run in devices that, like naturally intelligent agents, are so constructed as to be causally affected by, without cognitively representing, those factors constituting their contexts. Such devices would instantiate programs incorporating scripts that would assume control just in case the contextual factors relevant to the proper selection of those scripts were to happen causally to impinge on sensors or reactors figuring in the devices' hardware but not in their software. These artificially, even if not genuinely, intelligent agents would, then, be remarkable simulations of naturally intelligent agents.

Much the same can be said differently. Dreyfus's argument can be taken as a challenge to build a device that simulates natural learning.[14] Learning certainly must be the paradigmatic solution to the frame problem. No doubt, learning involves an impressive host

13 Dreyfus (1981, pp. 202–3) goes farther, saying not only that no one now knows how to describe completely the constituents of contexts sufficient for fixing the proper selection of scripts but also that it is in principle impossible to formulate such descriptions. Nevertheless, I find no compelling argument to substantiate this very strong claim.
14 See Boden (1977, pp. 247–97) for a survey of artificially intelligent simulations of learning.

of relations between an agent and his or her world. Still, Dreyfus has not given us reason to suppose that this system of relations could not, like other complicated relations, be artificially simulated.[15] And if it can be, then there is reason to suspect that his argument against the possibility of Artificial Intelligence ever coming upon a solution to the frame problem is itself mistaken.

2.3. MODULAR COGNITIVE SYSTEMS

Dreyfus is not alone in his conviction that the frame problem represents an insurmountable difficulty to Sententialism. Fodor (1983, p. 112) too, but for reasons of his own, worries that the nature of belief fixation may preclude a computational explanation of the frame problem consistent with Sententialism. According to Fodor, there is reason to suppose that an agent's system of belief, like the body of scientific principles and facts, is, as he says, isotropic and Quinean. A system of belief is isotropic if any belief within the system can affect the confirmation of any other belief. Such a system is Quinean if its method of belief confirmation is typically conservative and sensitive to systematic properties such as simplicity. In contrast to isotropic and Quinean information systems are encapsulated, modular systems in which only differentially selected bits of information already stored in the system can be deployed in confirming any new bit of information. Fodor takes the natural process of belief fixation to be nondemonstrative inference that results in an isotropic and Quinean system of belief. If Fodor is right, this is what makes the frame problem so very intractable. Any script that marks off as relevant for processing a subset of beliefs is bound to be implausible as a solution to the frame problem.

15 Of course, simulation of intelligence need not constitute intelligence. I am not urging that a program that successfully solves the frame problem and so, for example, perfectly mimics a naturally intelligent agent in his or her analysis of a story, would thereby literally understand the story, i.e., understand the story in exactly the sense in which a naturally intelligent agent would. All that I am arguing here is that Sententialism requires a solution to the frame problem and that Artificial Intelligence may reveal that solution. That is, Artificial Intelligence may establish what sort of processes a naturally intelligent agent undergoes in order to establish a cognitive frame of reference. But this is not to say that anything that undergoes such a process must possess genuine understanding. Instantiating a solution to the frame problem, though necessary for intelligence if Sententialism is true, need not suffice. More on this, as previously promised, in Chapter 5.

For by the nature of scripts, it must ignore an arbitrarily large number of beliefs within the system. Yet these beliefs partially determine how modification of any belief within the system is to occur. The idea, then, is that the frame problem amounts to the problem of explaining the nature of scientific confirmation, something about which very little is known except that it seems immune to a formalistic solution (Putnam, 1983).

Fodor argues that belief fixation is isotropic and Quinean under the assumption that it is a process of rational nondemonstrative inference. That is to say that a cognitive agent settles on a belief by virtue of formulating a hypothesis to the best explanation relative to what information happens to be delivered from the agent's ancillary, modular information-processing systems in addition to whatever is already stored in memory. The details of this process are, flirting with understatement, not well understood. So Fodor supposes that we might be best served by looking at them in the light of what we do know of the formation of scientific theory, that paradigm of rational nondemonstrative inference. It is this that sanctions his claim that belief fixation is isotropic and Quinean.

We should notice here, however, that while science certainly *ought* to be isotropic and Quinean, it surely does not achieve its ideal. Actually accepted scientific hypotheses typically are not gauged against *everything* already known to science. Physicists simply do not normally attend to everything economists, zoologists, and linguists have to say. Although a scientific hypothesis ideally should weather exposure to everything antecedently known, in practice the separate sciences suffer from limited encapsulation. If, then, belief fixation is akin to scientific progress, we should anticipate that it is perfectly isotropic and Quinean only in the fiction of the ideal situation but much less so in the actual case. Supporting this is the well-known fact that we are less than epistemically ideal cognitive agents (Tversky and Kahneman, 1974). That our errors in belief fixation are systematic and susceptible to study indicates that the processes implicated in belief fixation are, at best, only imperfectly isotropic and Quinean. The processes actually governing belief fixation in nature are thus not to be confused with those that might determine epistemically ideal processes (Heil, 1985).

We should anticipate, then, that our processes of belief fixation are marked by some measure of encapsulation, that beliefs are in fact fixed in ways that ignore the actual epistemic significance of some antecedent beliefs on candidates for fixation. Tversky and Kahneman (1974) report, for example, that subjects typically respond to classification problems in ways that betray that they ignore crucial information they possess. Told of the distribution of professions across a designated population, subjects, when provided uninformative descriptions of members of the population, tend to classify the described members according to profession in ways that are oblivious to the known distribution of professions. This amounts to saying that it is likely that the range of beliefs that actually come into play in the fixation of any particular belief is constrained in some important way. Hence, the beliefs an agent deploys in evaluating for acceptance any given hypothesis are probably restricted according to some heuristic. Perhaps the demands of the task at hand somehow settle just which and how many of an agent's antecedent beliefs are called on in judging a hypothesis. It would be wild here for us to speculate beyond this since it is without doubt an empirical matter how, exactly and actually, belief fixation proceeds. The important point is that it would seem, in practice, not to be perfectly isotropic and Quinean but rather infected by significant encapsulation. This is especially clear when we look to actual rather than ideal scientific practice for a model for belief fixation. Once we see, however, that belief fixation is not purely isotropic and Quinean, it appears that scripts might be plausible, even if at present simplistic, models for belief fixation within the context of the frame problem. Scripts are, by their very nature, certainly nonisotropic and quite un-Quinean. What needs to be emphasized, then, is that cognitive agents bent on belief fixation are subject to various and varying limitations in cognitive resources, the effect of which is an apparent, though not necessarily severe, encapsulation of belief fixation.[16] Although little is known about

16 Certainly of vital importance here are questions regarding the ways in which belief fixation may be constrained, how, that is, belief fixation admits of encapsulation. This amounts to the question as to how the mind determines the range of beliefs that will, in fact, affect the confirmation of some hypothesis. And this devolves to the problem of specifying heuristics that may apply. Tversky and Kahneman offer suggestions, but the point is that, whatever these heuristics might be, they can only be exposed by empirical research on the patterns of reasoning cognitive agents actually display. The best bet is that, like science in progress, agents in practice confirm hypotheses for acceptance by adverting to only a fraction of antecedently endorsed hypotheses. Fodor (1983, pp. 115–16) is aware of all this but dismisses it on the grounds that no one now has any serious proposals regarding precisely how beliefs relevant to the assess-

the principles governing belief fixation, the clear possibility of encapsulation gives credence to the idea that scripts or their successors may have promise as models of belief fixation.

Additionally, suppose that Fodor is right, that belief fixation is as isotropic and Quinean as you please. Let belief fixation be just as it ought epistemically to be.[17] Nothing in this precludes the truth of Sententialism. For assume that Sententialism is also true, that beliefs are encoded as sentences in the brain and that the fixation of belief is nondemonstrative rational inference defined over Mentalese sentences. It is part of Sententialism that mental processing is a causal affair in which those properties of representations that cause their transformations are their syntactic properties. Belief fixation thus would turn out to be a causal affair in which the syntactic properties of Mentalese sentences standing as the conclusions of rational nondemonstrative inferences are the effects of those sentences from which they are derived. If the process of belief fixation is perfectly isotropic and Quinean, the premises of any given nondemonstrative Mentalese inference are all of the antecedent beliefs of the agent in whom the process occurs. Now, even if belief fixation does not ensure the truth of confirmed hypotheses, it certainly does provide for their high probability. Generally, that is, our beliefs are extended and revised so as to provide us with true beliefs. Evolution, we may assume, has seen to that. It is precisely this that makes it plausible to consider the causal process that underwrites belief fixation as an inferential process. Now since the properties of the representations germane to the causal process of belief fixation are identified with the representations' syntactic properties, any causal laws linking beliefs in the process of fixation are, ipso facto, inferential principles as well. That is, they are principles linking Mentalese sentences by reference to their syntactic properties so as generally to provide for the probability of the truth of the effected representation, given the truth of its causally antecedent representations. The point is that if Sententialism is true and belief fixation is a causal process, then we ought, in principle, to be able empirically to settle on the causal laws associating representations. Since we may take it that any causal process can be

ment of a hypothesis are to be culled from all the beliefs an agent might have. It does seem, however, that the findings of Tversky and Kahneman shed some dim light on this matter.
17 Thus, set aside for the moment the findings of Tversky and Kahneman.

66

artificially simulated (even if not literally replicated), we can, consistent with the basic tenets of Sententialism, hope for an account of the nature of rational nondemonstrative inference as actually occurrent in mentation. Understanding the causal processes that drive belief fixation would lead to a tidy account of how beliefs are extended and revised, an answer to the frame problem. Of course should it happen that we never can identify causally related neural structures sufficient to carry the putative computations, then Sententialism would be thoroughly falsified. But this would not be attributable to the interesting fact that Sententialism was in principle barred from solving the frame problem but rather to the simple, even if metaphysically important, fact that its ontological posits proved simply to be false.

There is also this: Fodor is content to allow that the frame problem does not arise in modular information-processing systems, such as perceptual and language processors, on the grounds that they are informationally encapsulated or domain specific. These systems presumably have access to only restricted stores of information in producing their informational output. The modularity of these systems does not entail that they cannot be nondemonstrative processes. Presumably they also approximate rationality in some interesting sense. That is, relative to the information to which they have access, the information they generate is reasonable. So modular systems, like the central processes of belief fixation, may be processes of rational nondemonstrative inference. If this is so, then, relative to the information to which they have access, modular systems may themselves be isotropic and Quinean. It is consistent with what we know of modular systems that any and every bit of information to which they have access can affect the confirmation of any bit of information they process. Equally, considerations of simplicity and conservatism may govern the confirmation of the information they produce. If this should be so, modular systems would function exactly as do the (apparently) nonmodular processes of belief fixation, the only important difference being that modular systems have access to restricted data bases in comparison with the central system of belief fixation. Why then should the frame problem not affect modular systems if it infects the central system? The only answer would seem to be that the restricted informational access of the modular systems saves them from the frame problem. But is this really plausible? How many bits of information must be swallowed before the frame problem erupts? Certainly, if, as is evident, the visual system classifies distal stimuli according to kind, it will need access to all the information necessary for such classifications. What must it need to know if it is to reveal that this is a cat and that a canary? Enough to distinguish cats and canaries from all the other kinds it discriminates. That means it must have access to no small amount of information. And this suggests that if central processes are subject to the frame problem, then so too for the peripheral, modular systems – especially considering that they suffer from limitations of computational time, space, and power unknown to the more generously endowed central system of belief fixation. Nevertheless, and this is the crucial point, according to Fodor, the modular systems escape the frame problem. Yet, if this is so, then, by modus tollens, it is unlikely that a sententially driven central system is felled by that same problem.

One more point, and then this chapter is done. Perhaps the lesson to be gleaned from all this is that, as cognitive agents, we are nothing but structured modular systems, that we harbor no central cognitive system responsible for belief fixation. Nothing now known about cognition precludes its being largely a matter of the concerted effort of interactive modules. It is common programming practice to structure complicated programs modularly so that the main program consists only of calls to subroutines – modules per se. Such subroutines can be interdependent, calling on one another (and themselves, if recursive) as the occasion dictates. The degree of subroutine nesting must be finite but may be very deep. And calls within a subroutine to other modules can, of course, be conditional and activated only on the satisfaction of antecedently specified conditions. Complicated and interactive modularization – when viewed from the outside in ignorance of the details of the structure of the encompassing program – resists easy comprehension. What is deductive and deterministic may seem inductive and spontaneous. A program, when assessed in terms of its inputs and outputs, may appear to be isotropic and Quinean in the extreme even though it is in fact doggedly narrow-minded and jerry-rigged.

Does the plasticity of our behavior demonstrate that our internal system of computation is not a system of interactive modules unhindered by the operation of a central system of deliberation and

68

evaluation? The answer is certainly not in yet. It depends, in part, on continued success in developing artificially intelligent programs adroit in handling ever-wider ranges of tasks. Meanwhile, nothing in principle precludes the hypothesis that we are more modular than we might suspect. And that feeds the suspicion that we are sentential cognitive systems that solve the frame problem in our own case by radical modularization (Maloney, 1988).

3

Intelligence,
rationality, and behavior

3.1. INTELLIGENT BEHAVIOR AND BRUTE REACTION

Fundamental to Sententialism is the thesis that beliefs are causally efficacious physical structures that can be construed as contentful sentences. Now if, internal to an agent, physical states $S_1, \ldots, S_{n-1}$ cause state S_n, then, if the former states can be construed as premises from which the latter state, viewed as a conclusion, is deducible, the states in question apparently qualify as contentful mental states. This is especially so if the state constituting S_n is interpretable as a description of an action. The intuition at work here is that mental processes are, at root, inferential or computational.

The problem with this is that all events, including those that patently are not instances of intelligent behavior, conform to causal or natural laws. And evidently the collected causes of any effect can be construed as premises from which the effect, taken as a conclusion, is derivable. More generally, physical laws determine alterations in the states of physical systems, and these states can, in turn, be mapped onto symbols so that state transitions correspond to symbolic transformations. Since the symbols can be interpreted as representing the states with which they are paired, the symbolic transformations can be construed as computations or representations of the states bound to be realized. Thus, using a familiar example, the planetary motions conform to Kepler's laws. So, since the states of the planets causally implicated in their motions can be treated as representing the relevant antecedents in the laws and their motions construed as representing the laws' consequents, the solar system, according to Sententialism, appears to be psychologically endowed. For it seems to compute its motions just as we plot our actions. The difficulty, then, to which the objection points is how Sententialism is to distinguish representational from nonrepresentational states. If the distinction is to be drawn with reference to the computational or rule-governed character of transformations of states, then Sententialism is hopelessly allied with panpsychism. All physical states, insofar as they conform to physical laws, would appear computational or rule ordered in the same sense assigned to mental states. If this is right, then Sententialism would have blurred the difference between behavior and brute physical reaction. Behavior presumably is physical reaction whose cause includes mental states. And so, but contrary to plain fact, it would seem absurdly to follow that all physical reaction qualifies as behavior.

Fodor (1975, p. 74) meets the example of the pseudointelligent planets by saying that what differentiates unintelligent but rule- or law-governed activity from geniune behavior is that among the causes of behavior there must be a representation of the rules or laws supposedly implicated in the derivation of the behavior. But no account of planetary movement appeals to structures in the planets encoding Kepler's laws. Thus intelligence is not, if Fodor is right, forced on the planets.[1]

Fodor's (1975, p. 74) way of removing this burr, as Dennett (1978b) notes, pulls out too much fur. The difficulty is that many nonverbal organisms capable of intelligent behavior appear insufficiently intelligent to represent the rules or laws germane to producing their behavior. Dennett allows for the possibility that someday hamsters will be discovered to decide in accordance with a version of the Bayesian calculus. But it is hard to believe that hamsters could have the cognitive resources sufficient for encoding such complex principles. By extension, it may well be that we ourselves cogitate along the lines of rules or principles either at present undiscovered or so complicated that it is dubious that, given the apparent differences among ourselves in what we know and can learn, we could all represent such principles. Hence Fodor's way out constitutes a dilemma. Either the inability of selected cognitive agents – or types thereof – to represent complicated, subtle, and profound laws is, contraintuitively, only apparent, or much of

1 Those who, with Chomsky (1980), think of our linguistic competence as rule guided, typically suppose that we mentally represent grammars that determine our linguistic behavior. This, of course, is just a special case of Fodor's more general thesis that intelligent behavior derives from the mental representation of rules from which descriptions of the behavior are derivable. See Stabler (1985) for an argument to the effect that linguistic competence does not presuppose the mental representation of a grammar.

what we think of as genuine behavior is, like planetary motion, actually unintelligent reaction.

Surely it helps the Sententialist not at all to respond that indeed hamsters do represent whatever rules, including Bayes's theorem, that may be necessary to explain why they behave as they do, so long as these representations are unconscious or otherwise not properly considered among hamsters' conscious occurrent beliefs. The objection does not hinge on whether relatively unintelligent, nonverbal organisms can be said consciously to believe or understand the likes of Bayes's theorem. Rather, the issue is whether hamsters and their close cognitive cousins have the ability to represent *in any way at all* complex principles whose representation appears to presuppose a representational system as expressively endowed as, say, English supplemented with mathematics. That relatively unintelligent nonverbal organisms could aspire to such representations is, the objection rightly maintains, beyond disingenuous. And failing this, it is difficult to appreciate how Sententialism could consistently maintain, as any theory of cognition should, that hamsters can act intelligently although the planets cannot.[2]

In order to move Sententialism off the horns of this dilemma, we had better acknowledge that intelligent behavior does not, contrary to what Fodor says, require that representations of the rules, laws, or principles relevant for its computation occur among its causes. Not only do hamsters fail to represent the rules they follow in behaving as they do but so too might we, at least in producing much of our intelligent actions. What, despite the problem of the pseudointelligent motion of the planets, distinguishes genuine behavior from unadorned reaction is that only behavior counts mental

---

2 Stich (1978) distinguishes between doxastic and subdoxastic states. Both are information-bearing states, but, unlike doxastic states, subdoxastic states are not generally accessible to consciousness and do not exhibit the inferential connections that beliefs manifest. Subdoxastic states, Stich suggests, might encode grammatical information determining how linguistic agents are able to distinguish grammatical from ungrammatical sentences. Nevertheless, attributing to hamsters subdoxastic states encoding Bayesian principles in order to accommodate the possibility of their acting as accomplished Bayesians seems unwarranted for the same reason that cuts against hamsters (consciously) believing Bayes's theorem. Subdoxastic states encode information, and hamsters presumably are in no way capable of representing principles encoding information pertaining to the determination of probability assignments. Stich, by the way, does not argue that subdoxastic states suffice to preserve the intelligence of cognitive agents at the level of hamsters.

representations among its causes. These causes, in order to be mental representations, must also stand as premises in an inference, the conclusion of which specifies the relevant bit of behavior. But such does *not alone suffice* for making them beliefs and desires. Otherwise the planetary system would constitute a cognitive agent. Not just any sequence of physical states operant in the causation of some selected type of motion qualifies as a cluster of Mentalese sentences, even if we theorists can construe the states as sentences from which a description of the activity is deducible. In order that a physical state be a genuine mental representation it not only must be interpretable by cognitive theorists as an intentional state but also must be, *in rerum natura*, an intentional state.

So the question is what establishes the natural contentfulness or intentionality of a physical state? In Chapter 1, Section 1.5, the idea was broached that the intentionality of a state may reside in its physical character, that the very contentfulness of a state might ultimately be reducible to some aspect of its physical nature. Call this the hypothesis of the Material Basis of Cognition. Here we see an additional reason for Sententialism to adopt this hypothesis. If it is true that only states of a certain physical structure qualify for membership in the intentional club, then it is easy to see why, on the one hand, humans and hamsters are capable of having intentional, contentful states and why, on the other hand, the planets are not. Humans and hamsters possess states so materially composed that they constitute intentional states. The planets lack the material endowment requisite for content.[3] Accordingly, although

3 Is it not philosophically irresponsible to maintain that intentionality is materially based and thereby to saddle the physical scientist with the chore of isolating this intentional stuff? How is the scientist to know what to look for? What things have it? Philosophy has introduced the term. So is it not unfair for a philosopher who hesitates to say which things are intentional to ask the scientist to assay intentionality? Will not the scientist look upon this as a wild goose chase?

Well, philosophy is indeed responsible for 'intentionality', but this is just the technical term for what folk psychology aims at when it speaks of contentful states and propositional attitudes. In this sense, 'intentionality' is like 'star'. Long ago people noticed, or thought they noticed, bright objects in the night sky. These they called stars. Although much that might once have passed as star lore is now known to be false, astronomy has verified that stars exist and has had much to say about them. Similarly, long ago people noticed, or thought they noticed, contentful states within themselves. These we now call intentional states. Although much that now passes as intentional-state lore is very likely false, it may turn out that one of our sciences will someday verify that intentional states exist, constitute a natural kind, and conform to various laws. Humans and many other

73

humans, hamsters, and planets all may have sequences of states that can be conceived of by us as if they were, respectively, natural deductions of their final from their former states, we would err if we were to take as actual what we merely conceive. A sequence of states constitutes an actual mental deduction only if the states in the sequence do indeed have content, only if the states are actually intentional. And this, the hypothesis of the Material Basis of Cognition supposes, requires that the states comprising the sequences in question themselves be made of the matter essential to or constitutive of intentionality.

The lesson to be learned from the example of the pseudointelligent planets is that not everything that seems to be a mental deduction is what it appears to be. A mental deduction in the sense required by Sententialism is, first of all, a relation among contentful states. True, such deductions have their formal properties that invite characterizations of the sort familiar from systems of formal logic and, of course, computer science. Nonetheless, a necessary condition for a chain of states to count as a mental deduction is that the states be, in their own right, content-bearing states. That, by hypothesis, is a matter of their matter. In advancing this thesis, the Sententialist must be cautious to explain that the idea is not that the *specific* meaning or content of any particular representation is a straightforward function of its material nature. That may be so, but it is not implied by the hypothesis under consideration here. Rather, the suggestion is that what accounts for the fact that a mental state is contentful or intentional, regardless of what, specifically, might be its content or meaning, is its material structure. According to the hypothesis, only states composed of certain kinds of matter can be intentional structures, although that they are so materially composed does not determine what their content actually is. Again, additional reasons supporting the hypothesis of mental stuff must await development until Chapter 5. Still, the central idea here is that what prevents us from attributing beliefs, desires, and,

mammals have intentional states if folk psychology is right. Presumably, neural states are intentional states. Which neural states? Those, if any, that admit of experimental manipulation affecting propositional attitudes in predictable ways. Should, finally, neural science be unable to isolate such states or, once isolated, these states exhibit no common material base, then the hypothesis that intentionality is materially based is just plain false.

Isn't it nice for once to have a philosophical thesis that admits of empirical disconfirmation?

for that reason, genuine behavior to the planets is that, unlike ourselves and, presumably, hamsters, the planets do not contain the material necessary for the formation, much less the fixation, of belief.

Should the hypothesis of the Material Basis of Cognition prove correct, the very same would distinguish behavior and reaction within a cognitive agent. We explain Abelard's seduction of Héloïse by attributing to him various beliefs and desires that, in concert with certain (but not necessarily internally represented) rules of inference, entail the appropriateness of the actions constituting the seduction. We do not look to similar explanations for all of Abelard's activities. Some – for example, his stumbling as he crosses the threshold to Héloïse's chambers – we take to be unintended reactions to his environment. The stumbling is indeed partially the product of states internal to Abelard that we might construe as sentences. These, together with certain general rules, entail a description of his stumbling. Nonetheless, the stumbling is simple reaction rather than intelligent behavior. This is because not all of the states productive of Abelard's stumbling possess the physical features, whatever they might be, requisite for being a representational state.

The version of Sententialism before us thus denies that in order for an agent to behave intelligently he or she must internally represent rules of inference that rationally relate the behavior to its mental causes as a conclusion to its premises. In order that an agent's activity – described as it is – have a psychological explanation it is necessary that it result from intentional states *in accordance with* rules. Although these rules need not be internally represented in the agent, they must be specifiable by theorists attempting to explain the occurrence of the activity as a bit of behavior. This is not to reject the possibility of an intelligent agent actually mentally representing the rules that in fact connect his or her beliefs and desires as premises to their resultant behavior as conclusion. People sometimes overtly deliberate, even mentioning the premises on which they act as well as the rules they apply to those premises in order to determine their courses of action. That, if anything, *appears* to be an example of agents explicitly representing the rules rationally underwriting their behavior. The point here is that the actual representation of such rules by an agent is unnecessary for the agent's activity to be behavior rather than sheer reaction. This should cheer both hamsters and us. We both produce activity correctly describable as having occurred in conformity with rules. And we both enjoy behavioral episodes arising from genuinely intentional states.

Nevertheless, one might protest that if, in order to preserve the intelligence of hamsters and the stolidity of the planets, it must be denied that intelligence requires the internal representation of rules taking mental states into behavior, then the price of Sententialism is too exorbitant to bear. For if an agent need not internally represent these rules, then it is completely mysterious how or why his or her beliefs and desires result in the specific behavior they do. After all, if something like modus ponens is not represented in Abelard, why does he try to arrange a private tutorial with Héloïse? Yes, he believes that if he wants to be alone with her, then he ought to attempt to arrange a private tutorial, and he does want to be alone with her. So he internally represents a conditional Mentalese sentence and its antecedent. But unless he also somehow represents modus ponens, nothing ensures that he will generate a representation of the conditional's consequent and, thereby, attempt, as he in fact does, to arrange a private tutorial. Hence, if rules transforming mental states into their consequences are not represented in agents to whom they apply, what accounts for the typically *rational* relation between behavior and its causal antecedents?

First, we should remember that computational relations among mental representations are parasitic on their causal relations. Causal relations tie mental states to their results and, thereby, ensure that the specific behavioral results of mental states follow as they do. The natural order provides, then, for the activity that ensues on the realization of those physical states doing duty as cognitive states. If the behavior in question is guaranteed to occur in the same sense as in any natural event, Sententialism need not fear for repudiating the necessity of agents internally representing the rules revealing the rational relation between mental states and behavior. In order to behave, it is no more necessary for agents to represent the rules to which their behavior conforms than it is for the planets to represent Kepler's laws in order to move as they do. The behavior is bound to occur once its mental causes arise. For the agent's representation of rules applying to his or her mental states is causally irrelevant to the production of the behavior that those states induce.

So far we have it that behavior, as opposed to unintelligent reaction, is physical activity caused by representational states in accordance with certain rules. Still, even this is not quite enough to preserve the separation between behavior and simple reaction. The representational states that cause the occurrence of some bit of behavior, say, Abelard's trying to arrange a private tutorial with Héloïse, may have nonbehavioral results as well. Indeed, they normally do. They typically cause, perhaps as by-products of the behavioral episodes they generate, various neurological and physiological states in Abelard to occur. They might also have serendipitous effects outside his body, none of which appear to be properly considered instances of behavior despite being the results of representational states internal to Abelard. For example, while he speaks with Héloïse's father to arrange a private tutorial with Héloïse, a firing of a sequence of neurons in Abelard's brain and a particular flapping of his tongue may coincide with and result from the same cause as his trying to arrange the tutorial. Why are neither of these two former events, *simply so described*, behavioral episodes although, by assumption, they have the same cause as that genuine bit of behavior, Abelard's trying to arrange the private tutorial?[4]

It is only the least informative of answers to reply that behavior, as opposed to another sort of event in which the agent is implicated, is activity that an agent intends. There are at least two senses of 'intend' that might be relevant. In one sense, to 'intend' means to plan; in another, it means mentally to cause behavior. Patently the latter sense takes us not at all beyond our present impasse, and the former requires an explication of what it is to plan, where this is taken in a thoroughly mentalistic sense. Surely to plan cannot mean consciously to plot the course of one's activity. If it did, very little of what deserves to be dubbed behavior could be so nominated. Your having flipped the light switch in the room as you entered is a bit of your behavior, but you can hardly be said consciously to have plotted it. And neither is it an advance in understanding to take intentionally produced activity to be activity consciously or unconsciously plotted. What can it be so to plot other than to desire what is plotted, to believe how to achieve it, and to decide to act on that desire and belief? And this brings us full circle, since we now need to know how it is that some of the events caused by states constituting decisions to act are behavior whereas others are

4 Philosophers have kept publishers busy over this question. See Davidson (1963), Goldman (1970), Sellars (1973), Hornsby (1980), and Brand (1984).

not. So to say that behavior is intended activity is, even if true, hardly an answer to our question.[5]

An agent's behavior, but not the nonbehavioral events involving the agent, is the consequence of the agent's mental representations in accordance with rules of, what we might call, rational deliberation. These are rules that advert only to the content of the agent's representational states in explaining the reasonableness of the agent's behavior. An event is a bit of behavior, then, only if it is caused by mental representations whose contents rationally imply the occurrence of the event under some description. Abelard's trying to arrange a private tutorial with Héloïse is, as an event, a bit of Abelard's behavior because it is evidently reasonable for this event to occur given only the content of his beliefs and desires. For Abelard wants to be alone with Héloïse and believes that arranging a private tutorial would, ceteris paribus, probably be the most effective way of securing time alone with her. When we take his

5 Brand (1984) offers a sophisticated account of action in which intention occurs as a basic explanatory concept. While Brand argues that the cognitive element in intention is not belief (pp. 148–52), at least as it is generally understood, he also admits that the cognitive component of an agent's intention to act involves representations of the agent's similar past actions, current situation, and future actions as well as representations monitoring and guiding the agent's ongoing bodily movements (p. 153). Brand is surely right. In behaving, an agent typically draws on an extensive array of information, far more than simplified philosophical examples of action normally indicate. But what are these various representations if not sundry beliefs? Brand answers that these representations are too complex and fleeting, besides being typically unconscious, to be beliefs, popularly construed. (On this score, compare Stich's [1978] notion of subdoxastic states.) Now the dispute here is largely a terminological tussle over the extension of 'belief'. At most Brand's argument shows, as he himself is well aware (pp. 157–8), that popular wisdom errs in restricting belief to conceptually simple, stable, and consciously accessible representations. Belief, as we have characterized it, is not restricted in the way that Brand takes it to be circumscribed by the common conception of belief. (Brand's preferred way of transforming the relevant popular cognitive concepts into scientifically respectable ones can be found in Brand [1984, pp. 201–36].) Nothing in his argument prevents a scientifically minded psychology from extending the commonplace concept of belief to encompass representations of the sort current in (what Brand calls) intentions. This is especially so if it thereby purchases explanatory power while reducing the categories it uses in explaining behavior. But Brand also adverts to representations that guide the activity constituting behavior. And what exactly is involved in an agent's guiding his or her movements? Guidance cannot, except circularly, be explained as intention. If so, guidance seems to be nothing other than the causal influence of belief and desire on bodily movement. Thus, even in Brand's analysis of action, it appears as if action or behavior is finally to be explicated as activity caused by belief and desire, so long as these notions are sensitive to the demands of scientifically reputable explanation. With this, I suspect, Brand would not disagree.

trying to arrange the tutorial to be behavior, we implicitly suppose that there is an explanation of this event's occurrence that refers to the content of the representational states that cause it to occur. That amounts to saying that its occurrence conforms to rules of a certain type, rules that exhibit why it is rational for Abelard to act as his representational states cause him to – why it is rational, given the content of his efficacious mental states, to try to arrange the tutorial. In attributing rationality in this way to Abelard, we do not insist that he be perfectly rational. It is unnecessary that his course of action be the very best way of achieving his ends, given his beliefs, or even that the action necessarily serve its purpose. Nature can frustrate the best-laid plans. Nevertheless, in the standard case, what is requisite for an agent's action to be comprehended under rules of rational deliberation is that there be rules from which the action, or a description thereof, is derivable from the contents of the mental states that in fact cause the action to occur.

The topic of rationality deserves much more than its own monograph.[6] Still, we can venture to say that there are at least two senses of rationality that may emerge in discussions of the relation between behavior and its mental causes. In the first sense, an event caused by an agent's beliefs and desires is the rational consequence of its mental causes if, granted only that the contents of the beliefs are all true, it is probable that the event will fulfill the agent's desires. Hamsters and humans can both satisfy this conception of rationality without representing the laws, principles, or rules that underwrite the probability of the success of events satisfying their desires. The idea is that the rationality inherent in behavior derives from the fact that an event that constitutes behavior is likely to slake the desire from which it emanates if the beliefs about the world that drive the behavior should prove to be adequate representations of the world.

This conception of the rationality of a behavioral event relativizes the probability of the event's accommodating its associated desires

---

6 See Bennett's (1964) discussion of rationality for an excellent philosophical analysis of the concept. The literature on decision theory is also relevant. See Nozick (1969), Putnam (1981), Lewis (1981), Eells (1982), Jeffrey (1983), and Horwich (1985). Dennett (1978c, 1978g) has been careful to point out the necessity of attributing rationality to cognitive agents, although he worries that this amounts to referring to embedded cognitive agents and thus undermines any psychology in which beliefs and desires play a fundamental explanatory role. But we have already seen that Sententialism is able to deflect the problem of embedded agents.

to the truth of the beliefs operant in its production. Thus, the event's satisfying its associated desires, while probable relative to the truth of the efficacious beliefs, need not be at all probable relative to noncognitive factors. Still, this first notion of rationality needs amendment. Suppose that an agent knows that the only way, if indeed there is any way, of achieving some highly desired end is not likely to be successful. The agent's acting in the hope of success and the knowledge of the high probability of failure can still be quite rational, especially if the end is especially desirable or fundamentally important. Casual gambling for entertainment or even enrichment is not patently irrational, and leaping from a high window in a burning building to save one's life may be the only open rational option. Acknowledging this, we amend the account of the first sense of rationality.

> (R.1) An agent's mentally caused activity is the rational consequence of the beliefs and desires that cause it should either one of the two following conditions hold: (1) given only the truth of those beliefs, if there is any activity whose occurrence would, in all probability, slake the agent's operant desires, then it is probable that the activity in question will satisfy the desires from which it emanates. Or, (2) given that the agent believes that so acting (though improbably successful) is still the most probable way of being successful, the value to the agent of satisfying the desires causing the activity outweighs the influence of the belief that so acting is not likely to bring success.[7]

This is not the only sense in which an event might be the rational consequence of the mental states that cause it. What should we say of agents who, for one reason or another, happen occasionally to cogitate under the auspices of unreliable principles of reasoning? Action predicated on such reasoning cannot be counted on to put to rest the desires out of which it arises. If agents who reason fallaciously do misguidedly trust their unreliable principles, how-

7 I do not have anything to say about weighing values of satisfying desires or measuring the influence of beliefs. And something ought to be said by way of constraining the desires that spawn rational activity. Any action arising from a person's desire to be the first flying hippopotamus to win a Nobel prize in economics is, at best, of dubious rationality. So perhaps we should insist that there be some probability of the success of the action. Also, we will need to worry about actions predicated on perverse, unnatural, and perhaps immoral desires. Could an action predicated on the desire to annihilate all living things be rational? Not knowing what to say about this, I say nothing and suppress throughout the problem of restricting the range of desire in rational activity.

ever, might not their actions based on those principles yet be rational? What, after all, would be rational if not to act on the basis of what poses as a reliable principle of reasoning? How can we do better than that? What practical difference is there between cautioning someone to reason only validly and advising that person to reason in only those ways he or she takes to be valid?

Some of the work of Tversky and Kahneman (1974) and Wason and Johnson-Laird (1972) seems to show that, in certain restricted circumstances, people typically reason invalidly (Goldman, 1986). We may assume that the invalidity of the principles upon which such reasoning rests is not immediately evident to the agents employing them. Also by supposition, any agent adhering to such principles (but at present ignorant of their invalidity) would endorse them if told *only* that his or her reasoning follows such principles. This invalid reasoning produces activity, activity that intuitively qualifies as behavior even though it cannot be depended on to satisfy the desires that partially cause it. But since it does not meet either of the conditions imposed by the first sense of rationality, it would be disqualified as behavior unless it aspires to another legitimate notion of rationality. Thus, yielding to intuition's attraction, we might well introduce a second sense of rationality, one that, in effect, takes the rationality of a behavioral episode to be rooted in an agent's belief that the undertaken action will likely succeed.

> (R.2) If an agent believes or is disposed to believe that a rule of reasoning is valid, then events caused by the agent's beliefs and desires that are derivable by that rule from the contents of those beliefs and desires are the rational results of those beliefs and desires.[8]

And regardless of which of the two senses of rationality that may be operant, the rational result of belief and desire is, of course, full-blown behavior.[9]

Only those kinds of cognitive agents endowed with the ability to have beliefs about subjects as abstract as principles of reasoning

---

8 For a distinction parallel to that separating the two senses of rationality marked off here, see Heil's (1985) contrast between internalist and externalist conceptions of rationality.

9 Stabler (1985), drawing on Quine (1969), notes in the spirit of naturalized epistemology that the rationality of the processes productive of behavior might best be determined by scientific psychology. The idea is that rationality is whatever such a psychology might find to be characteristic of those situations in which what we call 'behavior' arises.

can meet the second sense of rationality. This may, on reflection, seem odd. This notion of rationality is weak in that it requires no logically valid connection between behavior and the desire it aims to satisfy. The appearance, however, is not to be trusted. In attributing the second sense of rationality to an agent we recognize that the agent is able or disposed unwittingly, to *excuse*, if not *justify*, the failings of his or her behavior to fulfill its associated desire. By virtue of being disposed to endorse the fallacious principle of reasoning on which his or her behavior rests, the agent displays an appreciation of the interplay of rules of reasoning, behavior, and mentation. This is exactly what we expect of a cognitively sophisticated agent. It is, after all, the first step toward being able to modify one's behavior intelligently in order to consider the principles that may underlie it.[10] Hamsters are not up to this; humans occasionally are. And that partially distinguishes them according to cognitive kind.

We were induced to survey the rational relation between mental representations and the events they cause in order to see why Abelard's trying to arrange the private tutorial with Héloïse, but neither the firing of the specified sequence of his neurons nor the flapping of his tongue, qualifies as behavior. The trying, firing, and flapping are all caused by the very same mental representations. Why is only the trying a bit of behavior? Only Abelard's trying is, in either of the two senses of rationality, a rational result of his mental representations. Although the neuronal firing and the tongue flapping, simply so described, happen to be caused by representational states, no explanation of these events refers to a rule of reason according to which they are presented as the rational outcome of their contentful causes. No doubt, given the natural or causal order of things, the firing and the flapping will lead to the satisfaction of Abelard's desire to be alone with Héloïse. Nevertheless, given *only* the content of the representational states that cause these two events, it is not at all probable that either of these two events, described as they are, will satisfy any of Abelard's desires, including his desire to be

10 By the same token, agents who refuse to repudiate invalid principles of reasoning once the unreliability of such principles is made plain lose their claim to rationality and with it their status as cognitive agents. Of course, patterns of reasoning can be entrenched and difficult to slough. In requiring an agent to avoid styles of reasoning he or she knows to be invalid, we insist only that the agent approach the goal of validity asymptotically, not that the agent achieve it all at once or completely.

alone with Héloïse. And certainly Abelard desires neither the firing nor the flapping. So, although his beliefs and desires are causally related to these two events, neither the firing nor the flapping is, in the first sense of rationality, rationally related to the same. The two events cannot be counted as behavior on that score.

The firing and the flapping also fail to rise to the level of behavior relative to the second sense of rationality. Abelard neither believes nor is disposed to believe in any rule according to which either the firing of his neurons or the flapping of his tongue is derivable from the contents of the beliefs and desires that happen to cause these two events. That is, in denying that the firing of the neural sequence and the flapping of Abelard's tongue count as behavior, we recognize that the explanation of these events is complete without reference to the content of any of the mental states that might fall within their etiological history.

Now qualification. Were Abelard to believe, say, the firing of his specified neurons to be implied by the contents of his current mental states, then the firing would, by way of the second sense of rationality, be the rational product of his mental states. It would, therefore, count as a bit of his behavior. And this is perfectly correct. The firing of the neurons, because it is the effect of Abelard's mental representations, would be, under the present assumption, as much within his power to control as would his trying to arrange a private tutorial with Héloïse. More on this next.

3.2. RATIONALITY AND BEHAVIOR

The type of Sententialism before us takes behavior to be the causal product of mental representations in accordance with rules of rational deliberation. This amounts to saying that an agent's behavior is generally guaranteed to be rational relative to his or her beliefs and desires and, thus, perilously mimics the Socratic paradox of *akrasia* (Irwin, 1977, pp. 78–82; Heil, 1984; Mele, 1983, 1986). Even if Sententialism is silent on whether an agent can behave in only morally correct ways, it nevertheless does tend to deny that an agent's behavior, *properly so called*, can be less than rational. This may not jibe with the popular notion that agents in the grip of powerful emotions often behave in ways that are manifestly irrational. Perhaps even more importantly, some of the findings of psychologists appear to undermine the idea that behavior is the

83

rational product of mentation (Tversky and Kahneman, 1974, 1983; Wason and Johnson-Laird, 1972). So we had better take a close look at rationality in the hands of Sententialism.

Remember that when Sententialism construes behavior as rational, the rationality of a bit of behavior is relative to only those beliefs and desires actually implicated in the etiology of that specific instance of behavior. Thus, if all of an agent's beliefs and desires are not, in the relevant sense, collectively consistent, it may – but harmlessly – well be that the agent's behavior is not rational relative to some of his or her beliefs and desires not involved in the production of the behavior. A chain smoker may know that cigarettes are potentially very harmful to himself or herself. Smoking may then appear to be paradigmatically irrational for this agent, since it will probably thwart his or her presumed desire for a long and healthy life. But the appearance of irrationality can be shown for the illusion it is if the rationality of a token of behavior is tethered only to those beliefs and desires that actually cause it to occur. What presumably causes the smoker to smoke is the desire for cigarettes and the belief that there are cigarettes at hand. The smoker's desire to live long and healthily and belief that cigarettes are potentially harmful are presumably not engaged in the causal process leading to his or her smoking. The desire for a long and healthy life and the belief that cigarettes are potentially harmful may indeed affect the smoker's behavior, perhaps causing the smoker to discard the smoldering butt in self-disgust. But that is a different bit of behavior from the smoking itself. Smoking might, then, be rational relative to the specific desires and beliefs that induce it, though it may not ring rational relative to whatever else the smoker may happen to believe and desire. The thesis defended by the Sententialist is simply that an agent's behavior is the rational result of its specific mental causes, not of the totality of the agent's mental states.

For all that we now know, it may be that the mental representations that cause a bit of behavior are themselves inconsistent. In such a case, truth-functional validity being what it is, it seems the behavior might be deemed rational on the grounds that any action is degenerately rational relative to such logical incongruity in the history of its production. Perhaps even paranoid behavior might in this way stand the test of rationality, although we would want it marked with an asterisk. In any event, although we take an agent's behavior necessarily to be rational relative to those of his or her beliefs that cause it, we do not thereby maintain that an agent's behavior is necessarily rational relative to *all* the beliefs and desires that might occupy the agent. Behavior that remains rational when measured against the totality of an agent's mental states might be characteristic of an Oxford don, but it is not the norm for mere mortals.

What should we say in the case that selected representations cause an agent to act in such a way that it is *unfathomable* how that activity could be understood to follow rationally from the content of the representations? Suppose, for example, that we find Abelard standing in the middle of Notre Dame at vespers singing in full voice one of Ovid's love poems while the rest of the congregation tries, though scandalized, to continue with the Divine Office. Strange indeed, and even more so if it should turn out that Abelard's salacious singing is caused solely by those of his mental representations respectively encoding his desire someday to have a good translation of Aristotle's *Metaphysics* and his belief that Plato was wrong about universals. Here we have absolutely no rational connection between Abelard's apparent behavior and its presumed mental causes. If this situation is a real possibility (and there may be reason to doubt that it is), then Sententialism would seem mistaken in construing behavior necessarily to be the rational product of the mental representations that cause it.

Well, if Abelard's singing is not just a spurious possibility, Sententialism must maintain that it is best taken not as behavior at all but merely as some noncognitive, serendipitous effect of the mental representations that cause it. Abelard's singing, as an effect of the specified representational states, must be quite independent of the content those states happen to have. In considering this type of case, we do not deny a priori that beliefs and desires could cause the weirdest of events. Still, in the face of Abelard's bizarre activity brought about by the designated representational states, Sententialism maintains that the syntactically realized semantic properties of the causally active representations play no role in causing Abelard's strange singing. The hypothesis, then, is that when mental representations produce irrational or nonrational activity, perhaps activity that is finally strange, they must do so by virtue of some of their nonrepresentational properties. This is just as a line from *The Magic Flute* sung at a high pitch may, by virtue of its pitch rather than any of its semantic properties, cause a crystal to shatter.

85

That the causes of utterly irrational events involving an agent happen to be contentful mental representations is simply irrelevant to the causal explanation of the activity. This would remain true even if the best way to control such peculiar activity should be to modify the beliefs whose realizations cause the activity. Although the contents of the beliefs are not germane to the production of the singular activity, it may be that the only practical way to eliminate the offending causes is to modify the agent's beliefs, thereby removing, accidentally as it were, the genuine causal, albeit nonintentional, properties.[11] By analogy, it could be that the only effective way of saving a prima donna's crystal is to prevent her from singing some particular lyrics. The point, as Sententialism would have it then, is simply that ultimately anomalous activity, should there be such, is not activity properly traced to the content of those representations that may happen to cause it. This is why an agent's nonrational activity is, at best, counterfeit behavior (Heil, 1985).

If we want to distinguish behavior and unintelligent reaction consistent with the Sententialist program, we are required to advance the hypothesis that behavior is activity caused by those properties of mental representations that constitute the syntactic properties of the representations. These properties presumably encode the representations' semantic properties or content. Activity so caused is real behavior. It is the rational consequence of the content encoded by the properties of the representations that cause it. Consequently, an event is a bit of behavior only if it occurs in accordance with rules of rational deliberation, rules that render the event rational relative to the contents of its representational causes. Activity not so caused cannot be behavior, at least if Sententialism is right.

Nevertheless, by way of objection, we might be asked to reconsider. Abelard, we know, desires to be alone with Héloïse and

---

11 According to Sententialism, an agent's reasoning is a causal chain of mental representations wherein the inferential structure rides on the back of the causal sequence. This entails that reasoning is a thoroughly deterministic or mechanistic affair, as deterministic or mechanistic as causal processes generally are. Thus, since argumentation with an agent can lead the agent to change his mind (i.e., to undergo changes in his pattern of reasoning), argumentation can bring about changes in causal sequences. Consequently, the sheer fact that an agent's mental processes are causally regulated does not imply that they or the agent are immune to rational influences. See Dennett (1978g) for a related discussion concerning the compatibility of mechanistic and intentional explanations of behavior.

believes that the best way to achieve this is to try to arrange a private tutorial with her. This desire and belief are, according to Sententialism, encoded as Mentalese sentences or representations within Abelard. As such, they exhibit syntactic properties serving both to fix their content and also to cause certain behavioral events. These Mentalese representations cause Abelard to try to arrange a private tutorial with Héloïse. Evidently this bit of behavior is rational relative to its mental causes. But suppose (perhaps wildly but to make the point) that the *very properties* of the mental representations in Abelard that cause him to try to arrange a private tutorial with Héloïse also cause him to flee Paris, this precluding his meeting privately with Héloïse. We are to conjecture here that the syntactic properties of the presentation that encode their content have, as causes might, various effects. On the one hand, they cause the event by virtue of which Abelard tries to arrange a private tutorial, an event presumably identical with the flapping of his tongue as he speaks with Héloïse's father. On the other hand, these very same properties of the mental representations are also said to cause the event of Abelard's fleeing Paris, an event identical with, say, the scurrying of his feet. And, of course, we are to assume that under any interpretation these events are, as bits of behavior, rationally incompatible. Both events seem to be bits of behavior since they are assigned exactly the same cause. But contrary to the thesis that behavior is rational relative to the representations that produce it, they surely both cannot be rational products of their common representational cause.

Now even if we were to accept the extravagant assumption built into this objection, we are not by that coerced into repudiating the essentially rational relation between behavior and the representations that cause it. For it remains to be argued that there are indeed no descriptions under which the events in question can be taken as the rational results of the same representations. Ascriptions of behavior are, if strictly correct, attributions of *attempts* to act in some particular manner. Literally correct behavioral ascriptions are not necessarily attributions of successfully completed attempts to act. For example, Abelard's tongue flapping is, from the psychological perspective, best described as his *trying* to arrange a private tutorial rather than his *successfully* arranging the tutorial. The tongue flapping (i.e., the event instantiating the behavior) occurs exactly as it does regardless of Abelard's success in securing the tutorial.

Whether or not he achieves his end, Abelard behaves as he does. Thus, given the occurrence of the tongue flapping, Abelard's behavior is guaranteed to occur. What is thus guaranteed to happen is that Abelard will attempt to arrange a private tutorial, not that he will succeed. An agent's behavior is, accordingly, best conceived as an attempt to act in some way, that being what is assured causally to result from the influence of the relevant mental representations.

What description, then, best fits the event constituting Abelard's scurrying, supposing with the objection that the event actually is a bit of behavior as opposed to brute reaction? If the event is a behavioral episode, the proper description presumably will advert to the content of the representations that cause it and whatever else we may know of Abelard. The objection maintains that the cause of Abelard's scurrying is exactly the same as the cause of his trying to arrange the private tutorial. Both events are presumed to result from those syntactic properties of the same mental representations that encode the representations' content. The objection allows that included in our knowledge of Abelard is his trying to arrange a private tutorial with Héloïse. So far as the objection goes, nothing else of what we know of Abelard is relevant. Given these suppositions, we are free to describe Abelard's scurrying as an *attempt* to do something consistent with his trying to arrange the tutorial. Lord knows that his actually departing Paris is not in harmony with his trying to arrange a private tutorial. Still, should the scurrying be either Abelard's extraordinarily ill-executed attempt somehow to advance the arrangement for the tutorial or his effort to do something simply not germane to arranging the tutorial, then the objection is stalled.

Perhaps the retort to this reply is that we are not at all entitled to describe Abelard's scurrying as an ill-executed attempt somehow to advance the arrangement for the tutorial or as an effort otherwise not antagonistic to the tutorial. Rather, the complaint proceeds, the objection lays it down in advance that Abelard's scurrying is, as a bit of behavior, best described either as his fleeing or as his attempt to flee Paris, both descriptions indicating that the behavior is rationally incompatible with Abelard's trying to arrange a private tutorial.

If this is the point of contention, then the Sententialist may rightly reject the objection as a simple *petitio*. So construed, the objection now merely assumes what is in dispute, namely, that agents need not behave in rational accord with their beliefs and desires. If the objection is to have any bite at all, it must argue for that conclusion. One cannot simply assume that Abelard's scurrying is most appropriately described in some way rationally incompatible with those of his beliefs and desires that cause it. The deep problem with the objection so conceived is that unless agents generally behave consistent with their beliefs and desires, there simply is no way to attribute beliefs and desires to them. We typically adduce an agent's beliefs and desires from his or her actions. In this we are guided by the supposition that an agent's actions betray the content of the representations from which the behavior results. This practice would be hopeless were an agent not generally to act consistent with his or her beliefs and desires. Thus, as long as it is conceded that beliefs and desires give rise to behavior – and the objection does not question that – it remains that agents typically act consistent with those of their beliefs and desires that cause them to act.[12]

But still, the objection does serve to illustrate Sententialism's conditions on attributions of behavior. Sententialism, at least as here conceived, takes behavior to be action caused by the syntactic properties of mental representations according to rules of rational deliberation. The objection assumes that Abelard's scurrying is behavior because it has the very same cause as his attempt to arrange the tutorial. The example featured by the objection challenges the idea that behavior is activity sententially caused even if the example does rest on the dubious supposition that the relevant properties of the representations in Abelard could cause him to attempt both to arrange the tutorial and to flee Paris. Nevertheless, the objection needs support when it takes the events in question necessarily to be mutually antagonistic behavioral installments. For such requires that there be reason to suppose that no description applies to the event realizing the scurrying that would render it rational relative both to the content of the representations by which it is caused and to Abelard's trying to arrange the tutorial.

12 Compare Davidson's (1974) Principle of Charity governing radical translation. There the idea is that translation from an alien into a familiar language presupposes attributing to speakers of the alien language generally true beliefs. Here we have it that ascription of belief predicated on observation of behavior requires the assumption that the behavior is the rational product of the beliefs and desires that cause it.

We certainly must acknowledge the significance of descriptions under which events are presented. Assume that Abelard tries to arrange the tutorial by speaking with Héloïse's father. Already supposed is that Abelard's so trying is, as a physical event, identical with the flapping of his tongue. Described as Abelard's *trying*, this event is the rational result and effect of his mental states. Described as his tongue's *flapping*, the event is not the rational result, but only the effect, of Abelard's mental states. This relativization to descriptions is not unique to the demands of cognitive science. Natural laws generally apply to events only under some of their descriptions. Microbiology may explain and predict on occasion the cloning of a virus but it is of no help in understanding the same event should it be described only as the event occurring in the building named for the university's wealthiest alumna. The laws of rational deliberation, like the principles of scientific inquiry generally, thus depend for their application to events on the descriptions under which the events are represented. Consistent with this, it yet remains that at least two conditions must be satisfied in order that an event be deemed behavior. The event must be caused by the properties of contentful states that encode the states' content, and there must be available a description of the event under which the event is rationally derivable from the content of the states that cause it.

It should not go unnoticed here that, in an important sense, rational derivations of behavior are analogous to formally valid inferences in logic. Just as events are rationally derivable from their mental premises only under certain descriptions, so too for the consequences of formally valid arguments. 'Abelard ought to try to arrange a private tutorial with Héloïse' is, by modus ponens, formally deducible from 'If Abelard wants to be alone with Héloïse, then Abelard ought to try to arrange a private tutorial with Héloïse' and 'Abelard wants to be alone with Héloïse'. This trivial derivation of English sentences holds only if the sentence standing as the conclusion is described as syntactically the same as the consequent of the conditional in the premises. Were the conclusion described, as may be correct, simply as a sentence recorded in black ink, the formal validity of the argument would be masked. The point is thus that whether something stands as the proper conclusion in an inference, be the inference practical or formal, depends on how the conclusion is described relative to the premises of the inference. We should not be surprised that such applies in distinguishing behavior – the result of rules of rational deliberation applied to intentional mental states – from sheer physical reaction. It is, of course, for cognitive science to determine exactly what the rules of rational deliberation actually are. But these will necessarily be rules that, by implicating the content of mental states in explaining the occurrence of selected events, thereby render the explained events behavioral episodes.

Behavior is just activity caused by mental representations according to rules of rational deliberation. Behavior also is most appropriately described as an agent's attempt to do something. Together, these points suggest, though apparently contrary to fact, that every effect of a sequence of mental representations meets the conditions on behavior. Reconsider the *firing* of Abelard's neurons. Like his attempting to arrange a private tutorial with Héloïse, the firing results from those of Abelard's physically realized mental states that represent his desire to be alone with Héloïse and his belief that the most effective way to isolate her is to arrange a private tutorial. Perhaps the neuron firing is itself a physically necessary condition of Abelard's tongue flapping, which itself constitutes his speaking with Héloïse's father about the tutorial. Apparently it would be misguided to construe the neuron firing as a bit of Abelard's behavior. But what properly prevents us from describing it as Abelard's attempt to do what is necessary to speak with Héloïse's father about the tutorial? After all, there surely is a rule of rational deliberation according to which it is reasonable for Abelard to do whatever is necessary to arrange the tutorial. And it seems that that would be just the sort of rule of rational deliberation that sanctions the description of Abelard's speaking with Héloïse's father as his attempting to arrange the tutorial. If that suffices for designating the speaking a bit of behavior, then it should also establish the firing of neurons as behavior.[13]

No doubt some will be troubled by the prospect of the firing of

13 We might, under the prevailing assumptions, think of the neuron firing as analogous to those basic actions collectively constituting an action undertaken by an artificially intelligent system. Winograd's SHRDLU, for example, undertakes to move a block by placing its (imaginary) arm in position, opening and then closing its digits, moving its arm, and, finally, opening its digits. Each of these elementary actions is necessary for SHRDLU to move a block, and each possibly deserves to be designated a bit of SHRDLU's behavior. Analogously for Abelard's neuron firing. Note also Schank's (1982) decomposition of complex into elementary actions.

Abelard's neurons actually qualifying as a bit of his behavior. To this quite legitimate complaint several things should be said. First, Sententialism does not entail that every event within an agent is a behavioral episode. Rather it more modestly, but still expansively, allows that more events occurring within an agent meet the conditions on behavior than popular lore tolerates. Any effect of the syntactically encoded intentional properties of a sequence of mental representations turns out to be a behavioral occurrence if it also fits some description under which it is derivable by rules of rational deliberation from the content of the mental representations that cause it. Given this, we have a choice. Either we can respect as sacrosanct the intuitive, commonsense sifting of bits of behavior from the chaff of nonpsychological events, or we can endorse Sententialism's culling of behavior, supposing that its more bountiful selection can be attributed to theory superseding folklore. Sententialism is a considerably more articulate characterization of the domain of psychology than that afforded by undisciplined common sense. It is natural, then, that they differ in how they parcel their domains. Here we are best advised to opt for the method that offers the deeper understanding of mentation. And thus we are most likely better served by Sententialism. Still, we ought to be prepared to welcome a different, perhaps leaner, designation of the realm of behavior should Sententialism itself fall to the scythe of a more powerful theory of the mind.[14]

Be this as it may, although Sententialism admits of a more expansive sweep in its determination of the range of behavior than does the popular notion of behavior, its reach is not too wide. There is nothing in principle confused in Sententialism's allowing that selected sorts of neuron firings and certain other instances of *apparently* nonbehavioral episodes are in fact bits of behavior. The only events it designates as behavior are those that result from mental states in pretty much the way that common opinion had vaguely anticipated. Sententialism deems behavior just those events caused by, and rationally derivable from, the intentional properties of mental states. These, of course, are just the kind whose occurrence can be controlled and modified by varying the content of an agent's mental states. What else could behavior properly be? Sen-

14 Pylyshyn (1984, p. 263) argues, as have others (e.g., Fodor, 1975, 1983), that, as cognitive psychology matures, its delineation of psychological phenomena will strikingly differ from that of tradition.

tentialism recognizes that specified behavioral episodes, such as certain sorts of neuron firings, are events of which agents are normally unaware. Agents thus may be ignorant of much of their behavior. But this is a fact all but the most benighted notions of behavior accept. We are all familiar with the experience of being on "automatic pilot," acting in routine ways, such as walking along a familiar route without consciously attending to what we do, even to the point of being unable correctly to report such recent bits of behavior. And therapists are quick to convince us that much of our activity is unconsciously undertaken behavior serving our goals and conforming to our beliefs. It simply turns out that, when the conditions on behavior are clarified by Sententialism, more of our activity ascends to the level of unconscious behavior than had been anticipated. Nonetheless, here there is nothing unduly shocking.

Such, according to Sententialism, are the presuppositions of attributing behavior and distinguishing it from brute activity. Nevertheless, this is not, as already remarked, to endorse the idea that we read behavior off the content of the mental states internal to the behaving agent. Rather, in practice, we notice an event, the flapping of Abelard's tongue, and suppose that, given all that we know of Abelard and agents of his kind, this tongue flapping might be describable as his attempt to arrange a private tutorial with Héloïse. This is plausible because we already allow that Abelard enjoys certain internal representations and are willing to subsume his activity under what, perhaps intuitively and provisionally, we take to be the rules of rational deliberation. We are constrained in applying behavioral descriptions to events by the assumption that bits of an agent's behavior arising from the same mental representations are generally consistent. This recognizes that the totality of an agent's behavior may admit of radically inconsistent episodes. But it is intolerant of rationally incompatible behavioral occurrences emanating from the very same (consistent) mental representations. Thus we typically infer the content of supposed internal representations from a prior commitment to certain behavioral descriptions of specified events and designated rules of rational deliberation. Our inclination to describe the event as we do and to apply to it the rules that we do itself rests on the assumption that the agent in question possesses internal contentful states or representations. That, in turn, seems to require that the agent have a certain physical nature, one that admits of intentionality.

Evidently, then, what we take to be the content of the internal states of an agent depends on what rules of rational deliberation we think may apply and how we have described the events that we construe as behavior. In Abelard's case, we begin with the idea that the activity is properly described as his attempting to arrange a private tutorial with Héloïse. By describing the event as an attempt, we implicitly suppose that the event can be adequately explained within the conceptual framework of cognitive psychology, explained, that is, by reference to both the contents of the mental representations that cause the event and also the rules that apply to those representations. Hence the rules that apply to the postulated mental representations must themselves produce, as a consequence of those representations, Abelard's attempting to arrange a private tutorial with Héloïse. Put differently, determining what rules apply is partially settled by the assumption that the rules must sanction a description of Abelard's tongue flapping according to which it is an attempt to arrange a private tutorial with Héloïse. Formally we have the conclusion of an inference, and our task is to discern both the rules that generate that conclusion and the premises to which those rules apply. These constraints do not suffice to generate a unique solution to our problem. Various rules applied to various internal representations would entail the conclusion we have. The evidence applied in determining representational content, as is characteristic of evidence deployed in scientific investigation generally, underdetermines the hypotheses sufficient to explain the phenomenon. The best we can hope for is to adduce rules of rational deliberation and ascriptions of content to the agent's internal representations that best enable us to explain a wide range of what we take to be the agent's behavior. All this, it should be acknowledged, is subject to the general conditions as to what, in any field, qualifies as excellence of explanation.

3.3. CAUSAL WAYWARDNESS

With all this in hand, we can turn to what Brand (1984, p. 19), with acknowledgment to Chisholm (1966), has called the problem of causal waywardness for accounts of the distinction between behavior (or action) and brute activity. With only nominal modification to Brand's example, suppose that Abelard and Héloïse have agreed that Abelard's winking of his right eye during dinner with

Héloïse's family is to signal to Héloïse that all is in order for a secret rendezvous later that evening. Abelard's belief that all is in order together with his desire to see Héloïse are the mental states that presumably cause the winking at the appropriate moment. Abelard is understandably quite nervous whenever he is around Héloïse's family, especially her brothers. As it happens, because he is nervous, his belief that all is in order and his desire to be alone with Héloïse induce in Abelard a twitch in his eyelid, a twitch that, like a wink, constitutes a rapid closing and opening of his right eye. The twitch and the wink are, from the physical point of view, completely indistinguishable. Héloïse notices the closing and opening of Abelard's right eye and, thereby, comes to believe that a rendezvous is in the offing.

It is part of Brand's point that Abelard's twitch, though a wink caused by his mental states, is obviously and intuitively not a bit of Abelard's behavior. How can this be since it is caused, albeit waywardly, by the very mental states that should serve to establish its credentials as behavior? For the twitch, after all, is an event caused by Abelard's mental states from which it is apparently rationally derivable.

There are two points to make at this juncture. First, given the description of the case, it is not obvious that the cause of the twitch or wink is actually Abelard's belief that all is in order and his desire to be alone with Héloïse. We are told that he is nervous. Is this nervousness a mental state of Abelard's? Is he perhaps nervous or afraid *that* Héloïse's brothers are aware of his planned rendezvous with her? If so, it appears as if it is this mental state of Abelard's that actually causes him to twitch. If twitching is the rational product of this mental state, then the twitching, winking that it is, is a bit of behavior. But it would not be Abelard's attempt to signal to Héloïse since it does not have the cause proper to an attempted signaling.

Second, even if the twitch is caused by Abelard's believing that all is in order and by his desire to be alone with Héloïse, it remains to be established whether it is caused by those syntactic properties of these mental states that encode their content. It is only if so caused that the twitch can be construed as behavior. If the twitch were caused by properties of Abelard's belief and desire that are irrelevant to encoding their content, then it fails to meet one of the conditions on behavior. It is only as caused by the representational properties of the mental states that the twitch can be construed as the rational result of the mental states. It is just this, however, that is dubious when we are told that Abelard's nervousness is a factor in the occurrence of the twitch. Should it be true that the content-encoding syntactic properties of Abelard's belief that all is in order and desire to be alone with Héloïse in fact cause the twitching of Abelard's eye, then it is indeed his signaling to Héloïse their rendezvous. If that is the situation, the winking is the rational product of Abelard's belief and desire. It would then be a bit of his behavior, and, importantly, his nervousness would be irrelevant to the production of the winking, even if it should have other effects on Abelard. In this case, the waywardness of the causal chain would itself have been illusory.

Well, perhaps the complaint revolves around the transitivity of causation. Abelard's belief and desire cause him to be nervous, and his nervousness causes the twitch. Hence the belief and desire cause the twitch. That would force Sententialism to count the twitch as a genuine wink signaling the rendezvous. Nonetheless, the objection concludes, if nervousness thus enters into the production of the eye closing, the eye closing is at best a twitch – never a wink – and so not a bit of behavior.

This simply will not float. Winks are eye closings in which nervousness plays no causal role. In the present case, Abelard's nervousness, regardless of its own cause, is what finally brings about his eye closing. So that event is not a wink, even though somewhere in its etiology occur certain of Abelard's beliefs and desires. Another way of putting this is that genuine behavior must be brought about in a *characteristic way*, a way in which mental states play a certain sort of causal role. No doubt lots must happen inside a person in order that he or she behave. Still, for behavior to ensue from what does occur internal to an agent, the internal events must have a certain sort of structure, a structure in which beliefs and desires occupy a designated niche.

Let us be clear about one thing: I have no idea whatsoever, and neither does any other philosopher (qua philosopher), as to the detailed nature of the structures from which behavior ensues. That is a problem to be solved in the laboratory, just as is the problem of revealing the composition of any sort of efficacious physical structure. The point worth emphasizing here is that Sententialism, at least in its present incarnation, is betting that behavior is restricted to that class of bodily events whose causes exhibit, at some yet to be specified level of generality, a similarity defined in terms of the role beliefs and desires play in their generation.

Much the same can be put this way: Abelard's designated beliefs and desires play only a subsidiary role in causing his twitch. They do not suffice for causing him to be nervous. If they did, his being nervous would be, which it is not, a universally necessary by-product of just these mental states. Rather, Abelard's nervousness is actually caused by his belief that all is in order and his desire to be alone with Héloïse *plus* his fear of her brothers and belief that they are easily given to uncontrollable rage. Thus the alleged transitivity actually fails. Although Abelard's twitch is caused by his nervousness, his nervousness is not wholly caused by his belief that all is in order and his desire to be alone with Héloïse. These mental states must be supplemented by others before Abelard's nervousness can arise. Hence, we cannot concede the objection's cavalier assumption that Abelard's nervousness has as its cause exactly what his genuine winking might take as its cause.

Still, sometimes behavior is the delayed result of a complex of mental states, and that may be problematic for the account of the relation between mentation and action offered here. Abelard might adopt a complicated plan first to kiss Héloïse. Perhaps he believes that she will walk with her sister in the garden in the late evening and that if he hides in the shadows behind the rose trellis, he will be able to kiss her as she pauses to enjoy the flowers' fragrance. He hides; Héloïse and her sister appear. Abelard watches them approach but, because of the poor light, confuses Héloïse with her sister. The women pause at the roses, and Abelard swoops down on the sister, who happens at that moment to stoop to pick a low blossom. Abelard's motion carries him over the top of the sister and, in full tumble, into the open arms of the startled Héloïse. With a crash the lovers fall to the ground, embracing one another in self-defense, their lips, as luck would have it, taking the full impact of Abelard's plunge. Abelard's *simple* plan has been fulfilled in exactly the *simplistic* way he intended. His plan was *merely* to emerge from the shadows and kiss the unsuspecting Héloïse. Indeed, this seems to be exactly what he did.

The question here is not whether Abelard's activity is behavior. It is. What we need to know is what Abelard has done. Has he done what he intended, namely, kiss Héloïse? Or has he, rather, failed to do what he intended? Did he not try, yet fail, to kiss the woman who stooped? Strictly speaking and as earlier noted about descriptions of behavior, Abelard's present behavior is properly described neither as his kissing Héloïse nor as his failing to kiss the woman who stooped. Given the case as portrayed, his behavior is rather his *attempting* to kiss Héloïse. This is what is rationally implied by the content of his mental states that cause him to act. Given Abelard's mental states, it is his attempting to kiss Héloïse that is guaranteed to occur. As it turns out, Abelard's attempting to kiss Héloïse is contingently identical with his failing to kiss the woman who stooped. It is also accidentally identical with his successfully kissing Héloïse. Described as such, neither of these latter two events qualifies as Abelard's action or behavior. Neither is rationally implied by the contents of his operant mental states. Certainly his failing to kiss the woman who stooped is not a rational consequence of his plan. Nor is his successfully kissing Héloïse, that event not being ensured simply by the mental states that launched Abelard.[15] The contingent identity of the events in question is consistent with Abelard's behavior being limited to his attempting to kiss Héloïse. For it is only as so described that this event is comprehended under the rules of rational deliberation.[16]

Should all this prove correct, we can see why ascriptions of belief and desire are inextricably entangled with attributions of rationality. Behavior is what follows from belief and desire, together with other sorts of mental representations, according to rules of rational de-

---

15 We must be careful here. The example has it that Abelard's behavior is caused *only* by the mental states constituting his plan. And the plan is so described as to exclude Abelard's present perceptual beliefs as he watches the women approach the trellis. Of course this is not at all plausible. We expect Abelard's perceptual beliefs to be among those mental states causing him to act. Indeed, plans characteristically, perhaps necessarily, are sensitive to the flux of perceptually encoded information. Once we allow for this, it is clear that Abelard's attempting to kiss the woman who stooped is a rational product of his *whole* plan, including his current perceptual beliefs. The behavior we should really attribute to Abelard is his attempting to kiss the woman he took to be Héloïse. For it is *only* this that is assured to occur by the causal powers of those of Abelard's mental representations collectively constituting his total plan. His attempting to kiss a woman he takes to be Héloïse is all that is implied by the content of his complete, realistically enriched plan. That is why his attempt, so described, is properly considered to be his behavior in this context.

16 See Castañeda (1972, 1975) for Fregean arguments to the effect that all three events in question here are fundamentally and ontologically different, albeit peculiarly related, particulars. Compare Clark (1978) and Rapaport (1978).

liberation.[17] As we have just seen, ascriptions of belief and desire are constrained by a specification of rules of rational deliberation. A doxastic agent thus is one whose mental states determine his or her actions in accordance with reason, even if the agent is ignorant of the actions and does not mentally represent the rules of reason that apply. An agent's representations are thus standardly guaranteed rationally to produce actions. Some creatures' activities are typically rigidly constrained and fail to manifest the plasticity characteristic of intelligence.[18] These activities thus seem not to conform to principles of rational deliberation, and we therefore suppose them to be without beliefs and desires.

3.4. EMPIRICAL TESTS OF RATIONALITY

Psychologists (Wason and Johnson-Laird, 1972, 1977; Tversky and Kahneman, 1974, 1982) have questioned the notion that behavior is the rational product of deliberation. Wason and Johnson-Laird report experimental results apparently showing that people often reason in ways that would seem to defy an intuitive conception of rationality, and Tversky and Kahneman argue that in a surprisingly large range of cases the inference patterns we depend on are patently fallacious. In proposing the second of the two senses of rationality introduced in Section 3.1, I have already tried to indicate that such empirical findings need not compromise the thesis that behavior is the rational result of mentation. Nevertheless, Stich (1985) has argued that these and similar experiments call into question the ancient Aristotelian idea that man is a rational animal, that the subject matter of psychology is rationally produced activity. Let us address

17 Compare Quine's (1960, Section 13) argument that no adequate translation scheme can assign the standard truth-functional connectives to an agent's language while also attributing truth-functionally inconsistent assertions to the agent. Dennett (1978c) takes Quine's point to suggest that, in attributing beliefs and desires to an agent, we cannot both preserve the rational connection between belief, desire, and behavior and also ascribe beliefs that are, for the most part, inconsistent. Otherwise there would be no way of inferring belief and desire from behavior. See also Davidson (1982).

18 Dennett (1978g) draws on Wooldridges's (1963, p. 82) description of the wasp *Sphex* to exemplify a creature whose apparently intelligent behavior is easily unmasked for the simple tropism it is. This wasp, after depositing its eggs in its burrow, will repeatedly, but pointlessly, check the condition of the burrow each time the food it is about to place in the burrow is moved a negligible distance by an interfering experimenter.

Stich's aptly put question and ask, "Could man be an irrational animal?"

Wason and Johnson-Laird report that subjects typically fail to answer correctly questions involving apparently straightforward reasoning about conditionals. In one situation that proved typical of others despite significant variation in experimental design, subjects were presented with four cards, labeled (a)–(d). Half of the facing surface of each card was masked so that subjects could not see what figure, if any, was printed on the portion of the card under the mask. The other half of each card was unmasked and was either blank or displayed a salient mark, such as an X. The right halves of (a) and (b) were masked, as were the left halves of (c) and (d). The left half of (a) and the right half of (c) displayed X's, whereas the left half of (b) and the right half of (d) were blank. Subjects thus saw cards like those represented on the facing page.

Once presented with the cards, subjects were asked to identify the cards whose masked parts would need to be exposed in order to determine whether the presence of an X on the left half of a card should ensure the same on the right half. The task amounts to determining the truth-value of a conditional sentence. That is, subjects were requested to designate the cards relevant for decisively answering the following question: Is it true that if there is an X on the left, then there is an X on the right? Subjects had only one opportunity to answer and were told that they could not examine cards individually. The relevant cards are (a) and (d), yet relatively few subjects designated those cards. Typical responses favored either (a) and (c) or only (a). The results are sobering since they would seem to indicate that subjects reason poorly when determining the truth of simple conditionals.

Tversky and Kahneman argue that people, when faced with certain types of problems, typically rely on particular problem-solving strategies or heuristic principles that, in selected – perhaps contrived – circumstances, produce systematically incorrect solutions. In one representative experiment subjects were found generally to violate the probability calculus in determining class membership for certain types of people. Subjects were acquainted with personality profiles of various types of target persons, lawyers, and thereby taught to estimate the likelihood of a particular person described in a designated profile being a lawyer. The subjects were similarly taught how to estimate the likelihood of a profiled person's being a Re-

100

(a)

(b)

(c)

(d)

101

publican. Once instructed, subjects were given a profile and asked to determine the probability of the profiled person's being a lawyer. This fixed, subjects were then to ascertain the likelihood of the same profiled person's being a Republican. After the subjects ventured these two estimates, they were then asked how likely it was that the profiled person was both a lawyer *and* a Republican. It is a theorem of the probability calculus that the probability of two (independent) situations both holding is the product of the probability of each situation. Thus, the probability of a person's being both a lawyer and a Republican can be higher than neither the probability of that person's being a lawyer nor the probability of that person's being a Republican. Yet subjects routinely estimated the probability of a profiled person's being a Republican lawyer as higher than that of the person's being a lawyer.

The implication of these studies, Stich urges, is that whether people are rational agents is to be determined empirically and that the data seem to run against the prospects of rationality being ingrained in humans. Fallacious reasoning of the sort teased out in the experiments apparently is more pervasive than formerly thought. If this is so, then Sententialism had better not hold out for behavior's being the rational result of the interaction of propositional attitudes. That or, perversely, Sententialism would need to insist that *much* of what passes as behavior is false coin. In the preceding section I allowed that utterly anomalous events posing as bits of an agent's behavior might, for the sake of Sententialism, be construed as pretenders within the cognitive domain. Could we now deny that the apparently vast range of activity generated by an agent's use of fallacious principles of reasoning is properly counted as genuine behavior?

Suppose it is true that a stunningly large amount of what passes for human behavior is actually activity that is not tied to antecedent propositional attitudes by way of valid chains of reasoning. Indeed, imagine that this activity ensues from propositional attitudes only by way of *characteristically* fallacious inference patterns. What would this situation be like? It would be quite analogous to a malfunctioning calculator, a calculator that characteristically yields false responses to arithmetic problems. Such a device, since it characteristically errs, could hardly be counted a calculator. It might look like one; it might even operate on chips from Silicon Valley. But it would not be a calculator. A calculator is something that, by virtue of its design, characteristically yields the right answers to arithmetic problems. Nothing else will do. Yes, things can go wrong. A functioning calculator might be dropped or its circuitry altered with dire consequences for its ability to do arithmetic. It would be broken, and a broken calculator is no more a calculator than a shattered vase is a vase. Similarly, if we were to find that humans *characteristically* are unable to solve arithmetic problems correctly, we would be ill advised to count them as calculators, that is, as engaged in the doing of arithmetic. And if we were to come to realize that humans are not calculators, what should we then say that they are *doing* when they regularly respond incorrectly to questions of arithmetic? Either we should deny that they are *doing* anything at all – in which case we would say that their activity is not, contrary to appearances, really behavior. Or we should allow that they are in fact behaving but deny that what they are in fact doing is arithmetic. We would need to reinterpret their responses as something other than false statements of arithmetic.[19] So, if we do not reinterpret, we cannot construe arithmetically deprived humans as doing arithmetic. Suppose, then, that for some reason we do not reinterpret. Would it then be finally somehow misguided to deny that the pseudoarithmetic activity is behavior? Hardly, for what should we say that they are doing? It makes little sense to say that they are falsely thinking of and responding to questions *about* arithmetic. What is the detectable difference between saying, on the one hand, that their answers are characteristically false and, on the other hand, that their answers are not about arithmetic at all?

The idea is that if we were experimentally to isolate a domain of activity or thought in which there is no logical or rational connection between the propositional attitudes attributed to an agent and the agent's activity, we would have no reason whatsoever for construing the activity as behavior. And if scientific progress should, astoundingly, show that, within a specified domain, humans are hopelessly alogical, then, regardless of our present intuitions, it would be utterly retrograde to continue to insist that the activity is cognitively controlled. Indeed, should it somehow be shown that, amazingly, human activity is *generally* alogical, then the inevitable conclusion would be that humans no more fall within

19 The point is, of course, Davidson's and Dennett's. See notes 12 and 17 to this chapter.

the domain of cognitive science than do broken calculators. Sententialism thus allows that in principle cognitive science could *discover* that humans are not rational, that they do not fall within the bounds of psychology, that 'human psychology' is an oxymoron.

But, of course, the state of affairs is not so serious as to warrant despair over human rationality. Consider the experiment by Kahneman and Tversky. The incontrovertible fact is that people will typically be unable to estimate correctly the probability of a compound situation obtaining if they know only the probability of the situations jointly constituting its components. The reason is simply that they do not know the rules of the probability calculus, at least in the weak but appropriate sense that these rules do not dictate the transformations of their propositional attitudes. When subjects are required to estimate the probability of a compound situation, they do the best they can. They guess or attempt to reason through to a conclusion. Here, however, there is nothing nonrational. Rather, it is just a special case of people trying to overcome ignorance. Problem solving is error ridden, but that certainly does not render the process irrational. Otherwise, the entire program of science itself would be irrational. Science progresses fitfully. Most of its attempts to solve its problems prove wrong. Over time, recognition of error produces recalibration, which with plenty of patience, ample funding, and lots of luck may finally secure success. Rationality admits of error so long as it is embedded in *self-correcting* processes.[20] This is why the malfunctioning calculator ultimately has no claim on rationality; it is incapable of reform. Genuine cognitive agents seem, however, generally to be capable of revising their habits of problem solving that they discover to be deficient.[21] What marks such revision as rational is that, depending on the importance of the problem to be solved and the available resources, it ceases only on satisfactory solution of the problem.[22] Thus, even

20 A potato is phototropic and so will correct the growth of its foliage away from a false light source and toward true light. Does this self-correcting activity render the potato rational? No, not even Mr. Potatohead is rational. According to Section 3.1, a precondition of a system's being rational is that its activity be driven by internal representations. Potatos do not, then, pass rational muster.

21 Within a cognitive agent the process of self-correction presumably occurs through manipulation of representations; i.e., the agent "figures out" what to try next.

22 So what marks a system as rational is a representation-fueled approach to truth

long-term failure to solve problems is consistent with rationality, so long as recognized failures lead, with the passage of time, to novel attempted solutions. What is necessary to show nonrationality in a type of cognitive agent is to show an inability to vary recurrent unsuccessful attempts to solve the problems of survival. Thus, were it empirically to be demonstrated that people could not be taught to apply the probability calculus or that they could not strike on new ways of reestimating probabilities known to be wrong, only then would the evidence begin to weigh against the rationality of humans within a domain. That card, however, seems not to be in the deck.

Nevertheless, suppose it should happen that people are typically immune to education pertaining to the rules of right reason. Assume, that is, that regardless of exposure to the theorems of the probability calculus, people persist in errors of the sort noted by Tversky and Kahneman. Such systematic errors must be laid to entrenched patterns of reasoning, patterns that are less than deductively or inductively valid. But nothing follows from this *alone* regarding rationality. What remains to be shown is that the patterns of reasoning involved do not in an important array of instances serve human needs. If these patterns are entrenched, then they would appear naturally to have evolved. Given that the patterns of reasoning in humans are the results of evolution's culling, they very likely once did, and perhaps continue to, contribute to human survival by allowing for prompt belief fixation when speed is advantageous. Evidently the cost of such speed is liability to the kinds of error and bias experimentally isolated. But the survival of the species is some evidence that the benefits resulting from adopting such patterns of reasoning compensate for the costs they extract. If this is so, then these patterns of reasoning are manifestly rational by virtue of furthering an advantageous allocation of cognitive resources within humans.

There was once in the wind an argument, which Stich (1985) has taken the care to formulate and repudiate, to the effect that rationality is necessarily inherent in naturally evolved cognitive agents. The conclusion, then, is that the rationality of naturally evolved

or satisfaction of needs. The notion is not, then, the circular one of rational changes' being whatever changes are rational.

cognitive agents cannot be impugned by the findings of cognitive science. This is to follow from two premises:

(3.4.1) Natural selection favors inferential policies that typically produce true beliefs, true beliefs being more adaptive than false ones.

(3.4.2) Inferential policies that typically lead to true beliefs are rational.

Natural selection thus favors rational inferential policies.

Stich takes both (3.4.1) and (3.4.2) to be false. Let us revisit his reasons. In assessing (3.4.1), Stich appeals to the experiments of Garcia, McGowan, and Green (1972) showing that aversions to a certain unfamiliar but innocuous food can be induced in rats exposed to harmful radiation after eating the food. Apparently the rats, which become ill after eating, employ a belief-forming policy that leads them falsely to believe the food they ate to be harmful. We may suppose that this policy is characteristic of rats in their natural habitats. Thus rats affected by disease after eating unfamiliar but harmless food will typically but falsely believe the food to be harmful. Natural selection might then opt for a belief-forming policy that usually yields false beliefs, especially if, as in the case of the rats, there is a severe penalty for false negatives. The adaptivity of rats would probably have been significantly compromised if they did not have a policy that ensured their avoiding food that really is harmful. Nature appears to have endowed rats with a typically misleading belief-forming policy that induces them to avoid a wide variety of safe foods in order to protect against any deadly mistakes.

Stich's use of experimental evidence is wonderfully ingenious, but two replies are possible. First, one might concede that (3.4.1) is false while adding that it can nevertheless be recast to retain what is important. Premise (3.4.1) might be so revised as to say that, where survival is at stake, natural selection favors inferential policies that typically produce true beliefs. Rats, if they have beliefs at all, apparently do employ a doxastic policy that leads them to believe correctly of poisonous food that it is harmful. And this suggests that we take (3.4.1) as relativized to situations bearing on survival. The weakened but still significant conclusion that this revision would underwrite would be that, where survival is at stake, natural selection favors rational inferential policies.

Second, and more important, one might wonder whether the

inferential policy the rats possess is in fact the one Stich assigns to them. For all that the evidence shows, it could well be that the computational practice leading to the food aversion actually produces true beliefs. The rats may come to believe not simply that the unfamiliar food is harmful but rather that it *might* be harmful and, so, is best avoided. That is, we can fancifully imagine a rat suffering from radiation poisoning thinking, What could have made me so agonizingly ill? Perhaps it was that strange food I ate. For all I know, it could have been. So, since I cannot think of anything else to blame and in order to be on the safe side, I had better stay away from that damn stuff. Hence, if the rat believes either that the food might be harmful or that, given what it knows, it had better not risk eating the food, it believes truly. The behavior of the rat is then explicable without attributing to it a systematically misleading doxastic habit.

Beyond this, it is essential to see how rats behave in the long run. Can rats learn to discriminate harmful from healthful food? If they can, then estimates of the epistemic systems operant in rats should be judged with this in mind. The inferential process that guides rats' beliefs about foods may well be one that, over time, does indeed tend to produce true beliefs. In other words, and as already noted, when judging the rationality of a type of agent, we must look to the plasticity the agent naturally exhibits. Where agents bend to survive, we very well may find, as in the case of rats, inferential policies naturally designed, given ample time, to select for truth.

The problem with (3.4.2), according to Stich, is that an inferential policy that typically yields true beliefs may occasionally fail with dire consequences, thereby calling into question the rationality of adopting the policy. Reconsider the rats and suppose, counterfactually, that they typically were to infer that unfamiliar foods are safe to eat even if ingestion is followed by illness. This belief might serve the rats well if food is typically unrelated to illness. Such a habit, one that typically produces true beliefs, may seem rational. Occasionally, however, rats would die from eating poisonous unfamiliar food. And thus the exorbitant cost of error may impugn the rationality of a typically reliable inferential policy. Moving away from the counterfactual, Stich notes that frogs, much to their detriment, will mistake rolling lead BBs for nourishing food. Apparently the practice that typically produces in frogs true beliefs about what is edible is at work when they ingest BBs, and this makes (3.4.2) dubious.

Or does it? BBs are alien to the habitat of frogs. That frogs can be tricked into mistaking BBs for food surely does not compromise the rationality of their generally reliable inferential policies regarding food. That policy was developed in the absence of BBs. This particular policy presumably would not have developed had BBs been natural to the environment of frogs. Additionally, we can recognize the rationality of a generally reliable belief-producing policy even if it suffers occasional disasters if it is the best that the type of agent employing the policy can achieve. Frogs must find food by using their sensory organs. It may well be that the only features of their food to which frogs are sensitive happen to be shared by certain rare poisons. The inferential policy frogs depend on in selecting what to eat will generally serve them well, though it will occasionally cost some frogs dearly. But because of their sensory limitations, frogs may have no alternative policy open to them. And if so, the rationality of their inferential policy is hardly suspect.[23]

23 Questioning (3.4.2), Stich points out that the experimental literature documents that people are prone to apply an inferential strategy that has proved *useful* in one domain to another. The results can be disastrous. Nevertheless, this is quite beside the point. What Stich needs to show here is that such strategies typically produce *true* beliefs and yet generate problematic consequences when applied in alien domains. Stich simply does not specify an actual situation in which an inferential policy that generally produces true beliefs in people in one domain so thoroughly fails in another domain as to establish that the policy is rationally bankrupt. In any case, the whole idea of the domain of an inferential policy wants clarification. Suppose we begin with the assumption that the natural domain of a generally reliable inferential policy is D. We might also find that, when applied to domain D^*, the results of the policy undermine any claim to rationality it might have, because in D^* it typically produces false beliefs. Or we might take the policy's failure in D^* to show that the domain of the inferential policy is only arbitrarily taken to be D and that it is properly the union of D and D^*. In this event, the policy would not typically produce true beliefs in its (now natural) domain of the union of D and D^* and, hence, would not be an inferential policy sufficient for undermining (3.4.2).

4

Along the cognitive spectrum

Perhaps the most natural, spontaneous objection to Sententialism is that it outlandishly supposes that all interesting cognitive phenomena are ultimately to be laid to the interaction of sentences encoded in cognitive agents' central and, perhaps, peripheral nervous systems.[1] What plausibility does this proposal have once we recognize that nonverbal animals are capable of cognition?[2] And besides, how likely is it that all of the neural processes necessary for the processing of information within ourselves are properly linguistic?

Sententialism does not require that all interesting psychological episodes in all creatures must be rooted in computational processes defined over mental sentences. The idea is, rather, that insofar as behavior is properly traced to propositional attitudes, it results from sententially driven computational processes. And of course, together with this goes the assumption that a great deal of what we do, and some nonnegligible amount of what many animals do, admits of explanation drawing on propositional attitudes. This is quite compatible with some of our psychological activities, as well as those of various animals, being explicable in terms of noncomputational, nonsentential models. A pigeon may peck because of prior conditioning; and a rat, because of its history of reinforcement, might press a lever. Nevertheless, this does not preclude the pi-

---

1 Although it is again relevant here, space still precludes a discussion of mental imagery. See the references cited in note 9 of Chapter 1.
2 C. A. Hooker (1976) was among the first to charge Sententialism with the inability to accommodate cognition in the nonverbal. For at least the last ten years, Paul Churchland and Patricia Smith Churchland have complained on similar grounds that sentential models of cognitive operations are woefully inadequate. See Paul Churchland (1975, 1979, and 1981), Patricia Smith Churchland (1978, 1980a, b), and Paul Churchland and Patricia Smith Churchland (1983). Kitcher (1984), Eckardt (1984), and Horgan and Woodward (1985) have defended selected cognitive constructs against the Churchlands' arguments.

geon's taking wing for fear of an approaching dog and the rat's remaining holed up in the hope of avoiding the cat outside. The point is that various kinds of activities of various kinds of organisms might have various kinds of explanations, such explanations applying differently as the specified organisms scale the phylogenetic tree. Sententialism is locked to the thesis that a significant portion of all this activity, especially as found in highly intelligent organisms, is explained by sentential encoding of information.

The Churchlands (Paul Churchland, 1979, p. 137; Patricia Smith Churchland, 1980b) press Sententialism for being too *parochial* a psychology ever to comprehend the behavior of nonverbal agents. Sententialism's modeling of psychological processes against human language must fail, they contend, with respect to nonverbal but intelligent agents. The intelligent processing of information displayed by a dog can hardly be sentential since the dog is nonverbal. So sententialism cannot pretend to be a start on a comprehensive psychology.

The reply to this objection should be plain by now. That a type of agent lacks overt language shows absolutely nothing about the nature of its psychological processes. It certainly does not establish that the processes could not essentially involve the interaction among sentences in an unspoken language encoded in the agent's brain states. In any event, this much is clear. The senses present the brain with a stunning amount of information measured simply in terms of electrochemical states the sensory systems enter consequent to stimulation. For the brain to use this massive and unwieldy amount of information, it must distill and categorize it. Nothing, however, precludes the possibility of such categorization's being of the same sort achieved linguistically. That is, it is consistent with the fact that the brain must abstract from the information in which it is awash that it does so by deploying states that function as predicates. A predicate is, among other things, a vehicle of categorization, and a system of predicates functions as an organizational scheme in the form of a language.

Certainly, verbal animals are distinguished from intelligent but nonverbal creatures by their manifest ability to use language to communicate. There is, however, no a priori reason to suppose that the division of animals according to their abilities with overt languages of communication perfectly, or even approximately, parallels the gulf between animals whose behavior ensues on com-

110

putations couched in a mental language and those whose behavior does not. Sententialism does not entail that only verbal creatures can enjoy a mental language. Neither does it presuppose that an intelligent creature's language of thought must be its language of communication, supposing the creature is verbal. What Sententialism does insist is that the propriety of predicating a language of thought to a type of intelligent agent depends on whether attributing a mental language to agents of that type best enables explanations of a wide range of such agents' behavior and whether their nervous system is sufficiently complex to carry the computational processes through which the postulated sentences are transformed. Nothing so far, then, seems to preclude the possibility that selected types of nonverbal animals possess mental languages whose expressive and computational powers are set by their environments and nervous systems.

It is no complaint against Sententialism, then, that it is forced to violate the quite reasonable demand for a unified psychology applicable both to verbal creatures and their intelligent but nonverbal evolutionary predecessors. Sententialism allows for mental languages of computation in verbal organisms as well as their nonverbal ancestors.[3] Certainly Sententialism is contingent on an account of how language, overt and mental, evolves.[4] This obli-

---

3 Patricia Smith Churchland (1980a) complains that Sententialism's willingness to assign covert mental languages to nonverbal animals is nothing short of an "infralinguistic catastrophe." However, in this charge, as Kitcher (1984) argues, Churchland simply begs the question against Sententialism. Whereas she supposes that nonverbal animals cannot have a covert mental language, Sententialism allows that they must. Churchland maintains that nature abounds in intelligent but fundamentally nonlinguistic activity. But the examples she cites, such as the intelligent activity of preverbal infants, can be differently construed by Sententialism. More on this in Section 4.2.

4 With this in mind, Kitcher (1984, p. 101), citing Ernst Mayr (1960), says, "A complex novel structure, capable of supporting linguistically mediated cognition, could have arisen in at least three different ways. Suppose the primitive forms of this structure had little adaptive value. Then the structure could have evolved via the mechanism of 'pleiotropy,' that is, by being carried on an adaptive structure that shared the same genetic determinants. Another possibility is that a structure capable of supporting linguistically mediated cognition arose via 'intensification of function.' Like primitive eyes, a primitive system of representations may have some adaptive value, and that value may increase incrementally with refinements of the system. The most common mode of producing evolutionary novelty is via 'change of function.' A primitive form of our cognitive system might have supported some other adaptive function. As the structure evolved, it became able to support the new function of linguistically mediated cognition."

111

gation does not underwrite an objection in principle to Sentential-ism. Even if the evolution of language is yet fully to be explained, it is certainly a fact that overt language somehow evolved. And we may anticipate that an account of the evolution of overt language may also shed light on the evolution of mental language.

Granted the possibility of Sententialism, how plausible is its premise that a substantial amount of the information that highly intelligent creatures process is sententially encoded and inferentially manipulated? Not at all, according to Patricia Smith Churchland (1980a, p. 160). She holds that the Sententialist picture perversely entails that concept learning is but an illusion, that human knowl-edge is necessarily static, and, consequently, that scientific advance is impossible. She argues thus: The Sententialist supposes that learn-ing involves processing sententially structured information. To learn a concept involves, on this model, confirming a hypothesis regarding the extension of the concept. In order, then, to learn what, for example, a bear is requires confirming a hypothesis to the effect that a bear is whatever has some specified property or set of properties. By way of Sententialism, an agent bent on under-standing the concept of being a bear must verify a Mentalese sen-tence such as:

> (4.1.1) Something is a bear if and only if it is F, where 'F' expresses a concept the agent already understands or a (truth functional) compound predicate constructed from antecedently familiar predicates.[5]

Thus in confirming (4.1.1), an agent would need antecedently to understand the concept (or cluster of concepts) expressed in Men-talese by 'F'. Yet, assuming (4.1.1) to be confirmed, being a bear turns out to be equivalent to being F. Thus, any agent who confirms (4.1.1) must already have the concept of being a bear (or the ex-tension of the same), that simply being F. This holds for any con-cept, and hence Sententialism is committed to the idea that an agent cannot expand his or her repertoire of concepts. An agent might thus come to discover that some *particular, individual* creature is a

---

5 Or to put the problem in terms of learning a new predicate, the Sententialist is said to have the agent confirm a truth rule such as

(4.1.1*) 'x is a bear' is true (in English) iff x is F.

Compare Fodor (1975, p. 59).

bear – that is, F – but could not discover the concept of being a bear. Should knowledge be so severely hobnailed, it would, but contrary to fact, be fundamentally static. A special, and important, case of this is that scientific progress would be beyond possibility, since it is certainly an instance of conceptual expansion.

Churchland is certainly right in repudiating any theory of mentation with so thoroughly wrong consequences. Sententialism, however, is not fused to the assumptions from which these consequences are wrung. Although it must concede that learning, as a cognitive process, essentially involves transformations of Mentalese sentences, Sententialism need not insist that concept learning involves confirmation as depicted by (4.1.1). Sententialism is consistent with a more expansive, holistic notion of concept acquisition. Concepts are understood by degree (Putnam, 1975). As an astronomer, you understand the various exotic properties of comets. I know only that comets are passing lights with tails. But we both can detect Halley's comet and recognize it for what it is. This is largely because, expert that you are, you predict its appearance and position and advise me where and when to look. Surely we both have the concept of a comet, although only you are authoritative on the subject. We both have the concept since we both know certain truths about comets. You are the authority because you know more of these truths than I do. You, but not I, know some of the laws comets obey and how these laws interact with the principles of astronomy generally. This suggests that in order to acquire a concept, it suffices to be able to use correctly an indeterminate number of nontrivial sentences predicating the concept. It is not necessary to confirm any sentence expressing a definitional or nomic equivalence between the concept to be acquired and ones already in hand. Otherwise, few of the concepts we suppose ourselves to possess would we actually comprehend. Since conceptualization comes in varying degrees, there is not, for any given concept, a principled, nonarbitrary specification of sentences predicating the concept that must be confirmed if the concept is to be understood. Suppose that 'F', 'G', and 'H' are predicates understood by an agent and that 'C' is a predicate expressing a novel concept. Then, depending on the concepts expressed by 'F', 'G', 'H', and 'C', it may suffice for understanding 'C' that an agent confirm or otherwise come to believe truths such as

113

(4.1.2) If x is F, then x is C.
(4.1.3) If x is C, then x is G.
(4.1.4) If x is H and G but not F, then x is C.

Indeed, depending on the concept in question and the importance of accurately identifying its instances, it probably suffices minimally to understand a concept simply usually to be able correctly to identify samples of the concept.[6] Even here slippage within certain ill-defined limits is probably permissible. Now, if we suppose that (4.1.2)–(4.1.4) are Mentalese sentences, then we can see how, according to Sentialism, an agent might acquire a genuinely novel concept, a concept not strictly equivalent to or definable in terms of any antecedently possessed. C, the acquired concept, is related in various, but nonequivalent, ways to the previously understood concepts, F, G, and H. Surely, however, acquiring a new concept does not require that its connection to known concepts be completely masked. Its novelty is ensured so long as it is embedded in a system of familiar concepts without being introduced as equivalent to any of them. If this is granted, then ever-newer and increasingly alien concepts can be added to an agent's system of concepts by virtue of the newer concepts' being variously related to previously introduced concepts with the result that an agent's final conceptual scheme may far outstrip the scheme from which it arose. Evidently, if being able simply to identify instances of a concept suffices for a rudimentary understanding of that concept, then it is possible, by Sentialism's lights, that an agent could acquire a concept that is disconnected from others the agent already has, although its utility would be practically nil until it is integrated with other concepts. Still, if various concepts are acquired in this ostensive way, they may increase in utility by virtue of their collective implications apart from what other relations they might in fact happen to have to the agent's aboriginal concepts. What is more, nothing in Sentialism prohibits the removal of concepts from a scheme.

The idea, then, is that Mentalese predicates function as concepts complete with extensions. A novel concept is thus a predicate newly

---

6 Although I do think that one might acquire some concepts by simple ostension, I do not want to push this line hard here, and I am at present content to say that confirming the likes of (4.1.2) – (4.1.4) suffices for learning a concept. See Chapter 6 for discussion of related matters.

114

added to an agent's Mentalese stock. Importantly, the manner in which new Mentalese predicates are introduced allows the extension of a new Mentalese predicate to be distinct from any of the extensions of those predicates to which it is explicitly related by way of introduction. The manner of introduction serves only to specify some extensions that include or are included by the extension of the introduced predicate. The extension of an introduced Mentalese predicate is, then, typically not completely determined on its introductory association with antecedently available mental predicates. Thus, subsequent to its introduction, a new predicate can be discovered to apply in surprising ways. In sum, if C is introduced by way of (4.1.2) – (4.1.4), it may subsequently be determined that falling under C implies or is implied by falling under some concept other than F, G, or H. Sententialism, thus, is consistent not only with the introduction of new predicates or concepts but also with their ever-novel ramifications.

Moreover, it is also easy to see how the conceptual base of an agent could be jettisoned once new, presumably more sophisticated predicates or concepts have been added to the base. To capture the point, imagine, whimsically, that mental sentences have a brief radioactive half-life with the consequence that all tokens of a type of mental sentence are erased from memory when any token of the type has persisted ten years. The conceptual scheme of a middle-aged adult would include, then, none of the concepts garnered in adolescence. Talk of midlife crisis! Although no Sententialist would suppose this fancy to be fact, that it is compatible with Sententialism serves to show the extent to which Sententialism can allow for evolving conceptual schemes.

One consequence of all this is that an agent's learned overt language of communication can far outstrip the agent's mental language *originally* deployed in learning the conventional language. To learn 'comet' it seems necessary and apparently sufficient to confirm truths such as

(4.1.5) Comets typically have luminous tails.
(4.1.6) If a luminous heavenly object appears to move relatively rapidly against a background of stars, cyclically appearing and disappearing from view, then it is probably a comet.

Confirming these presupposes understanding 'luminous', itself a presumably learned term. But it should be clear now that Mentalese, at least as primordially present in an agent, need not contain terms for or otherwise equivalent to either 'comet' or 'luminous'. In order to learn 'comet' and 'luminous', an agent requires as mental terms simply terms (or compounds thereof) that imply or are implied by 'comet' and 'luminous'. If the implicational chains leading back from 'comet', through 'luminous', to the basic terms of Mentalese are long and complicated with many intervening *English* terms, then there is every reason to suspect that the expressive power of English greatly exceeds that of Mentalese, at least that fragment of Mentalese necessary for the computational processes involved in confirming truths involving the English terms to be mastered. This is a consequence of the fact that the novel concept expressed by a learned term typically will have an extension distinct from the concepts in terms of which it is originally introduced.

As for the possibility of science, that too is consistent with Sententialism. As earlier noted, science is a special case of concept acquisition, and since Sententialism is hospitable to new concepts, it can welcome scientific progress as well.

4.2. FROM INFANT TO ADULT

Paul Churchland (1979, p. 127) has argued that Sententialism, besides being parochial, is for other reasons a woefully misguided theory of mentation. He has marshaled a straightforward yet singularly impressive argument against the plausibility of Sententialism, charging that Sententialism is incompatible with the *continuity* in the psychological processes that take an infant into an adult. The argument can be simply put:

> (4.2.1) Cognitive activity in infants cannot be attributed to their processing Mentalese sentences.

Yet, apparently,

> (4.2.2) The type of cognitive processing enjoyed by infants and adults is substantially the same.

Therefore, in neither adults nor infants is cognitive processing at bottom sentential processing. Sententialism, accordingly, must be false.

The argument is certainly valid, but it is not evidently sound. Its first premise is unsubstantiated. We need not argue that infants

116

do, *in fact*, process information sententially. Rather, it suffices to establish that Churchland's reasons for supposing that infants *could not* process sententially are themselves insufficient for securing the truth of (4.2.1).

Infants, from the earliest age, exhibit an array of interesting behavior that we must suppose is contingent on their furiously processing substantial amounts of information. Churchland makes his case this way:

> The behaviour of an infant during the first several months after birth invites description/explanation in terms of specific perceptions, beliefs and reasonings no more than does the (more leisurely) behaviour of many plants, or the (more frantic) behaviour of many microscopic protozoa. The apparently chaotic economy of an infant's behaviour – and there is plenty of behaviour if one looks closely – is not rendered transparent or coherent by any such projection of familiar categories. The relevant organization in its behavioural economy has yet to develop. Were it not for the fact that infants resemble and eventually develop into thinking adults, whereas plants and protozoa do not, we would not even be much tempted to ascribe propositional attitudes and our usual cognitive concepts to them. (p. 129)

The idea seems to be that even if we closely observe selected bits of behavior of an infant shy of his or her fourth postnatal month, we will be unable to settle on a systematic attribution of beliefs and desires sufficient to explain the behavior. Unable to ascribe beliefs and desires, we must deny that the infant is processing information sententially since, for Sententialism, sentential processing is proposed as an account of behavior induced by belief and desire.

Nonetheless, we need not be persuaded by Churchland's argument. There are two reasons. First, consider the apparently chaotic limb movements in neonates. Do such movements exemplify the type of behavior that Churchland takes to defy explanation in terms of propositional attitudes? If so, the Sententialist may well agree without thereby abdicating Sententialism. In a plain sense such movements are best viewed as akin to reflex reactions, bodily activity beyond the cognitive control of the infant. The newborn's chaotic movements are, no doubt, reactions to neural activity, the neural activity itself perhaps resulting from sensory stimulation. Nonetheless, this falls short of showing that the movements are of a kind with the movements in the adult that instantiate full-blown, cognitively controlled behavior. If so, then the infant's random movements are no more within the domain of cognitive science – and, hence, Sententialism – than are an adult's spasmodic movements. But the fact that Sententialism fails to explain spasmodic movements in an adult no more establishes the falsity of the doctrine than does its inapplicability to the cognitively unmonitored movements of an infant.

Second, let us note those movements of an infant that seem not at all random but in perfect harmony with the intersection of the child's needs and environment. An infant sucks when put to the breast and stops when sated. What shall we say here? Either the sucking is a tropism and, as such, not a manifestation of intelligent information processing or it is an intelligent response to stimulation. If the former, then Sententialism is unworried by the phenomenon since Sententialism is proposed as an account of only intelligent behavior. If the latter, then what prevents the Sententialist from saying *of* the milk in the breast *that* the infant desires *it* and believes respectively *of* sucking and milk that *such* is how to get *it*? Here we predicate beliefs and desires to the infant by way of explaining its behavior at the breast. Indeed, it is hard to decline the invitation to ascribe such beliefs and desires to the infant once we grant that the behavior at the breast is just that, behavior. This ascription of propositional attitudes to the infant apparently renders the behavior intelligible, which is what Churchland says Sententialism, in predicating beliefs and desires, fails to do.

These attributions of desire and belief are de re; they attribute beliefs and desires to the infant but avoid fully specifying the content of the infant's propositional attitudes. A desire for what we scribes know to be milk is attributed to the infant. But this ascription is silent on how the child conceives of milk. So perhaps the complaint is that falling back here on de re ascriptions is tantamount to admitting that English is unable to express the content of the attitudes the child is supposed to have. That, in turn, would entail the inability of Sententialism to indicate exactly which Mentalese sentences are operant in the infant's cognitive processing. If so, this exposes the Sententialist response for the ad hoc, untestable hypothesis it is.[7]

---

7 Churchland puts the reply thus: "One could insist, as some will, that the young infant is none the less the subject of the familiar propositional attitudes, the claim being that the particular propositions that would express the infant's attitudes are inexpressible in our language, the infant's ideas or concepts being primitive ones quite different from our own. Our inability to make any systematic explanatory sense of their behaviour and development in terms of propositional attitudes is therefore not to be marvelled at. Thus, it will be said, one can embrace premiss

Evidently, it is quite false that English lacks the resources to express the content of the infant's hypothesized beliefs and desires. Concepts, we supposed in Section 4.1, come in degrees. Naturally we should anticipate that the concepts that begin to structure an infant's cognitive scheme are most rudimentary, that their interconnections are sparse and fragile. One way of acknowledging this in attributing beliefs and desires to an infant is to retreat to de re ascriptions. These ascriptions, when applied to infants, simply ostend, as it were, the concepts current in the infant's scheme. But it is certainly possible to do better than this. We can say the infant wants milk and believes that sucking will bring milk, so long as we provide a gloss to the effect that the infant's conception of milk and sucking is impoverished relative to ours. Yes, we do not know just what the infant understands milk to be beyond being, from the infant's perspective, *this* stuff with *that* taste. But then again, I cannot pretend precisely to know exactly what you understand milk to be. You might be a chemist employed by the American Dairy Association whose understanding of milk leaves mine far behind. So, once we recognize that concepts come in degrees and, importantly, appreciate that that does not prevent their attribution to our adult peers, we can proceed cautiously to ascribe them to neonates, restricting our ascriptions to those minimally sufficient to explain infantile behavior. And where such explanations go wanting, we may continue to surmise that there is no intelligent behavior, only noncognitively guided movement, to be explicated.

So much for the first of Churchland's premises. The second also is questionable. Suppose, for the moment, it to be false that the type of cognitive processing enjoyed by infants and adults is substantially the same. How might this cohere with the smooth, continuous development in behavioral repertoire as an infant develops into an adult? Conceivably this developmental continuity masks a continuous transition from brute to intelligent processes. To see how this might occur, it may help first to consider an example from another realm. Imagine a long train moving down a track at

(4.2.2) [my number] whole-heartedly, while rejecting (4.2.1) [my number]. Now it must be admitted that a position along these lines is in no immediate danger of empirical refutation . . . for it is the paradigm of an untestable hypothesis. A dispassionate look . . . will reveal it for what it is: an *ad hoc* assumption of negligible testability embraced solely to preserve the generality of the 'propositional attitude' conception of human intellectual activity" (1979, pp. 129–30).

a constant speed and powered by several steam engines, each encased in a separate car. The train consists of many cars, several of which house nonoperating diesel engines whose horsepower collectively equals that of the steam engines that are actually pulling the train. The energy supplied to one of the steam engines is slowly choked simultaneous to the gradual powering of one of the diesels. Diesel continuously replaces steam power resulting in no variation in the speed of the train. One by one the steam engines are replaced in this way by the diesels until finally the train, whose speed has never varied, moves under purely diesel power.

If we were to attend only to the constancy of the train's rate of movement, we might casually, but wrongly, dismiss the idea that the explanation of the train's early motion importantly differs from that of its later motion. Something similar might be true of the apparently continuous behavioral development transforming an infant into a mature verbal agent. That is, it could be that the neonate is utterly unintelligent, that all of its activity calls for a nonpsychological explanation in the style appropriate to witless objects generally. Thus the infant's early movements toward the breast might, as movements, be indistinguishable from those of later infancy. Over time, the infant's attraction to the breast may seem much the same as that it originally displayed. Yet this constancy in movement to the breast may mask a basic change in the source of the movement. Although originally it may have resulted from an unintelligent process, its cause may, as the infant matures, finally be laid to beliefs and desires welling up within the child.

Who knows whether this apparent possibility regarding infants is genuine? Still, it is worthwhile to pause to reflect that if this proposal should prove true, it would serve nicely to explain both the smooth behavioral curve traced by a maturing infant and why it is so difficult to discern when sentential dynamics begin to move a child. The behavioral curve would be smooth because brutish activity would give way to intelligent behavior only gradually, probably according to domain of activity. Indeed, it would be just this that taxes attempts to get the explanation right for any specific bit of the child's behavior.

Given the hypothesis that intelligent sentential mental processing gradually and progressively replaces unintelligent systems within an infant, it would evidently be wrong to say that the infant *learns* to use its sentential system, if learning itself is understood to be a paradigmatically intelligent activity. Rather, it would be necessary to suppose that the sentential processing of information is determined to blossom in the developing infant, perhaps in accord with some sort of radical nativism (Fodor, 1975; Chomsky, 1982) or perhaps along the lines of a more modest sort of nativism sprinkled with a bit of empiricism.[8] Regardless of which of these tacks should be taken, the central idea would remain that the finally correct account of the onset of intelligent sentential information processing may itself need to be consistent with the possibility that a maturing infant changes from a brute into an intelligent agent. Indeed, something like this seems guaranteed to be the case. A zygote reacts variously and appropriately to its intrauterine environment, and – I suppose – as it develops into a fetus, it displays no radical discontinuity in the type of sensitivity it displays. Yet surely sometime after conception and prior to the senior prom it is transformed from an unintelligent to an intelligent system. There seems then to be no conclusive reason preventing its entry to intelligence coinciding with its assuming sentential processing.

Some (e.g., Patricia Smith Churchland, 1978, 1980a) will not like this at all. They suppose that Sententialism is committed to a sort of profoundly mistaken nativism making it utterly incredible. In any event, they hold it wildly wrong to contend that genuinely intelligent activity is concurrent with the onset of the processing of Mentalese. They urge rather that the human brain has evolved a nonlinguistic way of processing information (Paul Churchland, 1979) that underwrites the acquisition of natural language while surpassing it in informational power. It is just such a nonlinguistic system, rather than Mentalese, that they suppose the infant enjoys in common with the adult. They would have it that, so equipped, the brain distills the overwhelming amount of information available at the sensory periphery into manageable and necessarily highly abstracted informational units.

Certainly the brain is extraordinarily adept at abstracting information from the ambient array, but let us issue two notes here. First, any language, Mentalese included, is a system of information distillation and abstraction. What critics of Sententialism must, but have yet to, show is that Mentalese, as a system of information

---

8 In Chapter 6 I will opt for the latter alternative, arguing that Mentalese is, for the most part, an acquired, even if unlearned, language.

distillation and abstraction, is *inadequate* to the demands of information processing in intelligent creatures. Second, but more important for present purposes, those who would assign to the brain a nonlinguistic system of information processing vastly superior in all relevant respects to linguistic systems are hardly in a position to criticize Sentimentalism on the grounds of its assigning to human infants a linguistic system of information processing bound to outrun their endogenous capacities. The Churchlands cannot, then, consistently say that Mentalese is too sophisticated for neonates while also maintaining, by virtue of (4.2.2), that infants (like adults) have a system of information processing whose reach exceeds the limited informational capacity of any linguistic system. In their eagerness to find naturally installed in the brain an information processor sufficient to spawn and support spoken language, the Churchlands appear to have undercut their own complaints about Sentimentalism's commitment to a linguistic system of mental representation in the infant. And that amounts to dislodging (4.2.1) and with it the conclusion opposing Sentimentalism to which it leads.

The Churchlands' dissatisfaction with Sentimentalism arises not only from their concern that it founders on the continuity of the psychology of infant and adult but also from a certain inherent rigidity that defies the *plasticity* manifest in intelligent agents. Following Quine (1953), Putnam (1969), and Feyerabend (1970), Paul Churchland argues that every sentence suitable for judgment is subject to epistemic revision. The apparent failure of empiricism is taken to show that no truth-values, neither those assigned to expressions of sensation nor the supposedly analytic principles of logic, are guaranteed. Let us also assume for present purposes that this is so. Churchland advances to the claim that Sentimentalism cannot account for the possibility that, over time, truth-values of any and all sentences vary or submit to recalibration. The argument for this last appears to take the following tack.[9] To reassign truth-values to sentences is to revise the beliefs expressed by those sentences. Revision of belief, according to Sentimentalism, amounts to Mentalese sentences being either exchanged for their denials or else simply deleted from the store of affirmed sentences. Extensive change in belief thus is, by Sentimentalism's lights, extensive alter-

---

9 Churchland's argument (1979, pp. 140–2) is not transparently plain, and so my interpretation of it is just that, an interpretation that might misrepresent Churchland's intention. *Caveat lector!*

ation in the stock of Mentalese sentences. Importantly, belief revision of the proposed sort can be quite rational. And this rationality is presumably to be gauged in terms of Mentalese sentences' being exchanged according to specified principles. The question is: What, given Sententialism, must these principles be? Minimally, Sententialism is committed to the idea that these principles must themselves be recorded as Mentalese sentences. Yet these are the very kinds of things that are themselves open to revision. So how could they account for the underlying, *stable* constraints governing the rationality typically inherent in belief revision? There is, accordingly, no alternative to admitting that the dynamics of rational belief fixation and revision depend on nonsentential psychological processes.

To this we might consider two replies. First, for this argument to succeed, it would be necessary that Sententialism require that the principles of rational belief fixation and revision themselves be encoded in rational agents. We have already seen (in Chapter 3, Section 3.1), however, in discussing what distinguishes the rule-governed, cognitive activity of agents from the law-governed but noncognitive movements of the planets, that Sententialism need not insist that the principles dictating belief formation and alteration themselves be encoded in rational agents. Second, suppose that, finally, Sententialism must take an agent's rational revision of belief to presuppose the encoding in the agent of Mentalese sentences expressive of rules dictating the rationality of belief fixation and revision. It may well be that while these very principles are all subject to revision, they are not *all at once* revisable. Belief revision on a massive scale is, in any account, a slow process typically spanning generations and requiring more than minimal social commerce. If this is the case, there is no reason to suppose that the process of belief revision could not occur consistent with the general tenets of Sententialism. The theme to fasten onto here is that if Churchland is right in assuming that the demise of empiricism does demonstrate that every apparent truth is open to reconsideration, then so too, by Churchland's own supposition, are the principles governing belief revision itself! That implies that belief revision could not be a process marked by the long-term stability based in a constancy of epistemic principles to which Churchland alludes. If this is so, then Sententialism is quite consistent with the actual practice of belief revision, even if the doctrine should be forced to allow that belief revision requires the encoding in Mentalese of principles (temporarily) guiding belief fixation and revision. The rational, albeit finally unstable, transformation of language and belief therefore constitutes no refutation of Sententialism.

4.3. DOXASTIC HOLISM AND MENTALESE AMBIGUITY

Sententialism is the doctrine that beliefs are relations to Mentalese sentences, structures with both semantic and syntactic properties. Stich (1983) has perceptively argued that Sententialism's insistence on a semantic component for Mentalese is probably mistaken. The problem, as Stich sees it, is if the cognitive structures that control behavior are taken to be contentful, it becomes all but impossible to individuate them with the precision required by a science of the mind. That is, ascriptions of beliefs, if Stich is right, are essentially vague if beliefs are semantic structures of the sort Sententialism supposes.

In order to establish his case, Stich presents challenging examples purporting to illustrate that an ascription of a belief to an agent implicitly acknowledges the implications relating the agent's beliefs. The content of a belief, if Stich is right, is largely a matter of its position in a holistically characterized scheme of beliefs. Thus beliefs with different implications are different beliefs. Yet, Stich urges, it is possible that the very same syntactic structures in different agents have different implicational relations. Such syntactic structures could not then encode the same semantic properties. Hence, syntactic and semantic identity need not coincide; tokens of the same syntactic type need not be tokens of the same semantic type. Should this prove correct, Sententialism would be undermined. For at least within agents of the same sort, Sententialism takes semantic properties to supervene on syntactic structures (Fodor, 1980a). In short, Stich attempts to show that Mentalese is radically ambiguous. If he is right, Sententialism is a dubious doctrine indeed.

Examples then. Mrs. T. has grown quite old and now suffers from a serious neural disorder manifested by extraordinary memory loss. As a child, she was shocked and greatly impressed by the news of President McKinley's assassination. Not surprisingly, when now questioned about President McKinley, she asserts that he was assassinated. Yet so severe is her disorder that she seems to recall almost nothing else about McKinley. Indeed, if asked whether

124

McKinley is dead, she replies that she does not know! In short, she has no, or almost no, understanding of assassination although she apparently insists that McKinley was assassinated. What are we to make of this?

Stich supposes that, since Mrs. T. asserts "McKinley was assassinated" in much the same circumstances that others would, there must, according to Sententialism, be in Mrs. T. a Mentalese sentence encoding this belief, which sentence is syntactically the same as that which produces similar assertions in others. Same effect, same cause – not an unreasonable hypothesis. The catch is that, given what we know of Mrs. T., we certainly cannot blithely assume that she in fact believes that McKinley was assassinated. Her belief does not cause her to agree that McKinley is dead, which it would, were it the belief that McKinley was assassinated. The Mentalese sentence 'McKinley was assassinated' encoded in Mrs. T. does not cause to occur in her the Mentalese sentence 'McKinley is dead'. That amounts to the former Mentalese sentence not entailing, in Mrs. T., the latter. This is so despite the fact that, in normal people, Mentalese sentences syntactically identical with Mrs. T.'s token of 'McKinley was assassinated' presumably do cause, and thus imply, Mentalese tokens syntactically the same as 'McKinley is dead'. So, it appears as if the semantic properties of Mrs. T.'s Mentalese token of 'McKinely was assassinated' differ from those normally associated with tokens of the same syntactic type. For if Mrs. T.'s token *meant* that McKinley was assassinated, it would cause her to agree that McKinley is dead. Put differently, Mrs. T. does not believe that McKinley is dead and therefore cannot believe that he was assassinated, regardless of what mentally encoded syntactic structure leads her to assert that "McKinley was assassinated."

There are several things to say about the case of Mrs. T. First and paramount is that she is neurally impaired. Sententialism can legitimately claim to be a theory about normal cognitive functioning and, accordingly, hold that Mrs. T. does not fall within its explanatory compass. An analogy may help here. Suppose that a chess-playing computer program plays well-conceived games when running on functioning computers of a certain manufacturer but fails to produce anything remotely like chess when mounted on a malfunctioning machine of the same design. With respect to the combination of the program and a normally functioning computer, we might (metaphorically) say that it plays chess and even perhaps that is has all sorts of beliefs about chess. But we had better not say anything of the sort about the program as installed on a malfunctioning device. Such a combination plays no chess and certainly believes nothing about chess. Indeed, it has no beliefs at all. The reason, evidently, is that the malfunctioning machine, by virtue of its condition, simply does not qualify as an (artificial) cognitive agent. The same *may* well be true of Mrs. T. Due to her neural disorder, she may, within certain domains, no longer be cognitively endowed. If so, Sententialism can hardly be held accountable for an explanation of her condition. That would be for neurology to explain, just as it would be an engineering, rather than a programming, problem to revive a damaged computer.

Another analogy may be of some use. Suppose that we have two quarters and place one each into two different change-making machines. From the first machine we receive in return for the inserted quarter two dimes and one nickle. The other machine is broken. Some of its coin slots and chambers are jammed. So it surrenders only a nickle in change for the quarter it swallowed. It would be madness to infer from the fact that the machines do not produce exactly the same change that they both could not have inside themselves coins valued the same. The problem is simply that the internal mechanism of one of the machines precludes the quarter it contains from unleashing the coins it would were the machine intact.

Mrs. T. is most likely similar to the malfunctioning machine. The Mentalese sentence in her really is semantically evaluated as representing that McKinley was assassinated. In this it is modeled by the coin inserted into the malfunctioning machine really being valued at twenty-five cents. That the representation in Mrs. T. fails to cause her to announce or even believe that McKinley is dead may be due not to what it does or does not represent but rather simply to the fact that Mrs. T.'s neural circuits are "jammed." Her situation does not, then, necessitate conceding that Mentalese is ambiguous.

Besides this, we should question Stich's assumption about the syntactic structure occurrent in Mrs. T. On the one hand, Stich supposes that it is syntactically the same as the structure that, in a normal person, produces an assertion of 'McKinley was assassinated', the reason apparently being that the same effect has the same cause. But if this serves to establish that Mrs. T.'s relevant Mentalese token is of the same syntactic type as found in a normal person asserting 'McKinley was assassinated', then why does it not have the same effects all around? In normal people, tokens of the designated Mentalese syntactic type also cause occurrences of Mentalese tokens of 'McKinley is dead' and, thereby, assertions that McKinley is dead. Still, if exactly the same cause is supposedly lodged in Mrs. T., why does it not produce the same effects here? The only answer available is that the Mentalese token of 'McKinley was assassinated' is not *solely* sufficient to cause the effects attributed to it. At best, it is but *part* of the real total cause of utterances taken to be its effects. But then it no longer is plausible to suppose that Mrs. T.'s asserting 'McKinley was assassinated' has exactly the same real total cause as assertions of the same in normal people. In other words, once we notice that the supposed cause of Mrs. T.'s utterance has different effects from the supposed cause of normally produced identical utterances, we no longer can uncritically accept Stich's assumption that the efficacious Mentalese structure in Mrs. T. is syntactically the same as that in normal people. It would appear, then, that it is not evident that Stich has shown that Mentalese is ambiguous in the way he charges.

Something of the same can be alternatively expressed. Sententialism takes behavior to be the product of the causal interaction of Mentalese sentences, where the causal interactions can be viewed as syntactic relations. So an agent's utterance of 'McKinley is dead' might be caused by the interaction within the agent of the Mentalese tokens

(4.3.1) McKinley was assassinated.

and

(4.3.2) If McKinley was assassinated, then McKinley is dead.

Presumably, (4.3.1) and (4.3.2) cause the agent to utter 'McKinley is dead' by virtue of first entailing, and thereby ensuring, the Mentalese encoding of,

(4.3.3) McKinley is dead.

The thrust of this is that if this is in fact the etiology of the utterance of 'McKinley is dead', then it is plain that the utterance depends on the encoding of not only (4.3.1) but also (4.3.2). Why, then, does Mrs. T. fail to believe that McKinley is dead? Perhaps she fails to encode (4.3.2), despite encoding (4.3.1). True, normal agents who encode tokens of the same type as (4.3.1) typically also encode tokens of (4.3.2)'s type. Nevertheless, this is no reason to deny Mrs. T. the belief that (4.3.1) serves to encode. Rather, if something like this explains why normal agents who believe that McKinley was assassinated also believe that McKinley is dead, we can easily understand exactly why Mrs. T. in fact believes that McKinley was assassinated without also believing that he is dead. She, unlike most, encodes (4.3.1) without also encoding (4.3.2). We may be sure that although Mrs. T. does not have the conceptual reach of normal people, she nevertheless believes that McKinley was assassinated. For she does encode (4.3.1), a Mentalese token of the syntactic type that in a normal person typically produces the belief that McKinley is dead, so long as the person also believes that if McKinley was assassinated, then McKinley is dead. After all, (4.3.1), when paired with (4.3.2), causes, and so implies, (4.3.3). Thus, (4.3.1) encodes the belief that it does because it is a token of the syntactic type whose tokens *typically* have, in *normal* people, the effects that they do.

Perhaps one lesson to be learned from Stich's examples is similar to that of Section 4.1. Beliefs, like concepts, occur along something like a continuous scale. Think of the belief that water is H_2O. I believe this, and so do my friends across campus in the chemistry department. However, my ability correctly to answer questions about H_2O is nil when compared to theirs. Still, I certainly do have a belief here, and so of course do they. The chemists and I all have the same belief but to varying degrees, where the degrees measure not intensity or tenacity of belief but rather its conceptual sophistication. I share the same belief with the chemists because in all of us there occurs the Mentalese sentence 'Water is H_2O'. This sentence has the same potential causal connections in all of us, in the sense that *it is the sentence that, in the same specified environment, in fact has the same determinate causal relations to stimuli, other mental sentences, and behavior.* In me this sentence does not cause all the assertions of the sort it produces in chemists. This is partially due to the fact that it partially depends for its actual causal connections on its immediate environment, including other mental sentences. The relevant mental sentences in me differ from those in the chemists. To say that I believe that water is H_2O to degree D is, in this sense, simply to say that in me the mental sentence serving as the object of my belief occurs in a certain environment that enables it to cause me to engage in certain specified bits of behavior. A chemist might believe the same but to degree D^*. And this would be by virtue of the chemist's encoding a mental sentence as the object of her belief that, occurring within the environment constituted by the chemist, causes her to engage in different, but overlapping, bits of behavior. The mental sentences occurring in both of us qualify as tokens of the same type because in the *same environment* they have exactly the *same causal* connections.

The case of Mrs. T. is a dramatic example of the familiar situation of children learning new concepts. The child first hears that $e = mc^2$ but knows little, if anything, of mass and energy. So suppose that the child encodes a Mentalese representation to the effect that $e = mc^2$ while encoding few, if any, other representations capable of interacting with it. Here then is an agent with a belief registering the minimal conceptual degree. Nevertheless, it qualifies as a belief and has the content it does because, as the child incorporates other Mentalese representations over time, it will come to interact with selected Mentalese inscriptions to generate others still.

We can see our way, then, through another of Stich's examples designed to scuttle Sententialism. Stich (1983, pp. 57–8) (perhaps with Dennett [1978d] in mind) imagines it possible that there be a future scientific culture so far more advanced and sophisticated than our own that its science defies any sentence-by-sentence translation into ours. Such a science would be well beyond the comprehension of a medieval. So imagine that a Mentalese token encoding one of the esoteric scientific beliefs common within this conjectured culture should, by some unspecified, but allowable, process, come to be encoded in our long-suffering medieval champion, Abelard. This Mentalese sentence, when encoded in the heads of the scientifically advanced, has myriad inferential relations with other mental sentences. The belief it encodes thus exhibits great conceptual depth within the future scientists. In Abelard, however, it has absolutely no inferential relations whatsoever. Sententialism must allow that Abelard, by virtue of incorporating a token of this Mentalese sentence, has a belief identical to the belief encoded in tokens of the same syntactic type current within those fluent in the future science. But, Stich urges, it is plain that we cannot say what, if any, belief Abelard would here enjoy.

This case is just a special instance of the situation of Mrs. T. and the young child. Nothing precludes Sententialism from reacting by treating Abelard as possessing a belief with the most degenerate conceptual connections, that is, as having a belief the same in content as its syntactic correspondents so prevelant among those steeped in the distant science. Abelard certainly cannot infer from his belief what the more knowledgeable might from theirs, but this does not show that Abelard does not share any belief with them. Rather, at most but quite innocuously, it demonstrates that Abelard could not share *every* belief with his scientifically sophisticated descendants.

What should we say, however, were Abelard, still mysteriously, to encode two Mentalese sentences from the future science. Suppose neither of these two Mentalese sentences were to have any actual inferential or causal connections to any other Mentalese sentences within Abelard. They would both have absolutely no conceptual depth in Abelard. So what would distinguish them according to content? Nothing. They both would have a conceptual degree of zero in Abelard. They would thus mean the same – nothing – in Abelard. And so Sententialism errs when it lays it down that difference in syntactic structure flags difference in semantic content in Mentalese.

Again the objection misses its mark. Recall our coin-changing machines. Consider the properly functioning machine emptied of its reserve of nickles and dimes. Would its failure to provide change for one inserted quarter and one inserted dime show that the inserted coins must really have the same value, namely, nothing? Hardly! We trace the failure of the machine to yield change for the quarter and dime not to any malfunctioning in the machine. Indeed, it is acting precisely as its design dictates when its coffers are empty. Neither do we find the inserted coins at fault nor assert that, in the machine, they have the same (no) value. The problem is simply that the machine antecedently does not contain coins to interact with the inserted coins.

Similarly for Abelard and his implanted Mentalese tokens. They mean what they naturally do but fail to cause in Abelard what they normally would in those in whom they are normally found. This is due to the sheer fact that Abelard does not antecedently contain Mentalese tokens suited for interaction with his implanted ones. Were Abelard filled with Mentalese tokens fitted, by virtue of their syntax, for interaction with his newly implanted Mentalese tokens, he would wax eloquent in the lexicon of the future science. At most what the objection shows is that Mentalese sentences are standardly encoded in great interacting groups, just as coin machines typically contain various types of coins. In principle, however, it is possible for Mentalese sentences to be recorded in isolation from others, just as coin machines can run low on reserves. Nonetheless, this no more compromises the semantic value of Mentalese sentences than it devalues coins in empty change machines.

We have been entertaining the idea that a belief with the same content can vary in conceptual depth across different agents, depending on what other beliefs are available within the different agents for interacting with the belief in question. Stich (1983, p. 137) has a wonderfully conceived example designed to test this thesis. The worry behind the example is that beliefs apparently can interact with too bewildering an array of other beliefs to admit to any kind of ordering in terms of anything like conceptual sophistication.

Consider, then, an agent woefully misinformed on some subject. Suppose that Abelard says, "The tree in the garden is an oak." Presumably, he says what he believes, and, thus according to Sententialism, there is encoded in Abelard some Mentalese sentence encoding this belief. Suppose that this Mentalese token is

(4.3.4) The tree in the garden is an oak.

Our question here is what, exactly, is the content of (4.3.4)? Or, more modestly, we might wonder what its truth conditions are. Now whether (4.3.4) is true or false partially depends on to what it refers. Since we currently adopt the illustrative fiction that Mentalese is just English, we know that in other agents, Mentalese tokens of the same syntactic type as (4.3.4) refer both to the tree in the garden and also to oak trees generally. That is, such tokens in agents other than Abelard are about both the tree in the garden as well as oak trees in general. But the case is not so clear–cut in Abelard. He, we suppose, is given to the most peculiar pronouncements. For example, Abelard is inclined to say, "Oak trees are highly intelligent, enjoy playing chess, and are filled with uranium-enriched gelatin." Indeed, with the exception of his comment about the tree in the garden being an oak, almost everything Abelard says about oaks would be roundly derided as being more than outlandish.

Given all that Abelard says, Sententialism will want to assign to him a variety of Mentalese sentences corresponding to his several beliefs. To keep matters simple, we can suppose that, besides (4.3.4), Abelard encodes these Mentalese tokens:

(4.3.5) Oak trees are highly intelligent.
(4.3.6) Oak trees enjoy playing chess.
(4.3.7) Oak trees are filled with uranium-enriched gelatin.

Together with (4.3.4), (4.3.5)–(4.3.7) cause to occur (entail) in Abelard the Mentalese token

(4.3.8) The tree in the garden is highly intelligent, enjoys playing chess, and is filled with uranium-enriched gelatin.

Given what Abelard says, how are we to interpret (4.3.4) – (4.3.8) as they are encoded in him? We would not hesitate to take (4.3.4) to be about the tree in the garden being an oak were it encoded in anyone knowledgeable about oak trees and not prone to Abelard's pronouncements. However, given all that we know of Abelard, we might begin to suspect that he could not be talking about oaks when he says what he does. For if we were to view him as speaking about oak trees, we would have to admit that all, or almost all, that he believes about oaks is false. We would need to insist that (4.3.5) – (4.3.8), as encoded in Abelard, are not true. Now, although this may seem the correct route to take, it is not without peril. As Abelard's false beliefs ramify and as the example is extended so as to attribute ever more bizarre statements to Abelard, we will be hard pressed to preserve Abelard's rationality. What finally distinguishes a rational agent with pervasively false beliefs and an irrational agent? Irrational action and action predicated on extensively false belief will be indiscernible in the end, both at last bringing an agent to a sad demise in an unforgiving environment.

Alternatively we can preserve the truth of Abelard's Mentalese sentences and their associated beliefs if we judiciously reinterpret at least some of the terms constituting his mental sentences. While that might keep Abelard a member in good standing in the society of rational animals, it would strike a mortal blow against Sententialism. That theory holds that syntactic identity of Mentalese sentences ensures their semantic congruence. The Mentalese term 'oak trees' encoded in Abelard cannot refer to oak trees if Abelard's editions of (4.3.4) – (4.3.8) are to have a chance at truth. Yet, by hypothesis, in other agents 'oak trees' refers to oak trees. This, after all, is why we allow that Héloïse believes truly when she encodes the Mentalese sentence 'Oak trees are unintelligent, do not enjoy chess, and are not filled with uranium-enriched gelatin'. So if we attempt to reinterpret Abelard's Mentalese sentences so as to ensure that they are generally true, we will be unable to maintain, as Sententialism must, that Mentalese is not ambiguous, that in Mentalese syntactic identity provides for semantic identity.

This dilemma is not really so hard on Sententialism as it may seem. If, as is to be assumed, Abelard is rational and manages to survive long at all, his beliefs must, in general, be true. But that is quite consistent with his having *topically* localized beliefs all or most of which are false, so long, of course, as these do not pertain to subjects crucial to survival. Certainly the notions of intelligence and rationality are tolerant of this kind of limited, contained error. Indeed, this would seem to be a plausible reaction to Abelard's situation. That is, Sententialism can allow that, in Abelard, (4.3.4) −(4.3.8) refer to oak trees, just as they would in other agents, and accept that Abelard is a font of false beliefs about oak trees.

If the objection to this is that the example is constructed so as to force the choice between viewing most, if not all, of Abelard's beliefs about anything under the sun either as false or as true but differing in reference from their syntactic clones in other agents, then Sententialism may fairly conclude that the objection describes an impossibility. We are now to imagine that Abelard contains, for the most part, Mentalese sentences of two sorts. His Mentalese inscriptions are either the negations of those normally found in others, or they are the affirmations whose negations are normally found in others. Mentalese inscriptions, it is agreed, cause behavior. Yet, once we recognize that Abelard's Mentalese inscriptions are as described, it becomes almost impossible to imagine that Abelard could survive at all. His inscriptions would produce in him behavior quite at odds with his environment – supposing that the complementary inscriptions in normal people produce behavior that meshes with the join of their needs and situations. Abelard's described circumstance seems, then, an empirical impossibility, a situation that Sententialism, as a proposal for the structure of an empirical theory of the mind, can be excused from exploring.

Perhaps this response in defense of Sententialism implicitly presupposes that the environments of the relevant agents are essentially the same. Putnam (1975), Burge (1979), and Stich (1983) have argued that Mentalese can be seen to be potentially ambiguous once we recognize that the reference of Mentalese terms is, like the reference of overt linguistic tokens generally, fixed in part by the environment, physical and social, of the agent who deploys the terms. This issue will occupy us in Chapter 6, but we can still profitably discuss here a modified version of Stich's way with the objection.

You say, thinking of Eisenhower, "Ike was a mediocre golfer." I say, thinking of Tina's former husband (someone not easily confused with Eisenhower), "Ike was a mediocre golfer." We are using syntactically the same English sentences to issue quite different assertions. You refer to one person; I to another. What we say can certainly differ in truth-value. The semantic conditions on our syntactically indistinguishable English sentences are, or at least could be, dramatically different.

Stich supposes that much the same might be true of Mentalese. It too might draw on tokens of the same syntactic type that, by differing in reference, possibly engender different truth conditions for syntactically identical Mentalese sentences in which they occur. Therefore, if you and I use different Mentalese tokens of the Mentalese sentence 'Ike was a mediocre golfer' to believe what we do, we would both deploy syntactically identical Mentalese sentences, and Sententialism would credit us with the same belief. But how could this be correct? Your belief refers to one person; mine, to another.

Stich is certainly right here. If Mentalese admits of the kind of referential ambiguity with which natural language is ripe, then Sententialism cannot hope to treat syntactically identical Mentalese sentences as agreeing in their semantic properties. But happily for Sententialism, there are no compelling reasons to think that this kind of example establishes the referential ambiguity of Mentalese.

The example trades on the assumption that Mentalese terms refer. Fair enough. That and how they refer is itself something to be explained. In any account, Mentalese terms are physical structures replete with their own etiological histories. How do such structures come to refer as they do? By being caused as they are. (Compare Dretske [1981] and Fodor [1984].) Mentalese terms with the same causal histories are presumably themselves physical structures of the same kind. Being physical structures of the same kind, they are terms of the same syntactic type. If so, Mentalese terms of the same syntactic type agree in reference. There is, therefore, no Mentalese referential ambiguity of the sort Stich describes *if Mentalese reference is a function of the etiology of Mentalese terms and if etiological identity is required for syntactic identity.*[10]

Since the issues here are so important, recasting them, as does Stich, in the light of kind terms may be helpful. Stich tells the tale of two men, John, an American, and Robin, an Englishman. Americans call 'chicory' what the British call 'endive', and what the Americans call 'endive' the British call 'chicory'. Neither John nor Robin have ever been presented with any chicory or endive. John, however, has heard certain reports descriptive of (American) chicory to the effect that it is bitter. In fact, what Americans call 'chicory' is bitter. Robin has heard reports descriptive of (British) chicory to the effect that it is bitter, but what the British call chicory is not in fact bitter. Assume that the reports heard by John and Robin are, word for word, the same and that these reports exhaust the information John and Robin have on the subjects. When asked about vegetables, both John and Robin typically assert, "Chicory is bitter."

Given that their information is identical, it appears that the Mentalese sentences encoded in John and Robin that cause them to assert 'Chicory is bitter' have exactly the same relevant causal relations and thus are syntactically the same. Sententialism must then take them as having beliefs with the same content. Yet this last is not evidently correct. For something feeds the intuition that what John believes is true, whereas what Robin believes is false. Thus it may seem as if Sententialism may, after all, err in mapping syntactic onto semantic identity.

This tale is not so telling as it may at first appear. If, on the one hand, we dwell on the fact that John and Robin are members of different communities with different verbal practices, we might be tempted by the idea that their Mentalese tokens suffer the sort of ambiguity Stich suggests. On the other hand, when we attend to the fact that John and Robin have indistinguishable sources of information, then the attraction of the Sententialist doctrine is not

10 Things are actually a bit more complicated than this. We certainly will need to relativize this naive and too facile account of Mentalese reference to kinds of agents. The physical effects of a referent on a human and Martian may differ if the human and Martian fall into radically different physical kinds.

negligible. Certainly, that their behavior exhibits no difference fuels the Sententialist program here. It is just this vacillation that suggests that we cannot be guided by intuitions in this matter. Rather, we are best advised to trust to theoretical considerations in settling the issue. The fact that Sententialism accommodates their identical behavior by assigning to them identical beliefs counts for something in the way of theoretical simplicity.

It is not an accidental feature of the case that neither John nor Robin has any direct perceptual information regarding the vegetables in question. If they were to have seen what, in their respective countries, is called 'chicory', they would have had markedly different perceptual experiences. This perceptual difference would presumably constitute a significant causal difference in the production of the information-bearing Mentalese structures respectively internal to John and Robin. That would ensure that they encode syntactically different Mentalese tokens, thereby routing the force of the counterexample, which depends on their having syntactically the same Mentalese tokens. Under these newly introduced perceptual circumstances, Sententialism would nicely subserve the presumption that John and Robin have different beliefs.

When we consider Stich's several examples designed to show the referential shortcomings of Sententialism, one element continually reappears, the notion that Mentalese tolerates referential ambiguity. From the fact that we might be inclined to ascribe different beliefs by embedding tokens of the same English sentence, for example, 'Chicory is bitter', within different belief attributions, say, 'John (Robin) believes that chicory is bitter', we might naively be inclined to infer that the Mentalese sentences occurrent in the attributed beliefs must be as syntactically indistinguishable as the sentences embedded within the belief attributions. Always in evaluating such examples we need to assess the plausibility of postulating syntactically the same Mentalese sentences within the relevant agents. The two points that call for emphasis here are: (1) If there are any salient physical (causal) differences between similar agents in their manner of information pickup, then there is prima facie evidence that their Mentalese sentences occurrent in their beliefs exhibit syntactic differences sufficient to secure referential differences;[11] and (2) if similar

---

11 If John and Robin believe what they do because they have been exposed to physically different kinds of vegetables, vegetables that have differential effects

136

agents behave the same in all possible relevant circumstances consequent on their ascribed beliefs, then we might well suppose that, other things being equal, their occurrent Mentalese sentences referentially coincide and their corresponding beliefs are indeed the same. Working either of these points, depending on the details of the examples, amounts to arguing that the relevant Mentalese tokens are not referentially ambiguous. They may, then, suffice to keep Stich's counterexamples at bay.

This said, let us look to Mentalese indexicals. I say, "I won the race," and you utter the same. If the belief that drives my assertion is syntactically the same as the one that causes yours, then, according to Sententialism, we have the same belief. But how can this be correct? At most one of our beliefs is true, and, anyway, yours refers to you, mine to me. This example, like the others before it, relies on the idea that Mentalese terminology must perfectly mirror English, in this case that Mentalese indexicals – if such there be – correspond to English indexicals. But who knows this? The postulate of Mentalese is surely consistent with the supposition that Mentalese indexicals are occasion specific, that, for example, each agent has a syntactically unique Mentalese first-person personal pronoun. If, in believing that this (the stuff before you) is paper, you issue the Mentalese sentence 'This is paper', perhaps the demonstrative Mentalese pronoun you use is syntactically distinguished from all other demonstratives. Indeed, if, as is likely, its demonstrative reference should be traced to something idiosyncratic in your perceptual experience, its causal connection with its referent would be unique, thereby ensuring its syntactic distinction. So there may be reason to suppose that Mentalese demonstratives are as syntactically distinct as Sententialism might require in order to preserve distinctness of beliefs featuring demonstrative reference. In short, if Stich's complaint is to be well founded, it must be based on an argument that Mentalese is as indexically impoverished as natural language. And that argument is not forthcoming.

We have been assuming that Sententialism takes difference in information pickup to secure a syntactic difference that, in turn, allows for a semantic difference in the Mentalese structure encoding the information. This is not quite correct, as Stich well knows.

on their sensory systems, then there is indeed reason to suspect that their Mentalese representations syntactically diverge.

There are situations in which it is plain that, for example, those who are color-blind can be said to share with the normally sighted beliefs about the colors of objects. If Martha is blind to the difference between red and green, she may nevertheless believe, as does normally sighted Mary, that the traffic lamp shows red. Martha may infer that the traffic lamp shows red since she knows that the highest light on a traffic lamp is red and observes that the highest light is lit. Evidently Martha and Mary arrive at their beliefs, and therefore their relevant Mentalese sentences, by causal routes that, at some level of analysis, count as different.[12] Thus their Mentalese sentences must syntactically differ, thereby rendering their beliefs different in content, at least according to an untutored rendition of Sententialism.

One way of appreciating the force of the example regarding the beliefs of the color-blind is to consider the effect of different causal pathways to the same belief within perfectly normal people. Suppose that you believe that either it is snowing or raining and also that it is not snowing. Probably you will infer, and so come to believe, that it is raining. I, on the other hand, believe that if it is not snowing, then it is raining and also that it is not snowing. Like you, I too come to believe that it is raining. My inference apparently relies on different Mentalese sentences as premises than does yours. Thus, given that inferential routes supervene on causal ones, the cause of your belief that it is raining differs from the cause of my belief of the same.

Different bits of information can obviously lead to the same result. This is the essence of the example from color blindness, and only the most simplistic edition of Sententialism would fail to appreciate this.[13] The instruction the example affords is thus that Sententialism must allow that the syntactic identity of a Mentalese sentence is fixed not simply by the causal relations it *happens* to have but rather by the causal relations it *could* have (presumably in agents of a specified, standard, perhaps ideal sort). My belief that it is raining is the same as yours since the Mentalese sentence en-

12 We will return to this theme in Chapter 6, arguing that there may be grounds for supposing that, at some other level of analysis, apparently distinct types of causes of Mentalese structures may qualify as causes of the same type.
13 It is important to keep in mind that there may be a relevant level of analysis at which what, at a different level, appear to be different bits of information are in an important sense the same. Again, more on this in Chapter 6.

coding my belief is a sentence of the same Mentalese syntactic type as yours. That our Mentalese sentences are of the same type is ensured by the fact that what could have caused yours could also have caused mine and whatever might be the effects of yours might also be the effects of mine. Conversely too.

Mary and Martha are in an analogous situation. They possess tokens of the same Mentalese type representing that the traffic lamp shows red, despite the fact that their tokens happen to have been produced differently. This is because their tokens would have all the same possible causes and effects were they installed in a normal agent.

5

The matter of intentionality

5.1. SEARLE'S ARGUMENT AGAINST ARTIFICIAL INTELLIGENCE

Sentientialism and Artificial Intelligence appear to be natural allies. Such, at least, is suggested in Chapter 1, Section 1.4, and Chapter 2. There we saw that Sentientialism construes thinking as essentially a parade of logically related Mentalese sentences encoded in the brain. We also acknowledged an objection: If these mental sentences are to be intelligible – if to think is to deploy Mentalese – then, but absurdly, it may seem as if there must be some intelligent agent within each agent, whose job is the reading and inscribing of the sentences constituting cognitive episodes. Since Sentientialism poses as a theory of intelligence, it must explain the intelligence of the embedded agent. Yet according to the Sentential scheme this in turn apparently leads to an unending succession of ever more deeply embedded agents.

This regress of embedded agents could perhaps wreck Sentientialism were it not that Artificial Intelligence offers dramatic evidence that it is unnecessary to posit embedded agents in order to explain how the intelligence of an agent can amount to the encoding of rationally related sentences within the agent. Artificially intelligent devices are commonly sententially driven machines under the influence of programs ensuring the logical character of their sententially characterized internal states. Such artificially intelligent machines stake their claim to intelligence on the ground that their internal states are logically related not only to one another but also to the stimuli to which they are engineered to be sensitive and the behavior they are designed to cause. We understand the engineering of these machines and know full well that they harbor no embedded agents. So, with a nod to Artificial Intelligence, Sentientialism might avoid the regress of embedded agents by denying that the intelligent use of mental sentences presupposes an embedded intelligent agent whose job it is to comprehend and control the passing mental sentences. Rather, it would suffice for an agent's mental sentences to be so causally related to stimuli, one another, and behavior as to count as the logical consequences of their causes and derivations of their effects. The sense in which mental sentences are to be logically related is precisely that in which sentences in purely formal logic are related. That is, the deducibility relation that binds them is to be characterized solely in terms of the formal or syntactic properties of the sentences, regardless of what the sentences represent (Fodor, 1980a; Stich, 1983).

The reasoning, in sum, runs thus: Sententialism holds that intelligence amounts to the encoding and transforming of Mentalese sentences. These sentences are representational or contentful structures for the agent in whom they are encoded. Artificial Intelligence shows, without reference to an infinite regress of embedded agents, how it is possible that mental sentences can be contentful for the agent who encodes them. For artificially intelligent devices are themselves intelligent by virtue of following programs that ensure that the linguistic structures they encode are logically related to stimuli, one another, and behavior by way of their formal or syntactic properties.

Of course, one possibly unwanted consequence of this is transparent. Any device whatsoever that is in fact under the control of a formal program sufficient for producing plastic behavior appropriate to a relatively wide range of situations is, ipso facto, intelligent. It is important to appreciate that this conclusion is not idiosyncratic to Sententialism. Exactly the same can be reached by much more generally accepted premises than those constituting the theses defining Sententialism.

In order to understand what to say in the teeth of this problem, it is helpful to survey some recent history. Not too long ago, some philosophers (Armstrong, 1968; Smart, 1969) were eager to explain how mentality could be incarnate and supposed that types of mental states were in fact identical with types of physical states. Abelard and Héloïse both believe that Paris is a large city and, therefore, both enjoy instances of the same type of belief. This would be possible if beliefs of the same type were necessarily made of matter of the same type. The material identity of the relevant beliefs could, in turn, readily be the case if, in believing what they do, Abelard and Héloïse were to be in brain states of the same type. Nothing

141

seems to obstruct this since Abelard and Héloïse, qua humans, do indeed have brains of the same material composition. Thus, the doctrine of type-type identity: Mental states of the same type are necessarily physical states of the same type.

Other philosophers (Putnam, 1975a, c, d; Fodor, 1968; and Cummins, 1983) objected, arguing that it certainly seems possible that there could be creatures who share our mental but not physical states. For example, it is apparently possible that there could be silicon-based Martians who, like Abelard and Héloïse, believe that Paris is a large city despite the fact that they, the Martians, could not occupy the same brain states as do Abelard and Héloïse. After all, brains are carbon, not silicon, based. If the situation of the Martians is indeed possible, then − but contrary to the thesis of type-type identity − mental-state types could not be essentially identical with types of physical states. What then could mental state types be?

Certainly each instance or token of a mental-state type must itself be an instance or token of some physical state. Instances of a mental type need not be instances of the same physical type, however. Rather, the reasoning continues, types of mental states must transcend physical types. So the type of a mental state must be determined by the functions it serves within a cognitive economy. Tokens of mental states are the same in type, the reasoning concludes, just in case they coincide in their typical causal histories and consequences. The stuff out of which mental states are made contributes not a wit to their being mental states. The only thing that does matter is not the matter of mental states but, rather, their functional relations to stimuli, other mental states, and behavior. Thus, since Martians and humans might contain functionally equivalent information-processing systems, they might enjoy the same types of mental states. It is also evident that the states of an artificially intelligent device that mimics the behavior of a naturally intelligent agent qualify as functionally equivalent to the agent's mental states. Thus, and again, emerges the idea that devices controlled by formal programs deserve inclusion in the cognitive circle as much as we do.

In opposition to this, Searle (1980, 1982a, b, 1983, and 1984) has argued that it is roundly false that the intelligence of an agent is secured sheerly by the fact that the agent operates under the influence of a formal program sufficient for producing what, for all the

142

world, appears to be intelligent behavior. That, with Searle, is to say that mental types are not at all functionally individuated by way of their typical causal connections. If Searle is correct – and, judging from the literature, not many who are positioned to judge think he is[1] – then much of what has recently passed in cognitive psychology, Artificial Intelligence, and the philosophy of mind is wrong. And more particularly, Sentialism cannot appeal to the workings of artificially intelligent devices to explain away the regress of embedded agents. So, on to Searle's argument.[2]

Assume for the moment that advocates of Artificial Intelligence rightly maintain that intelligence – genuine understanding – is secured through the instantiation of a formal program.[3] It would follow that our own understanding of the languages we naturally speak is itself simply our conforming to a formal program dictating how symbols of these languages are grammatically and reasonably to be exchanged. No one has yet had much success in actually composing a program adequate to the demands of full-blown linguistic competence, but if Artificial Intelligence is ever to achieve the goals it has set for itself, it must suppose that such programs are theoretically possible while trusting that someday they will be commonplace. A program for understanding English would, when instantiated in a computer, be indiscernible in its production of English conversation from any typical native speaker of English. It need not be able to converse long or very intelligently about everything under the sun. None of us can do that. But it must be

1 See the sections of peer review in Searle (1980 and 1982a) as well as Dennett and Searle (1982), Cummins (1983), Russow (1984), Cole (1984), and Maloney (1987).
2 At the risk of redundancy, let me make clear that although I shall argue with Searle that Artificial Intelligence alone cannot pretend to explain how it is that our mental states come to have content, I do think that Artificial Intelligence in fact has a great deal to contribute to the answer to this question. I am at present arguing for the modest thesis that the intentionality or contentfulness of a mental state is not a simple function of its interactions with other mental states being determined by a formal program. It is important to keep in mind that this is compatible with the hypothesis that formally specified relations of a mental state contribute to the determination of the content the state in fact has.
3 This is not to say that Artificial Intelligence is necessarily committed to this strong thesis. It may adopt the considerably weaker position that Artificial Intelligence is not the real thing, that it is *merely* a simulation of genuine intelligence. Construed this latter way, Artificial Intelligence is, as a research program, a branch of cognitive science in much the way that the simulation of oceanic processes is a branch of oceanography. As such, Artificial Intelligence will certainly have much of importance to contribute to the understanding of mentation, although it will not itself stand as the explanation of the deep nature of thought itself.

able to talk gracefully about lots of things with lots of different people. You might know much more about particle physics than your great-grandmother does, and in comparison to what she knows about life back home in Indiana, you might know almost nothing. Still, you both do in fact understand English very well, as is evident from your respective abilities to talk to each other at length and with mutual interest about various subjects. What here holds for English should, if Artificial Intelligence is the key to genuine understanding, hold for Chinese as well. Thus we English speakers should become fluent in Chinese immediately on instantiating a formal program for Chinese.

In order to test this hypothesis, Searle invites us to imagine what it would be like, for someone whose native language is English and whom we will call Marco, to master a formal program for Chinese. For the sake of simplicity alone, we may ignore spoken Chinese and focus exclusively on the language as written. First, we need to know about the program for Chinese. It is a set of rules, doubtlessly many and complicated, dictating how sequences of written Chinese characters are to be produced, combined, and exchanged so that the resulting strings of Chinese characters would be indistinguishable from transcriptions of conversations among naturally fluent speakers of Chinese. We can suppose that Marco is presented with a thick manual containing an exhaustive list of Chinese characters and rules, written in English, telling him how to manipulate strings of Chinese characters intelligently. Keep in mind that Marco's program, his manual, is completely formal in the sense that it identifies Chinese characters and strings thereof only by their shapes. In mastering the manual, Marco learns only which strings of Chinese characters can legitimately be exchanged for other Chinese characters that he may happen to receive from other people. Marco is, then, never given a semantics for Chinese characters; that would violate the condition that he realize a purely formal program for Chinese of the sort fit for realization in a computer. He need not be informed that it is a language, much less Chinese, of which his manual provides mastery. All that is required of Marco by way of his program is that he become adroit with written marks that, but possibly unbeknownst to him, happen to be Chinese characters.

After a great deal of boring practice, Marco masters the rules in the manual and becomes remarkably quick in exchanging Chinese characters. Indeed, he may no longer even need to refer to the manual when deciding on which strings of characters to produce for exchange. If a native speaker of Chinese records a question and passes it on to Marco, Marco will quickly produce a string of Chinese characters that, from the point of view of Marco's interlocutor, appears to be an intelligent reply. Does Marco then understand, really understand, Chinese? Would you? Proponents of at least one line of Artificial Intelligence insist that Marco does and that you would. Searle is appalled by what he takes to be the transparent absurdity of the position and concludes that neither Marco nor you would in any way understand Chinese. If Searle's evaluation of this thought experiment is correct, then Artificial Intelligence's claim to represent the true nature of genuine intelligence and understanding is exposed as a myth. If true, this is not only interesting in its own right but also bears on Sententialism's right to appeal to Artificial Intelligence in order to circumvent the regress of embedded agents. If Searle is correct, then it is difficult to see how Artificial Intelligence alone could serve to explain how the language of thought could have content.

5.2. ARTIFICIAL INTELLIGENCE AT BAY

Whosoever would defend Artificial Intelligence from Searle's objection must concede that Marco's situation is possible. For, as already remarked, it is among the discipline's goals to produce programs that replicate our linguistic abilities. There is no reason, then, for defenders of Artificial Intelligence to deny that a person could master a program after Marco's fashion. Rather, what appears necessary to maintain in order to preserve Artificial Intelligence is that the description of Marco's program somehow illicitly nurtures the intuition that he does not understand Chinese and that, contrary to untutored opinion, he does indeed comprehend this language.

In order to make their case, several of Searle's critics (Dennett, 1980; Fodor, 1980b; Lycan, 1980; Smythe, 1982; Russow, 1984) have maintained that the description of the power of Marco's program is itself flawed so as to obscure his understanding of Chinese. The complaint is that if Marco's program were of the sort that Artificial Intelligence properly envisions, it would not only enable Marco to converse in Chinese but also cause him otherwise to behave consistent with his conversations. For example, when presented with a request in Chinese to prepare tea, Marco's program would ensure that if he were to consent, he would then proceed to attempt to prepare the tea. Marco's program would, if it were to qualify as the sort of program necessary for language comprehension foreseen by Artificial Intelligence, need to be contextually sensitive. In the general case, it must register in Marco information available from the ambient array and, through him, drive devices to alter the environment consistent with the purely linguistic abilities the program bestows on Marco. What Artificial Intelligence anticipates is a formal program for Chinese that is fully integrated with programs for the cognitive capacities typically found in a language user. If, the defenders of Artificial Intelligence contend, Marco were to realize such a program, he would indeed comprehend Chinese, and we observers, appreciating his remarkably coordinated abilities, would not hesitate to attribute this comprehension to him.

Although this type of defense of Artificial Intelligence has enjoyed wide appeal, it mistakenly insists that a program for language comprehension must be able to produce changes in the environment of its realization or otherwise be integrated with environment-modifying programs. The error here is revealed by examples showing that the ability to affect the environment is not a universally necessary condition of language comprehension in naturally fluent linguistic agents. Hence, even if the ability to modify the environment in ways compatible with the current conversation is typical of naturally endowed language users, Artificial Intelligence cannot take this ability to be essential in emulating real linguistic understanding.

Examples, then. Surely Marco's understanding of English would not be compromised if, being disabled or otherwise prevented from acting as would a normal speaker of English, he were to fail to act as a current conversation might normally require. If, because he is physically handicapped or bound hand and foot, Marco does not attempt to open the door for you when you say, "Marco, please open the door," that certainly does not entail that he has not understood you, especially if he replies, "Sorry, I can't. Use the key hanging on the wall."[4] So Artificial Intelligence cannot require that

---

4 Evidence of Marco's understanding of English may be garnered from his illocutionary and perlocutionary acts.

Marco's program for Chinese must, if it is to be a program adequate for real linguistic comprehension, actually be implicated in causing him to operate in his environment as would a normal, naturally native speaker of Chinese. Thus, if Artificial Intelligence correctly assigns linguistic competence to a program, it must concede that this program can function in an agent although the agent happens to act atypically.

It is important to recognize that what consideration of impaired linguistic agents reveals is that although we normally appeal to an agent's manifest abilities to manipulate the environment to certify his or her linguistic competence, this competence can be realized apart from those abilities with which it standardly appears. An advocate of Artificial Intelligence cannot maintain, then, that a program for language comprehension must also drive nonverbal behavior. Hence, that Marco's manual for Chinese does not direct him to engage in much, if any, nonverbal behavior fails to demonstrate that his program necessarily falls short of what Artificial Intelligence is required to provide. After all, what if Marco's program provides him with the ability to produce strings of Chinese characters that, to an interlocutor fluent in Chinese, mean that Marco is excusing himself for not acting as expected? Would not such a program satisfy the conditions on intelligent language use that Artificial Intelligence hopes to realize? Once we appreciate that language comprehension is not essentially tied to nonverbal behavior, we can see that Artificial Intelligence, if it is minimally to emulate linguistic comprehension, is not required to provide a program that ensures both linguistic competence and a corresponding mastery over the environment. If this is the case, then it is no defense of Artificial Intelligence to say that Marco's program must, if it is to satisfy the demands of intelligence, prompt him to maneuver in his surroundings in a fashion normally expected of those naturally versed in Chinese.

Anyway, as everyone can agree, one's acting in accordance with the conversation of the moment is contingent not only on one's understanding of what is being said but also on one's *willingness* to behave cooperatively. Being willing to do this or that is, presumably, a mental state that, if Artificial Intelligence is right, ought to be programmable. Indeed, in nature there are instances in which agents who do comprehend language occasionally do not, because they are unwilling, act consistently with their conversational contexts. Thus programs that control language comprehension ought, in principle, to be independent of those determining overt behavior, even if as a matter of practical fact they normally interact. Artificial Intelligence cannot, then, dodge the example of Marco on the grounds that his program does too little to constitute what Artificial Intelligence takes to be required of genuine language comprehension. True, Marco does not do everything that we expect of naturally fluent speakers of a language. The present point, however, is that the ability to comprehend language can, in theory, be isolated from the ability to act in accordance with comprehended conversation. Artificial Intelligence cannot, therefore, rely on the claim that a formal program for language comprehension must also include a sophisticated motor routine. Accordingly, Artificial Intelligence is unable to deflect the force of the example of Marco by denying that his program is not of the sort that sober research in Artificial Intelligence would recognize as underlying linguistic comprehension.[5]

Undaunted, one might reply that what needs to be shown here against Artificial Intelligence is that it is possible for an agent to understand a language were the agent never to have had the ability to interact normally with the environment. In support of this is the fact that agents deprived of sensory stimulation and opportuni-

5 George Graham has noted in correspondence that, although natural linguistic agents may suffer disabilities preventing them from acting as is normal for others of their kind, the evolution of linguistic processes probably ensures that only creatures of *kinds* capable of intelligently directed movement are capable of language comprehension. With this I certainly agree. Marco, as a natural linguistic agent, is capable of intelligent activity normally coupled with the exercise of English, his naturally acquired language. Thus, if Artificial Intelligence is correct and the ability to use a language is reducible to a program, such a program in nature would be found only in kinds of things capable of intelligent movement that is causally connected to the exercise of the linguistic capability. What is so joined in nature may well be separated in art, however. Thus, Artificial Intelligence needs an argument to demonstrate that artificial linguistic agents must be of kinds capable of movement coordinated with their speech. Compare Lycan (1980), Russow (1984), and Cummins (1983, p. 108). Failing that argument, immobile Marco remains a candidate for artificially comprehending Chinese. Besides, even if Artificial Intelligence were to demonstrate that artificial linguistic agents must be of *kinds* capable of movement coordinated with their speech, it would remain that aberrant *individuals* of these kinds might be unable to make their movements conform to their messages. If so, such agents, like Marco, would still qualify as artificially linguistic. This would show that a program presumed to control language comprehension can be installed without producing linguistically coordinated movements. Artificial Intelligence seems committed to immobile Marco's understanding Chinese, contrary to what Searle's argument aims to show.

ties to act typically manifest signs of insanity. They fail, that is, to maintain normal cognitive functioning.

We must concede that it is difficult to demonstrate conclusively that an agent permanently deprived of a motor routine could nevertheless understand language. The best one can do here – and it is good enough – is note that it seems conceivable that there could be linguistic agents who neither sense nor act. God, according to some, is just so. But we are not forced to rely on questionable examples here. For since its inception, Artificial Intelligence has been happy to divide in order to conquer. The practice of the discipline has been to isolate distinct mental abilities – visual discrimination and sentence parsing, for example – for the purpose of artificial duplication. A program whose sole achievement is the ability to recognize and manipulate blocks (Winograd, 1971) is supposed literally to understand something about blocks. Analogously, a program designed simply but adequately to manipulate language must, by the lights of Artificial Intelligence, count as understanding the language it uses. So it is against the tradition of research in Artificial Intelligence to repudiate Marco's program on the ground that it does not prompt him to maneuver as would a native speaker of Chinese.

Still, to all this a proponent of Artificial Intelligence might retort that yes, language comprehension is properly distinct from the processes that produce nonverbal behavior and consequently can occur without accompanying nonverbal behavior. But since language comprehension is typically manifested in overt behavioral processes, we witnesses standardly rely on behavior epistemically to warrant our attributions of language comprehension. In Marco's case the attendant behavior has been artificially separated from the linguistic performance, leading the naive into Searle's mistake of supposing that inactive Marco is ignorant of Chinese. It is an error to confuse the absence of the nonverbal sign of language comprehension with the lack of language comprehension itself. What we ought to fasten on in determining whether Marco understands Chinese is whether the program governing his manipulation of Chinese symbols *could*, and *typically would*, contribute to the production of nonverbal behavior in those contexts in which it is *both* possible and appropriate. Presumably Marco's program, installed in a device designed to emulate all the intelligent capacities of a normally functioning person, could and typically would contribute to generating complementary verbal and nonverbal behavior. Once we realize this, then even though we recognize that language comprehension is only an element in the psychological process responsible for the production of nonverbal behavior, we can appreciate how very plausible the idea is that Marco in fact does understand Chinese and, therefore, how eminently reasonable Artificial Intelligence actually is (Dennett, 1980; Fodor, 1980b).

Even this will not restore Artificial Intelligence. Consider what ensues when we equip Marco with a program for manipulating written Chinese symbols that also produces behavior indistinguishable from that of normal native speakers of Chinese. If Artificial Intelligence were correct, any such program should ensure that Marco understands Chinese, just as do native speakers. Nevertheless, this is where it fails. There is reason to worry that just such a program need not necessarily provide for Marco's enjoyment of the linguistic comprehension characteristic of speakers of Chinese. Suppose that Marco's program somehow causes him to serve tea when he is requested in Chinese to do so. Would he thereby understand that he has been requested to serve tea?

Not necessarily. Marco acquires his program by mastering a manual written in English instructing him what symbols to display in response to symbols received and, now, how to behave in contexts of symbol exchanges. But this is quite consistent with the manual's being written in such a way as to ensure that Marco *moves* appropriately without his understanding what, in the Chinese scheme of things, he is *doing*. For example, the manual might describe tea and its service so as to conceal from Marco that that is what is thereby described. Having told Marco what symbols to exchange in response to symbols that (unbeknown to Marco) request him to serve tea, the manual might continue by instructing Marco thus: "Fetch the stuff in the green container, mix it with the stuff in the blue pot, and pour the combination into the four white receptacles."[6] Marco might fulfill this command without

6 These instructions identify the tea and its service by way of their accidental properties. One might worry that Marco could not regularly rely on such properties to locate and serve tea. Nevertheless, this is an inessential artifact of the example. The manual could identify tea by its chemical properties and Marco could be equipped with a device sensitive to such properties. He might, then, follow the instructions, use his auxiliary device, and regularly locate tea. But so long as he is not informed that it is tea that is so selected, he could well remain

realizing that dry tea and hot water are in the green and blue vessels, respectively; that the white receptacles are exquisite, rare tea cups dating from the Ming dynasty; and that he has acted the gracious host. Marco might then manage to serve tea without having the vaguest idea that he is doing so. That is, a native speaker of Chinese would, if acting as Marco, realize *that* he or she is serving tea. But Marco's program, even when supplemented with a motor routine, does not provide that he understand his activity as would a native speaker of Chinese. But that is precisely the sort of understanding at which Artificial Intelligence aims when it proposes to produce a language program that affects knowledge of Chinese.[7] Of course, this generalizes to all overt behavior since all such behavior can be described in nonstandard ways that obliterate what, from the relevant point of view, is being done.[8] If so, then, contrary to Artificial Intelligence, Marco would want what his Chinese counterparts have – an understanding of Chinese.[9]

The lesson to be learned from all this is that Artificial Intelligence cannot appeal to behavioral considerations in attempting to foil Searle's argument. Intelligent behavior, as opposed to brute movement, requires that the agent conceive of the activity constituting

---

ignorant that he is in fact serving tea. And it is *exactly this* that he is supposed to know if he understands Chinese.

7 It is worth noting here that Marco need not have even a vague idea *that* he is serving tea. His instructions might so craftily conceal that it is tea that is being served that Marco might conceive of his activity in a way alien to that characteristic of native Chinese. And yet, according to Artificial Intelligence, it is the understanding characteristically enjoyed by the Chinese that Marco is supposed to achieve by virtue of his program.

8 This argument seems more general than the one Searle (1980, 1982a) offers as his "robot reply" in that the present argument transcends considerations of robotic instantiation and ensures that regardless of the physical manner of its production and contextual appropriateness, an agent's activity qualifies as genuine behavior only if the agent properly conceives of the activity as would a native speaker.

9 Although Marco would not know *that* he is serving tea, it might remain that he knows *how* to serve tea, even if he has no idea what tea is. Robots might be said to know how to act without understanding that they are acting in any specified way. This is true enough, but it does not suffice to attribute to Marco what Artificial Intelligence promises. It maintains that Marco's program suffices for the sort of intelligence and understanding that native speakers of Chinese exhibit. And such speakers not only know *how* to speak Chinese but also know *that* they are so speaking. Native speakers of Chinese understand what they are saying; a verbal robot need not realize what it is saying although it knows how to speak. One might venture that *knowing that* is, in this context, to be explicated simply in terms of actual or potential linguistic behavior. But that would seem to beg the question in favor of Artificial Intelligence.

the behavior under the appropriate description. This is not guaranteed by Artificial Intelligence. The blind fact that activity resulting from the realization of a program in an agent can be described in a particular way does not ensure that the agent will conceive of it that way. If not, the activity need not be the relevant behavior. And so, when behavior is requisite for, or otherwise a reliable sign of, understanding, activity produced by a program does not suffice for establishing understanding. This is because the occurrence of the activity does not establish the occurrence of behavior – activity under an intentional description – of the appropriate type.

5.3. LANGUAGE COMPREHENSION AND TRANSLATION

Other considerations have seduced some into affirming Artificial Intelligence despite Marco's situation. On behalf of Artificial Intelligence, they note that Marco certainly does exchange symbols just as would a native speaker of Chinese, that he does display, to whatever degree desired, activity characteristic of people versed in (written) Chinese. Normally, when we discern activity of this type, we attribute understanding of Chinese and thereby explain and enable ourselves to predict the activity. To recall Dennett's apt phrase, we adopt the intentional stance. Why should we not follow suit with Marco, attribute to him an understanding of Chinese, and so begin to explain and predict his manipulation of the Chinese symbols?

The answer may appear to be that since Marco presumably would deny, in English, that he knows Chinese, it would be wild to attribute an understanding of Chinese to him. Certainly Marco is the best judge of whether he himself understands Chinese, and he denies that he does. Still, perhaps we should reassess Marco's self-analysis. After all, depending on how the instruction manual requires symbol sequences to be exchanged, Marco may appear to be an unreliable informant about himself. The manual could easily require Marco, when presented with symbols asking in Chinese, "What language are you now using?" to issue the symbols that, when translated into English say, "I am speaking Chinese." Would this not be significant confirmation from Marco's own hand that he understands Chinese? This evidently is much the same caliber

152

of information that Marco provides when he says in English, "I understand English, not Chinese."

We have a nasty little problem here: Should we accept Marco's English utterances as indicative of which languages he understands, or should we instead attend to his remarks in Chinese? We cannot cavalierly ignore his Chinese testimony. Depending on how the instructions in the manual run, Marco might conform to them by producing in response to the Chinese symbols asking whether he understands English the Chinese symbol for 'No!' Would Marco himself thereby confirm that he does not understand English? And importantly, is not this apparent disconfirmation of Marco's understanding English exactly the same kind of evidence to which we appeal to show that he does not understand Chinese? Artificial Intelligence's ploy here aims at undermining Marco's epistemic authority in determining which languages he may know. It looks to the hypothesis that Marco must speak whatever language that, if attributed to him, would best explain his otherwise curious behavior (Dennett, 1978; Wilensky, 1980; Cole, 1984).

It would be naive to suppose that Artificial Intelligence's rejection of Marco's testimony in determining the languages he comprehends is without warrant. In attributing an understanding of Chinese to Marco, Artificial Intelligence does explain his behavior, which is undeniably similar to that of native speakers of Chinese, in terms of the intentional theory used to explain the verbal behavior of those naturally fluent in Chinese. Artificial Intelligence is right to hold that if its construal of Marco's behavior fits best with our general psychology without otherwise compromising what we know to be true, then Marco's insistence that he does not understand Chinese should be ignored.

Nevertheless, Artificial Intelligence's assignment to Marco of an understanding of Chinese does indeed conflict with a solid fact about language comprehension indicating, contrary to Artificial Intelligence, that Marco is, after all, ignorant of Chinese. Marco does not understand Chinese because, for him, his Chinese expressions lack semantic content. This we know not only or merely because of Marco's disavowing any understanding of Chinese but also because we know that he cannot *translate* between English and Chinese. Marco certainly understands English, and if he also understood Chinese, he would be able to translate between the two. The ability to translate, to at least some degree, among known languages is essential to fluency in those languages. Here Marco stumbles, and that is why Artificial Intelligence is false. The idea is that Marco's inability to translate between English and Chinese evidentially overrides his own reports, in Chinese, that he does understand Chinese. The same also mandates an explanation of Marco's dexterity with Chinese character symbols that does not ascribe to him comprehension of Chinese.

Still, the connection between translation and language comprehension will not persuade all. Some argue that although being multilingual usually presupposes the ability to translate among the known languages, Marco's idiosyncratic failure at translation between English and Chinese does not yet betray his ignorance of Chinese. No doubt, they say, we generally learn a target language by learning, perhaps discovering, how to translate between a known language and the target. But there may be other ways to acquire a language that do not presuppose learning how to translate between known and new languages. Indeed, unless nativism is true (Fodor, 1975, 1981), there must be some way to learn a language, one's first, without mastering a translation scheme (Lewis, 1980). Although no one can say with certainty how first languages are learned, translation cannot play a part. Thus a process not involving translation between English and Chinese possibly accounts for Marco's acquiring an understanding of Chinese. Accordingly, Marco's inability to translate between English and Chinese does not lay Artificial Intelligence to rest.

Not at all. Although acquiring a second language need not presuppose *learning* how to translate between the first and second languages, one cannot *understand* them without *knowing* how to translate them. For example, knowing both English and French, you might learn Spanish by learning how to translate between French and Spanish. As a result, you would *know* how to translate between English and Spanish without ever having *learned* how to translate them. Knowing how to translate among known languages is a *consequence* of knowing the languages. Since Marco cannot, to any degree, translate between English and Chinese, he could not, knowing English, know Chinese. Again, Artificial Intelligence is at bay.

Russow (1984 and correspondence) contends, in defense of Artificial Intelligence, that Marco's inability to translate might be taken as showing not that his program itself fails to explain comprehen-

154

sion of Chinese but, rather, that he simply fails to instantiate the program properly. That is, were he to constitute a genuine realization of the program for Chinese, his skills with Chinese symbols would be coordinated with his linguistic abilities generally, and, thus, he would be able to translate between English and Chinese. Since Marco cannot translate, he himself must not properly instantiate the program. Russow reasons that the example involving Marco fails as a counterexample to Artificial Intelligence because the system supposed to instantiate the program has Marco as a proper part. Marco's involvement as a proper part of what poses as an intelligent system ensures the failure of the attempted instantiation because Marco is himself a fully intentional agent. Marco's participation in the system precludes the sort of orchestration of various cognitive abilities normally found in and essential to a truly intelligent system. That is, it is not simply that Marco is himself an intelligent agent that establishes that any system of which he is a proper part is bound not to be intelligent. It is rather that since Marco's mastery of the rules for Chinese is not properly integrated with his other cognitive skills (if it were, he could translate between English and Chinese), his acquisition of the Chinese program does not count as what Artificial Intelligence should insist on as an instantiation of a program for understanding a language. Accordingly, Artificial Intelligence is not required to count Marco's instantiation of the program for Chinese as knowledge of Chinese.

The objection, then, is that Marco fails as an instantiation of what itself is an adequate program for comprehending Chinese because he does not exhibit the proper coordination of cognitive abilities. It is especially his inability to translate between English and Chinese that marks this crucial lack of cognitive cooperation. In order to test this defense of Artificial Intelligence, we ask what the ability to translate requires of Marco. Presumably it involves the ability to exchange strings of Chinese symbols for strings of English symbols. And what marks this as translation is not only that the exchanged symbols are, at least roughly, semantically congruent but also, and importantly, that Marco understands this. For Marco actually to translate between English and Chinese, he must appreciate that the English strings he exchanges for Chinese strings are not *arbitrarily* related. Should Marco reliably trade semantically equivalent English and Chinese tokens without knowing them to be so related, he would not be translating in the ripe and relevant sense of the term but rather and merely playing at swapping English symbols for alien and empty marks. Marco's instructions could after all, be so written as to require him to exchange Chinese symbols for meaningless marks, marks not included in any language. Such a system of exchanges would be formally analogous to Marco's supposed formal translation between English and Chinese. But since the exchange of Chinese symbols for meaningless marks would not be translation, neither would be the envisioned formal exchange of Chinese and English symbols.

Alternatively, if Marco's manual explains to him that the exchange of English and alien marks effects a translation between English and Chinese, then he will in fact translate between the languages, and there would be no reason to deny an understanding of Chinese to him. But – and this is absolutely crucial – Marco's program would no longer qualify as purely formal in the sense demanded by Artificial Intelligence. For by virtue of clarifying the semantic relation between Marco's Chinese symbols and his familiar English counterparts, the manual would be trading on Marco's appreciation of the semantics of English. That is what full-blooded translation requires, and that is why it ruins the formal character of Marco's now altered manual.

Let us rehearse this. Marco can translate between English and Chinese only if he first understands English. So to say that for Marco to instantiate the Chinese program properly he must be able to translate between English and Chinese is to require that he understand English. But Marco's understanding of English evidently is itself an intentional ability, one for which Artificial Intelligence owes an explanation. It will not do for Artificial Intelligence to explain Marco's understanding of English saying that such is simply the mastery of a formal program for English symbols. That would beg the question against Searle's general argument, which itself questions this basic thesis of Artificial Intelligence.

In reply Artificial Intelligence might modify this account of translation and deny that Marco must – in any robust, nonformal sense – independently understand at least one of the languages under translation. It might then propose that the ability to translate is just the ability to exchange sequences of symbols in one language for those with which they are synonymous in another.

Nevertheless, this is not at all what we correctly comprehend under the concept of translation. Consider what we should say of

Marco were he to master purely formal programs for Japanese, Sanskrit, and Tibetan in exactly the same way in which he learns the program for Chinese. Let him also be equipped with a compiler enabling him to exchange strings of any one of these languages for semantically equivalent strings of another. Marco could then be said, in an attenuated sense proper to Artificial Intelligence, to know how to translate between these languages. His apparent cognitive abilities would be remarkably coordinated, but he would still fail utterly to comprehend what he might be saying in any of these languages. Thus, even if Marco is blessed with highly coordinated abilities to manipulate various languages, if his abilities are bestowed on him solely by the grace of formal programs, they do not merit canonization among the intentional. Artificial Intelligence cannot, therefore, be saved by denying that Marco is a legitimate instantiation of an adequate program for Chinese. And once we alter Marco's way with the Chinese symbols so as to incorporate this ability with the others that may be required, we still find that he continues to fail to comprehend Chinese.

5.4. FRAGMENTED AGENTS

Well, perhaps we should try to salvage Artificial Intelligence by conceding all of the above and allowing that Marco himself does not understand Chinese. We might nevertheless insist that Artificial Intelligence is, for the most part, the correct explanation of how internally encoded mental symbols qualify as real representations sufficient for genuine understanding. The reasoning begins with noting that Marco's Chinese character symbols are regularly exchanged according to Chinese grammar. This ensures that the formal program for Chinese recorded in the manual is unquestionably realized somewhere near Marco. But Marco himself does not understand Chinese. He does not instantiate the program. Therefore, there must be another agent, Polo, who does realize the program and thereby understands Chinese. To postulate Polo is, according to Artificial Intelligence, to offer a hypothesis to the best explanation of the symbol exchanges (Dennett, 1978; McCarthy, 1980). Our task is to determine whether this is a good, if not the best, hypothesis.

Nominating Polo is not as scandalously ad hoc as it may appear. We should remind ourselves that we do urgently want some explanation of what, in Marco's presence, closely resembles the phe-nomenon found in native speakers of Chinese and what we typically describe from the intentional stance. Given both that Marco himself does not know Chinese and that the symbol exchanges in which his hands are implicated do require a cognitive account, we seem forced to postulate a new agent as the seat of the relevant cognitive processes. According to Artificial Intelligence, if no agent there understands Chinese, then either the symbol exchanges are mys-terious or we are generally misguided in ascribing an understanding of Chinese to the billion human systems in China who manipulate Chinese characters (McCarthy, 1980; Wilensky, 1980; McDermott, 1982). Prudence, then, dictates introducing Polo.

Although it is undeniable that postulating Polo is not without reason, there remains an overwhelming difficulty with Polo that emerges on close examination. We need to know who Polo is. Perhaps he is the entire physical system constitutive of Marco's environment, including Marco himself. Or Polo might be a cog-nitive agent locked inside Marco's body. An empirical constraint dictates the second of these alternatives. For the Chinese program to be realized, it must be embodied in a mechanism of sufficient physical complexity to complete the computations required by the program within the time limits defined by the actual symbol ex-changes. As a matter of fact, the only device adequate to this chore, available to Polo, and in Marco's vicinity is Marco's brain. So, if Polo is the agent who knows Chinese, he must use Marco's brain to converse in Chinese. Similarly, since Polo needs to receive input conveying information about the presence of Chinese tokens await-ing reply, he must have an embodied information receiver. The only one ready and willing is Marco's sensory system, and Polo will have to borrow that as well. He also needs some tools enabling him to select and present the symbols he offers in reply to those received. Here again Polo will look to Marco's idle hands for help. In short, Polo, at least part of him, must be embodied in Marco's body. Actually, all of Polo has to be there. Polo cannot be the union of Marco's body and something extraneous. The reason is simple: Wherever Marco goes, Polo is sure to follow. Should Marco mem-orize the Chinese manual and travel to China and confront new tokens of the familiar Chinese symbol types, Polo would also be found there, up to his old tricks with the new symbol tokens. Polo must therefore be realized inside Marco's body.

158

This is our empirical constraint. Insofar as it makes sense for Artificial Intelligence to locate centers of cognition, Marco and Polo will both be wholly found in Marco's body. Only now it seems unbridled capitalism to think of the body as Marco's rather than their common caravan.

Now we at least know where Polo is. However, since, by assumption, Marco and Polo are distinct cognitive agents, they both could not be identical with the body they share. Neither does it seem that either alone could be identical with the body since arguments favoring the one could easily be recast to favor the other. That should make us worry that Artificial Intelligence is not only compatible with but also might imply some version of substance dualism since it appears to demand some fundamental cleavage between cognitive agents and their bodies. Hence, to avoid such a dualism, Artificial Intelligence must construe Marco and Polo as respectively identical with, or realized in, different parts or time slices of Marco's body.

Whether this is finally correct is, remember, subject to the empirical constraint. For Marco and Polo will both need to have access to the same necessary computing equipment, the same central and peripheral nervous systems. Assuming that dualism is false, access to this hardware presupposes embodiment in the nervous system. In order to squeeze both Marco and Polo into the same nervous system, Artificial Intelligence must accept one of two alternatives. Either Marco and Polo are cognitive systems sharing time on the same nervous system, now one using it, now the other. Or they must be genuine parallel processors, different programs simultaneously realized in different sections of the central nervous system, sharing time, when necessary, on the common peripheral appendages. In either case, there may need also to be an Operating System, the emperor OS, instantiated in some control center, monitoring Marco and Polo, assigning them time and duties on the system or their respective parts of the system. Quite a crowd is forming, but as long as the human nervous system is engineered consistent with all the software it is to accommodate, there will be room for all in the body. Artificial Intelligence avoids dualism in favor, apparently, of pluralism. Artificial Intelligence exposes the myth, if it is one, of the essential unity of the self. If Artificial Intelligence is true, the agent we identify as Marco is merely one among many agents (who knows how many?) housed in the same body. Call it what you will, it is not dualism, and with lots of luck, it may be a small step toward understanding schizophrenia. In any event, if correct, it makes it obvious why it is nearly impossible to place a long-distance telephone call on Mother's Day.

According to Artificial Intelligence, the "mistake" that ignites Searle's indictment of the thesis that the intelligent use of language is secured by a system under the control of a formal program is the unreflective assumption that the agent who understands Chinese must be Marco. This slip is to be traced to the plausible, but finally and profoundly misguided, presupposition that a human body necessarily realizes but one cognitive agent.

Sadly for Artificial Intelligence, the product of this unrestrained multiplication of agents must at last be excised. In finding Polo in the land of OS, Artificial Intelligence makes mush of some familiar facts. Marco, by our original assumption, is the agent who learned how to manipulate the symbols. The manual is written in English, and Marco, the English speaker in the system, read the manual. Marco learned how to manipulate the symbols in much the same way in which he has previously learned lots of different things, including poker. Now, according to Artificial Intelligence, understanding how to play poker can only involve mastering the proper program, just as understanding Chinese amounts to running the right formal routine. However, since Marco both learned how to play poker and also plays poker, that is, understands poker, why is it Polo rather than Marco who understands Chinese? After all, it was Marco, not Polo, who mastered the program for Chinese. When Artificial Intelligence introduces Polo, it introduces a mystery. It obscures why Marco understands poker but not Chinese. Given Artificial Intelligence, all that Marco did in order to understand poker was instantiate a program. That is just what he did when he acquired the program for Chinese. It is Marco, not the mythical Polo, who must realize the formal program for Chinese. If anyone here understands Chinese, it must be Marco, not Polo. But we have already established that, despite realizing the formal program for Chinese, Marco is ignorant of Chinese. Thus, Artificial Intelligence, we are forced to conclude, is an ultimately and thoroughly false theory of how content accrues to an agent's use of language.[10]

---

10 Lilly-Marlene Russow helped me to see this, although I do not want to suggest that she would endorse this point.

This point, or else its closest kin, can be made differently. When Artificial Intelligence renders intelligent behavior as simply movement driven by a program, it is blind to the semantic interpretation of the activity that makes it the kind of intelligent, typically purposeful, activity it is. Attending only to Marco's gross bodily movements when he exchanges his Chinese character symbols, we cannot attribute to him an understanding of Chinese as opposed to an understanding of how to follow certain apparently pointless rules. It is only on assigning an interpretation to the program-driven movement that we can ascribe to Marco understanding of any sort, be it of Chinese or mere symbol manipulation. Even if intelligent behavior is movement induced by a program under an interpretation, not every generally consistent interpretation of gross movement is guaranteed to be correct. If our interpretation of an agent's movements conflicts with the agent's own interpretation, we ought, at least, to be cautious in overriding the agent's interpretation, all the while recognizing that the agent is not infallible on the matter.

Behavior is manifested in bodily movement, and bodily movements of the same physical type can be realizations of different types of behavior. Artificial Intelligence ignores this when it construes the movements of Marco's body as behavior displaying an understanding of Chinese. Exactly the same symbol manipulations can be described as displaying an understanding not of Chinese but, rather, of how to exchange meaningless marks. Just which description is appropriate, precisely what sort of behavior we are entitled to attribute to the cognitive agent, depends on which description enables us best to explain *all* of the agent's activities across a large span of time in a wide range of settings. We can best explain Marco's behavior by attributing to him knowledge not of Chinese but rather of how to manipulate meaningless marks. Given that ascriptions of behavior (i.e., attributions of bodily movement under an intentional description) are inferences to the best explanation, behavior cannot simply be read off the program driving the bodily movements constituting the behavior. The program is specified in a purely formal way that is necessarily indifferent to the different ways in which the movements produced by the program can be interpreted (Fodor, 1980a; Rey, 1980). All this is to say that although Marco's body moves according to the rules of Chinese grammar, we cannot, on that basis alone, attribute comprehension of Chinese to him. If so, Artificial Intelligence stumbles when it takes conformity with a program to suffice for realizing behavior. The program is guaranteed to underdetermine the behavior too radically.

Neither does it promote Artificial Intelligence to locate intelligent understanding of Chinese in programs enhanced so as to learn. The appeal of adding a learning routine is prompted by the idea that what is wanting in Searle's thought experiment is complexity, that Artificial Intelligence ought to treat real language comprehension as possible only in concert with a wide variety of cognitive capacities. Lured by this, we might be tempted to conjecture that until Marco's situation is amended so as to include the coincident instantiation of formal programs for a full range of cognitive capacities, it will not stand as a counterexample to Artificial Intelligence. This would lead us to conclude erroneously that once these cognitive capacities are appended, it would be transparent that Marco understands Chinese.

We have seen the fly in this ointment. Artificial Intelligence takes a cognitive capacity to be determined by a formal, computational process mediating input and output. The liver satisfies that condition, and the whole digestive system together instantiates a highly complex interactive system of formal computational processes. But that certainly does not install understanding of any sort in the digestive system as a whole. And if the digestive system is insufficiently complex to meet Artificial Intelligence's condition on complexity, nature is not stingy in its array of ever more complex but unintelligent computationally characterizable systems.

5.5. COGNITIVE PSYCHOLOGY AS A FORMAL THEORY

Stich (1983) has argued that cognitive psychology is best advised to consider mental processes as defined over purely syntactic structures. The idea is to suppose that there is indeed a language of thought while denying that this language is a semantic structure. That is, the language of thought is to be viewed, if Stich is right, as an uninterpreted formal calculus of the sort studied under the rubric of proof theory in logic. Transformations among Mentalese sentences would then be characterized *solely* in terms of the syntactic properties of the sentences. Reference to the content of Mentalese sentences is to be banished because either Mentalese is, in rerum natura, a formal, uninterpreted, contentless language or the content

162

of Mentalese sentences is totally without relevance to their role in psychological explanation. Stich (1983, Chapters 8 and 9) distinguishes between the Syntactic Theory of the Mind (STM) and the Weak Representational Theory of the Mind. The former denies that psychological states have content, whereas the latter insists that if psychological states do have content, it is not germane to the purposes of psychology.[11]

Stich places his money on the STM. So, since it is clearly in league with the doctrine that Artificial Intelligence will map the character of the mind, we had better attend here to the STM as promoted by Stich:

The theorist's job in setting out an STM cognitive theory can be viewed as having three parts. First, he must specify a class of syntactic objects (types, of course, not tokens) and do so in a way which assigns a formal or syntactic structure to each of these objects . . . this is best done with a grammar or a set of formation rules detailing the ways in which complex syntactic objects may be built out of a finite set of primitives. Second, the theorist hypothesizes that for each organism covered by the theory, there exists a set of state types whose tokens are causally implicated in the production of behavior. He also hypothesizes that there is a mapping from these state types to syntactic objects in the specified class. . . . The theorist is not claiming that the mapping is the same for each subject, but only that for each subject there is a mapping. . . . The third part of a cognitive theory built on the STM pattern is a specification of the theory's generalizations. The core idea of the STM – the idea that makes it *syntactic* – is that generalizations detailing causal relations among the hypothesized neurological states are to be specified indirectly via the formal relations among the syntactic objects to which the neurological state types are mapped. Similarly, generalizations specifying causal relations between stimuli and neurological states will identify the neurological states not by adverting to their essential neurological types but, rather, by adverting to the syntactic objects to which the neurological types are mapped. Ditto for generalizations specifying causal relations between neurological states and behavior. (1983, pp. 150–1)

What is exciting and provocative in this is its defining proposal that psychological generalizations advert *only* to the syntactic properties of the relevant Mentalese structures. Sentialism is quite keen on the idea that the syntax of occurrent Mentalese structures is literally efficacious in producing behavior, but it wonders about

---

11 Fodor (1980a) is certainly known for a sympathetic presentation of a view of this sort, but as Stich (1983, p. 187) notes, it is not perfectly clear whether Fodor favors the Syntactic or Weak Representational Theory of the Mind.

the suggestion that psychology can eschew reference to the content of an agent's operant Mentalese sentences. In order to appreciate the significance of mental content to psychology, let us modify one of Stich's examples. Suppose that subjects who memorize the sentence

(5.5.1) Among the Moa people of New Guinea, it is common for a man to have several wives and several separate dwellings.

are more inclined to agree with

(5.5.2) Among the Moa people of New Guinea, it is common for a man to have several separate dwellings.

than are subjects who memorize

(5.5.3) Among the Moa people of New Guinea it is not uncommon for a man to have several wives and several separate dwellings.

Why? The STM postulates that encoded in subjects who memorize (5.5.1) there is an uninterpreted Mentalese sentence or syntactic structure of the form $(A \& B)$, whereas in subjects who memorize (5.5.3) there is a syntactic structure of the form $\sim\sim(A \& B)$. Subjects who agree with (5.5.2) do so because they encode a structure of the form B. The reason that subjects who memorize (5.5.1) more readily agree with (5.5.2) than do subjects who memorize (5.5.3) is that it happens that structures such as $(A \& B)$ are more likely to give rise to structures of the sort B than are structures of the form $\sim\sim(A \& B)$. This is because Mentalese conforms to the (supposed) general law of cognitive science that if a syntactic structure X syntactically entails structure Y, then the probability that subjects encoding X will also encode Y is higher than the probability that subjects who encode $\sim\sim X$ will also encode Y (Stich, 1983, pp. 155–7).

Very neat. Insofar as we can provide a syntactic theory for transformations among mental states, the STM is quite promising. Nevertheless there are some reasons to think that the prospects for such a purely syntactic theory are not good. Why do English-speaking subjects who memorize (5.5.1) come to encode a Mentalese structure of the form $(A \& B)$? In other words, why is memorization of an *English* conjunctive sentence sufficient for encoding a *Mentalese* sentence of the form $(A \& B)$, that is, a Mentalese

164

conjunction?[12] The answer is straightforward if we allow that the Mentalese and English sentences semantically agree and suppose that the relation taking the English into the Mentalese sentence is a type of translation relation. The STM theory cannot tolerate this, however, since it eschews semantically endowed mental structures.

This type of problem can be made more graphic if we ponder the austerity of formal systems of logic. We now know that, within certain limits and domains, axiomatic systems can be consistent and complete, first-order propositional logic being a case in point. Yet we have nothing that begins to approach an adequate syntactic theory of the general logic of entailment. For example, most English speakers who memorize

>(5.5.4) Socrates was a father.

will tend to agree with

>(5.5.5) Socrates was a male.

What does the STM make of this? Presumably it will respectively assign (5.5.4) and (5.5.5) to some encoded Mentalese syntactic structures, C and D, and take C syntactically to entail D. But what in the world accounts for the syntactic entailment from C to D? Apparently nothing.

Of course, the natural reply is to say that an encoding of C typically brings with it an encoding of $(C \rightarrow D)$ and that C and $(C \rightarrow D)$ together syntactically entail D. But this puts us back where we started. What explains why an encoding of C typically carries along one of $(C \rightarrow D)$ if not the fact that the semantic conditions on C ensure those on D, a fact that the STM cannot allow?

Stich is led to the STM because, as we have seen in Chapter 4, Section 4.3, he is convinced that any attempt to assign content to mental states is a journey to confusion, that ascriptions of mental content are bound to be hopelessly vague. But we also saw there that the case might not be as bad as Stich fears. Here it remains to

12 Appeal to a sheer syntactic homomorphism does not serve to explain why an English conjunction is mentally encoded as A & B. Such a homomorphism would be, at best, purely accidental. After all, there are various syntactic constructions in English for expressing conjunction, and different spoken languages employ utterly different syntactic structures to express conjunctions. So it seems unlikely that the phenomenon here is a function of a syntactic homomorphism between Mentalese and an agent's spoken language.

consider an argument advanced by Stich that seems to justify both the STM and its first of kin, Artificial Intelligence.

Assume that, as the STM anticipates, we someday manage to discern the syntactic structure of Mentalese. We would then have specified the class of primitive Mentalese types and the grammar that, when applied to the primitives, yields complex Mentalese configurations. Additionally, for agents comprehended by the theory, there would be a mapping from those of their states that cause them to act onto the syntactic types designated by the theory's grammar. This much Sententialism would welcome. Beyond this suppose that, besides being able to map the states of selected organisms onto syntactic types, we also devise a way of associating the states of computers with the very same syntactic types. Indeed, we might devise programs exploiting such mappings that perfectly simulate certain behavior patterns of designated kinds of naturally intelligent agents. We might, for example, come to understand the psychological processes that control a worker on an automobile assembly line as she welds pieces of passing metal and use this information to construct a robot that relies on the same syntactically characterized states to accomplish the same.

Although we might naively describe the worker's behavior by attributing to her contentful mental states – say, the belief that a frame and a strut have arrived and the desire to weld them – we are not at all inclined to attribute the same to the robot. After all, the program driving the robot to act could, in principle, be instantiated in another robot on a different part of the assembly line in order to weld motor mounts to engine blocks. Since the robots are, by assumption, in exactly the same psychological states, it would be patently wrong to attribute to the one a belief about frames and struts and to the other a belief about motor mounts and engine blocks. It would be much more plausible to refer only to the syntactic properties of the internal states of the robots when explaining what they are doing.[13]

13 Stich defends what he calls the Principle of Autonomy (1983, pp. 164–70), a thesis to the effect that "historical and environmental facts will be psychologically relevant only when they influence an organism's current, internal, physical state. So if a feature of the organism's history or environment might have been different without affecting the organism's current, internal, physical state, then that historical or environmental feature must play no role in the psychologist's theory" (pp. 164–5). Since attributions of content to mental states typically assign to psychological states referents that might vary as a function of the environment

166

The catch is that the same would appear to apply to the worker as well. She is driven to act by exactly the same syntactic type of states as are the robots. So, if the explanation of the robots' activity does not depend on characterizing the robots' efficacious states as contentful, neither should the account of the worker's behavior. There is no more reason to ascribe content to the mental states of the worker than there is to ascribe intentional states to the robots. And there is simply no reason to attribute intentional states to the robots.

The STM is, accordingly, undisturbed by Searle's argument. That argument relies on the notion that a genuinely intelligent agent is awash in contentful states, states of the sort missing in Marco's mastery of Chinese characters. From the perspective of the STM, to insist that content is essential to those psychological states that prompt behavior is to wallow in popular, entrenched, but finally mistaken dogma.[14]

The plausibility of the example featuring the robots as an argument for the STM depends in no small part on the assumption that the robots, simply by virtue of instantiating states with the same syntactic properties as the worker's psychological states, themselves enjoy psychological states, much less psychological states of the same sort as those of the worker. Of course, it is the contention of Sections 5.2–5.4 that this is false. Let us set that aside, however, and allow that the worker and robots do indeed possess psychological states of the same kind. Does that demonstrate that psychological states are contentless and thereby render the STM credible?

If we suppose, as may appear correct, that the robots are acting differently, one welding frames to struts, the other welding motor

while the structure of the psychological states remains constant, the Principle of Autonomy stands against ascriptions of content. It would seem that the syntactic properties of a mental state could remain invariant across different (apparent) referents, implying that the reference, and hence the content (if any), of the mental states is psychologically inert. Compare Burge (1979).

14 Now this is full circle! We began with the assumption that cognition requires a language of thought. That led us to worry about how, short of an infinite regress of embedded agents, such a language could have the content it evidently does. Artificial Intelligence appeared to have the answer, but Searle's argument serves to derail it. So, in order to preserve Artificial Intelligence, we find ourselves looking to the STM. And this completes the circle, for the STM denies that the language of thought need be contentful at all. We philosophers sometimes travel a very long way to get to where we already are.

mounts to engine blocks, then we may be disinclined to attribute to them the same mental content. Failing this, it seems retrograde to assign to their mental states any content whatsoever. Since their states are, by assumption, syntactically and, hence, causally the same, they will engender precisely congruent behavior patterns. But if their states were differently contentful, we should expect them to manifest some behavioral difference. So, following Stich, it appears that their states could neither differ nor coincide in content. They could not, then, have any content at all.

We should be cautious here. Although the robots do manage to weld different types of automobile parts, it may well be that the robots' activity to be explained is most appropriately comprehended under a common description. That is, we might well view the robots as both engaged in welding *things arriving from the left to things arriving from the right*. The robots perhaps do not distinguish fenders from motor mounts and struts from engine blocks. What the robots do differentiate, however, are things as arriving from the left and things as arriving from the right. If so, this would be why the robots would in fact be behaving in the same way; what each does satisfies the same behavioral description, namely, 'welding (or attempting to weld) things arriving from the left to things arriving from the right'. Once we recognize that the robots can be construed as engaging in the same type of behavior, assigning the same content to their operant states becomes plausible. Evidently, if we hold that the robots are in the same psychological state as the worker, we must assign to her state much the same content we do to theirs. Thus, we should drop our naive assumption that the belief that causes the worker to weld is the belief that a frame and a strut have arrived. Rather, the belief that induces her to act is, like the robots' belief, the belief that things to be welded are arriving from the left and from the right.

It is nearly impossible to overestimate the importance of the lesson to be learned here about revising our early attribution of belief to the worker. As hypotheses concerning the best explanation of behavior, belief attributions are sensitive to whatever current data the attributions are to explain. When we consider the worker in isolation from the robots, we may be justified in supposing that the belief causing her to weld a frame to a strut is the belief that a frame and a strut have arrived on the assembly line. Once, however, the data to be explained are expanded so as to include the activity of the robots, the warrant erodes for locating the cause of the worker's behavior in a belief that frames and struts are arriving.

When it is incumbent on us to discern a belief that will serve both the worker and the robots, we are forced to revise our original assessment of the content of the worker's state. But this is the way of abductive inference generally, and so we should not be especially alarmed by the volatility of ascriptions of content to mental states. In any event, certainly nothing here precludes the possibility of the worker's believing that frames and struts are at hand. It is consistent that she have this very belief without it being the case that it is among the states implicated in the etiology of her welding. It could be that she believes both that a frame and a strut have arrived and also that things from the left and from the right have arrived. And yet it may be the latter, but not the former, belief that contributes to the cause of her welding. This, of course, is contingent on the hypotheses that the worker and robots agree in efficacious psychological states and that the robots do not conceive of the things to be welded as frames and struts. All this conceded, we need not march to the tune of the STM. For we are not driven to grant that the case of the robots mandates that naturally intelligent agents must be void of content.

5.6. THE MUNDANE MATTER OF MIND

More might be said on behalf of Artificial Intelligence and its theoretical basis in the Syntactic Theory of the Mind. The point made by this chapter, however, is that Artificial Intelligence is not an especially promising research model for the intentional. Its apparent failure to explicate the nature of mental representation seems to devolve from its failure to recognize natural boundaries, those nature appears to have established on its evolutionary march, between intelligent and unintelligent objects and processes. Artificial Intelligence may be wanting as a science of natural intelligence because it effaces an important difference in nature itself between agent and object, action and event. Faced with this, we had better retreat from the idea that the purely formal properties of the mind account for its intentional or semantic features. Although we can look to Artificial Intelligence for instruction on the computational nature of mental processes, we cannot hope there to find an explanation of how, ultimately, our mental states come to have content. If this is correct, we will need, for the sake of Sententialism, to look beyond Artificial Intelligence for a final solution to the problem of embedded agents.

Well, what, then, is necessary for an agent to enjoy intentional states, states that really do have representational content for the agent? What does Marco have, as a speaker of English, if not just a capacity to move in ways orchestrated by a marvelously plastic, adaptive, complex, but purely formal program? If, as has been argued so far, the purely formal does not fix the intentional, the best explanation of the intentional must have it that intentionality is somehow dependent on realization in matter of a certain sort. No one now can say what this substance might be or what will prove to be the important laws governing it, but it certainly is possible to indicate who someday will. But let us first mark the trail with a little tale.

Once upon a very long time ago, when Philosophy was queen of the sciences (her kingdom was small and impoverished), there taught at the Majestic Institute of Tutelage an assistant professor of natural philosophy named Functatus Excessivus. Functatus marveled at all the wonderful things to drink, clear-liquids-in-green-glasses, clear-liquids-in-blue-glasses, clear-liquids-in-red-glasses and many others besides. But being a scholar of no mean scope, he was also taken with the abundance of games he found to play – guessing games, athletic contests, and, most exciting of all, tenure roulette. Functatus dedicated himself to studying these two kinds of wonders. Beginning with the liquids, he devoted several years to sampling as many clear-liquids-in-glasses as his NSF grant allowed, first hoping to detect, but then finally despairing of finding out, what made them all so nourishing. They seemed to have nothing in common, each obviously being of a different natural kind, red-glass, green-glass, blue-glass.

One day, after puzzling endless hours over his problem, Functatus wearily sat back in his chair and scratched his shoulder to relieve it from the relentless discomfort of his rough wool shirt, wishing he had worn his linen one instead. Then the solution struck him. Both his shirts were shirts despite the fact that they were not made of the same material. Indeed, a shirt could be made of most, if not all, kinds of cloth. What makes an article of clothing a shirt is not what it is made of but rather what function it serves. There certainly is no hidden physical essence common to shirts. Exactly

170

the same must also be true of the clear-liquids-in-glasses. Despite their obvious physical differences, each clear-liquid-in-a-glass serves much the same function. Each can slake one's thirst, revive wilted daisies, and so on. Inspired, Functatus concluded that a clear-liquid-in-a-glass was whatever had just such a network of relations. "Never mind the stuff! Look for the function!" How thrilled Functatus was. Not only had he made a profound discovery, but he also had a catchy slogan to boot.

Functatus won his round of tenure roulette and lived happily ever after. His discovery and slogan deservedly made his name known throughout Philosophy's kingdom. It launched research programs for a whole host of philosophers as the idea gained currency that the true nature of various kinds of things could be discerned without the necessity of probing deeply into their physical constitutions. Only in the far, far west was a single voice raised against Functatus, but it was drowned out by a large chorus of praise.

Once justly famous and secure, Functatus turned to his other interest, surprised to find that games were quite different from clear-liquids-in-glasses. All the games he knew were so much fun to play. Even tenure roulette had not been so bad, he thought in retrospect. So, Functatus reasoned (although he did admit it to be transparent), being fun to play was the physical nature common to all games. He even dreamed of founding a science, to be called chemistry, that would analyze all the different kinds of things, like games, into their basic elements. This would be an arduous, expensive science, one demanding examination in the laboratory of the physical constituents of its subjects. Functatus was too busy lecturing throughout the kingdom to achieve this goal personally. Still he was, and always would remain, proud to know that he had, at least, discovered the first and probably most important element in nature, being fun to play.

Poor Functatus, he had it all backward. He never realized that the glasses all contained H_2O and that chemistry would not favor his favorite element. In nature apparently diverse things may constitute a natural kind if they share a common, even if obscure, material essence subjecting them to the same laws. Similar artifacts typically lack common cohesive natures binding them into kinds. Functatus faced a difficult problem. It is extraordinarily hard to know when what does not seem to be a natural kind really is and when what looks to be a natural kind really is not (Paul Churchland,

171

1985b). Only mature science, as opposed to our common and popular intellectual heritage, is much good at elevating the true heirs and unmasking the pretenders. Attention to the history of science should teach us that, like phlogiston, many of the kinds we suppose to be natural are bogus and that, like the until recently unknown neutron stars, many of what we shall discover to be natural kinds are currently unknown to us.

Intentional states arise in nature, and it may not be a bad, even if not a sure, bet that they are comprehended by a natural kind (Paul Churchland, 1982). So, if we book this gamble and want to know about this presumed kind, we had best wager on our friends in the natural sciences to be first in with the answer. If, as the apparent failure of Artificial Intelligence to expose the essence of intentionality may indicate, intelligent, intentional states cohere as a natural kind, then *no amount of philosophical speculation uninformed by the results of neuroscience can hope to be an adequate theory of the mind.* To maintain otherwise, insisting that work outside the laboratory will discover the essence of intelligent understanding, would be as thoroughly wrong as holding out the hope that philosophical analysis alone could reveal the nature of combustion, gravity, or cancer.

Even if intentionality does turn out to be a natural kind fit for scientific dissection, there still may be work for Artificial Intelligence. It may well be, as earlier remarked, that intentionality is matter of a certain sort insofar as it realizes computational relations. Putting it baldly, it *could* be that intelligence involves a computationally structured mental language necessarily encoded only in tokens composed of neurons. That would be like discovering an alien language, all tokens of which had to be written in red ink in order to be tokens of that language. I am not arguing that something like this *must* be the case in order for there to be genuine intelligence but only that it may be. Should such be true, we would have a ready explanation as to why formal programs alone fail to install genuine understanding. They can be realized regardless of the material composition of their receptacles, whereas bona fide intelligent systems require instantiation in matter of some material type that is yet to be described. What would ensure, then, that Mentalese, when encoded in the human brain, is contentful would be that the material of the brain devoted to Mentalese is, by its very physical properties, exactly the stuff sufficient for supporting intentionality.

Should this prove to be so, then that the mental sentence 'Héloïse is beautiful' encoded in Abelard's head is a naturally contentful structure would be traced to the fact that it is encoded in the kind of material it is. Given the argument to this point, that the same structure specifically represents, say, *that* Héloïse is beautiful could be at least *partially* determined by the functional relations this inscription bears to stimuli, other mental inscriptions, and behavior. But since a condition of a structure representing at all is that the structure be composed of the type of material characteristic of contentful or intentional structures, it could not be, as Artificial Intelligence insists, that it suffices for a structure having content simply that it be enmeshed in a functional economy of a certain sort.

Well, isn't this a fine kettle of fish? Remember Marco? Isn't he made of the proper stuff for mentation? By assumption he has mastered the program for Chinese, so should not it follow after all that he does understand Chinese? And would not that undercut the argument on behalf of Searle that brought us to this embarrassing point of casting about for some hidden physical essence of intentionality?

Yes, Marco does contain the matter of mentation, and, yes, he has mastered the formal program for Chinese. Nonetheless, he does not understand Chinese. Explaining why forces a new wrinkle in the story to be taken up in the next chapter, but we can anticipate the gist of it here.

In the case of a mental language, especially a *natural, nonartificial*, language of thought, we will need to discern how the world causally impinges on an agent so as to produce in the agent an intentional structure with some specific content.[15] But the current lesson is that even if we were to concede that, from a formal point of view, Marco does instantiate in his mental matter just what a native speaker of Chinese does, that still does not suffice for his mental states to agree in content with those of someone fluent in Chinese. That he is flush with mental terms encoded in the type of matter that ensures that these terms do in fact represent does not itself suffice to settle their specific content. Something else is required for a mental term to come to mean what it does. What seems to be missing from Marco's situation is a guarantee that his mental structures have been caused to occur within him as they have been

15 This is the topic to which we shall turn next, in Chapter 6.

in those who do know Chinese. Before we can concede that Marco's mental terms enable him actually to understand Chinese, we must know whether the relations that connect Marco's terms to the world are essentially the same as those that link the corresponding mental terms in a native speaker of Chinese to the same world. Compare Putnam (1975), Fodor (1980a), Dretske (1981), Stich (1983), Maloney (1985b), and Graham and Garrett (1986).

Let us see what we have here. Consideration of Marco's situation with the Chinese characters provides us with evidence that Marco does not understand Chinese. The evidence may not be *absolutely* conclusive, but it certainly suffices to justify the hypothesis that, contrary to what Artificial Intelligence might hold, Marco's mastery of his manual does not suffice to secure for him an understanding of Chinese. Why not? Well, it is hard not to notice that one thing that differentiates Marco and other agents known to understand languages from the class of artificial systems capable of mastering (in the sense relevant to Artificial Intelligence) Marco's manual is that Marco and his peers constitute a natural kind whereas the artificial class does not. This fuels the hypothesis – not a demonstrated dogma of faith – that something in the physical nature of Marco and company is essential to intentionality. Since the artificial class is drawn without regard for what binds Marco's kind, there is no provision that the members of the artificial class will have the intentionality that Marco and his crew enjoy.

What Marco brings to the world, then, is a type of matter suitable for intentional states. What he does not bring to the world is a system of ideas. That is, although Marco is by nature equipped to have specific ideas, he does not come into the world with all, if any, of the ideas he will someday have. This must be, the working hypothesis continues, because specific ideas arise within Marco's intentional matter only on its being activated by its causal connections with his environment. Marco may share his environment with a rock. Both Marco and the rock may be exposed to heat. Marco, but not the rock, develops the idea of heat despite the fact that both are affected by the heat. This is because Marco, but not the rock, harbors intentional matter. Although Marco masters the formal manual for Chinese in the manner demanded by Artificial Intelligence, he may yet fail to know Chinese. This is because he has not undergone the causal processes necessary to implicate his intentional matter in the appropriate way.

174

We know that Chinese has certain formal properties; we may assume that the formal structure Marco comes to master is indeed a language with the same formal properties as Chinese. However, Chinese sentences, in order to be such, must also have meaning. And nothing we have learned of Marco ensures that the sentences he deploys on an occasion mean what their syntactic partners would mean when sincerely issued by a native speaker of Chinese. Without this insurance, we have no reason whatsoever to concede that Marco understands Chinese. Indeed, until we can be confident that Marco's manual provides a semantics for his syntactic structures, we are best advised to demur to the claim that what Marco has mastered is even a language.

To be sure, not nearly enough has been said to begin to count as an explanation of how an agent's mental terms come to mean precisely what they do. All that we now have are some hypotheses: that the intentionality of a mental state is drawn from its instantiation in a certain sort of matter; that the functional or formal relations among such states *may* contribute to the meaning of a mental term; and last, that the causal connections between the world and an agent's encoded mental terms seem to make some difference to what an actual mental structure represents.

But perhaps you have already had enough of this encroaching materialism and mock it, saying that it equates real understanding, which seems absent from Marco's realization of the Chinese program, with some inscrutable stuff – some secret, slimy secretion flowing in Marco's brain when he exchanges the Chinese symbols (Dennett, 1980). You recall the argument in Section 5.1 regarding the possibility of intelligent silicon-based Martians and contend that you can certainly *imagine* it to be possible that in some remote corner of the universe there is some sort of inorganic creature who writes novels and equations and understands *Finnegans Wake* and quantum mechanics. So you conclude that a neuroscience biased in favor of terrestrial chemistry is sure to fail in its search for the secret stuff of intelligence.

This kind of argument has been widely, but wrongly, touted as a refutation of materialistic identifications of mental processes. Its error is evident once we realize that we can also imagine that, possibly, wherever in the universe intentionality abounds it is *essentially* organic. Does this show that it is possible that intelligence is necessarily organic and, given that the possibly necessary is nec-

175

essary, that intelligence is therefore necessarily organic? This way of arguing about the prospects of a science is absurd, for it rests on imagination indiscriminately fueled by dogma and insight. Surely, although we can imagine that possibly water is not H_2O, it remains that chemistry rightly takes water necessarily to be composed of hydrogen and oxygen. Nothing else *could* be water, regardless of what we fancy.

Remember: Before the ascent of chemistry, a functionalist curious about water might have specified its functional relations, taking such to be the ultimate essence of water, and try to embarrass early, unsuccessful chemists into silence by deriding the idea that water could only be stuff as unlikely as a mixture of different types of, good Lord, gas! Fortunately that did not happen, and we have been rewarded with a clear conception of what water really is. Analogously, understanding what intentionality is may, if intentionality is a natural kind, amount to comprehending the stuff of which it is made. The continuous success of science generally and neuroscience particularly feeds the hope that the stuff of understanding, like that of earth, air, fire, and water, will find its place in the materialistic scheme. Should we someday discover forms of intelligence utterly alien from local types, that need not show, as functionalists often maintain, the vacuity of the materialistic account of intelligence. For such a discovery, while refuting the then-current materialistic conception of intelligence, could also energize further research into the finally basic stuff common to all intelligence, domestic and foreign, familiar and strange.

If, at last, you insist that these materialistic hypotheses are wildly wrong, then I can only suggest that for the moment you try to see it my way. Recall the situation on Putnam's (1975) Twin Earth, where each of us has a doppelgänger. Each doppelgänger looks exactly like his or her terrestrial partner and speaks and acts the same on similar occasions. But, departing from Putnam's tale, imagine they are made of some stuff other than what makes us intelligent. They say that the clear liquid they drink is water. Nevertheless, they are wrong; it is not H_2O. They say that they have intelligence and have convinced you of the same. But if, as I have urged, intelligence is a natural kind, they again, and now you too, are fooled. I certainly do not know what it is that they have, but since it is not the same kind of stuff as its Earthly reflection, it cannot be intelligence. How can it be? It is not the right stuff.

6

Fixing the content
of mental sentences

6.1. EMPIRICISM AND MENTAL REPRESENTATIONS

To think, if Sententialism should be true, is to deploy a mental language. Now a language, as a structure determined by a grammar, can be treated as an uninterpreted formal calculus when complemented by a set of axioms. But the mental language is more than a contentless calculus if the preceding chapter is to be believed. So, if this is right, we must anticipate that an agent's language of thought is, like familiar spoken languages of communication, a fully intentional structure, a system of interacting symbols, well-formed combinations of which are meaningful. What we need to pursue is an explanation of how content could accrue to Mentalese, how Mentalese sentences might come to mean what they do.

In rejecting the notion that the language of thought is an uninterpreted, formal system, we advanced the hypothesis that a necessary condition of a physical structure's having mental content is that it be composed of a peculiar type of matter. This hypothesis of the Material Basis of Cognition need *not* be narrowly construed so as to imply that only creatures conforming to what we *now know* of our own physiology can enjoy a mental language. It is consistent with the prevailing hypothesis to suppose that the study of cognitive processes will someday yield a radically new taxonomy of physical states according to which organic and inorganic devices are comprehended by a natural physical kind, membership in which ensures the possession of contentful mental states. That such a possibility is within the realm of reason should be clear from the history of biology and chemistry. For whereas once we struggled with a taxonomy that bifurcated the world into animate and not, we now have a different and more articulate classification scheme that eschews the contrast between animate and inanimate objects. Thus

177

it is with some reason that we may conjecture that developments in the sciences of the mind may someday make it necessary and compelling to posit natural kinds not familiar from other areas of inquiry.

Even if mentation should presuppose membership in a natural physical kind, it remains to explain how different Mentalese tokens fabricated from this kind come to mean what they specifically do. That is, pretending that Mentalese and English are orthographically identical, we need to inquire why, for example, the Mentalese sentence 'Héloïse is in the garden' happens to mean that Héloïse is in the garden.

Sententialism does not insist that all types of cognitive agents share the same mental language. Indeed, the converse seems much more likely; cognitive kinds may be distinguished by peculiarities of their distinctive languages of thought. So we shall suppose throughout that mental languages are species specific. Although mental languages may differ according to cognitive kinds, we will assume that the mechanisms that fix the content of mental languages are fundamentally the same. And to keep matters simple, we will focus on the language of human thought.

Thought naturally bifurcates into sensuous and nonsensuous. Some of our cognitive episodes are the direct result of sensation; others are not.[1] We might begin by attempting to indicate how sensuous cognition is representational. That is, assuming that sensation is a variety of cognition, we might try to explain how sensory states, Mentalese tokens occurrent in sensation, represent what they do. If Locke's hope for raising a general account of cognition from sensation is generally sound, and what we survey here is at all close to correct, then we may hope that a complete semantics for the mind is, even if not yet within reach, at least on the horizon.[2]

1 The distinction is difficult to draw with precision. Roughly, however, the idea is that some mental representations must be the effects of our sensory organs. Within a computational model of the mind, these are representations that are encoded within a computational system without themselves being the inferential or causal consequences of other representations. In other words, sensuous representations are akin to undemonstrated premises in a deductive system. A deductive system must start from some premises that are not the consequences of other formulas; otherwise no deductions can be constructed.
2 See Fodor (1981c) for reservations about empiricist programs for explaining mental representation.

Let us assume throughout that nativism is false, that cognitive agents are not endogenously versed in Mentalese. This is a purely empirical assumption that may well be false and whose truth can only finally be settled by a completed cognitive science. Still, it would be a boon to Sententialism were it not necessarily wedded to nativism (Patricia Smith Churchland, 1978, 1980a).[3] Accepting Mentalese is tantamount to recognizing a mental lexicon replete with mental predicates. In denying nativism, we especially want to repudiate innately meaningful Mentalese predicates, physical structures whose sheer existence ensures their content. This evidently is consistent with recognizing, though it certainly does not presuppose, an innate mental grammar that operates on acquired Mentalese terms. In rejecting nativism, we impose a constraint on our explanation of sensuous content. If we turn our backs to nativism, we cannot try to explicate the content of an agent's mental states generally by reference to what the agent may happen antecedently to believe or otherwise think. That would be to refer circularly to cognitive states themselves ripe with content, which is what awaits explanation. In other words, it would violate the spirit of empiricism ultimately to explicate an agent's acquisition of primordial mental terms by reference to a process that depends on the agent's "figuring out" the significance of his or her mental terms. This is because, by Sententialism's lights, such a process would involve the inferential use of meaningful mental sentences, sentences whose meaning awaits explanation.

6.2. A CAUSAL EXPLANATION OF SENSUOUS REPRESENTATION

To sense is to suffer a specific type of representational state, a state that registers in a cognitive agent information gleaned from the ambient array. So much is noncontroversial and also true of at least some nonsensuous mental states. What, then, distinguishes sensuous cognition? Certainly in humans, and probably in other species of cognitive agents, sensation is typically laden with qualia; sensing

3 See Fodor (1975, 1981a) for an argument that representationalism entails nativism. If our way with sensuous cognition proves plausible, it should show a way of accepting representationalism without thereby being coerced into accepting Fodor's nativist conclusions.

has a characteristic feel or phenomenology.[4] Most likely, sensuous qualia vary across, and perhaps even within, cognitive species, and it is in any event unclear whether these qualia are essential or accidental to the intentional or representational character of sensory states. So we might reasonably hesitate to appeal to qualia in characterizing the semantics of sensory states. If we ignore the phenomenological nature of sensation, our best hope in ascertaining the nature of sensuous representation probably rests with the physical sciences, neurology in particular. Sensation evidently is an essentially physical process necessarily involving a specific sort of biochemistry. No one now can pretend to know what the hard sciences may one day find to be characteristic of all sensory systems, but we can lay it down as a working hypothesis that sensation is an essentially physical process, a process possible only in certain kinds of physical structures, a way of processing information open only to cognitive agents endowed with selected, probably neurological, properties.

Sensory states are effects produced in cognitive agents by surrounding, typically external, objects.[5] These same states themselves participate in the production of cognition and behavior appropriate to the agent's milieu. There can be no doubt that the environment influences an agent's behavior through the medium of the agent's sensory states. It is this simple, undeniable fact that drove the classical causal theory of perception, fuels the more recent causal theories of reference, and propels the basic idea to be propounded here. With abundant qualifications, the argument will be that sensory states represent their causes, that the content of a sensory state is the state of affairs by which it, the sensory state, is caused.

To begin, recall that sensory states, besides being states of a certain general physical kind, are Mentalese tokens. Minimally,

---

4 We shall look at the whole issue of the phenomenology of consciousness more closely in Chapter 7. For a variety of views see Nagel (1974), Block and Fodor (1972), Block (1980b), Patricia Smith Churchland (1980b), Churchland and Churchland (1982), Paul Churchland (1985a), Davis (1982), Dennett (1978a), Graham and Stevens (1985), Jackson (1982), Maloney (1985a), and Shoemaker (1975).

5 When I talk of objects as causes, I mean to attribute causal efficacy to specific properties of the objects, or, putting the same differently, to attribute causation to the objects by virtue of specific properties they have. Beyond this, I ignore the whole issue of whether causation is, finally, a feature of events, states, properties, or objects.

then, sensory states refer and predicate.[6] So in a sensory state there must be an element that refers and an element that predicates. To explain the content of a sensory state is to explain both its referential and its predicative components, what they are, and how they represent. Suppose that on one occasion an apple's being red causes Abelard to be in sensory state S, whereas on another occasion a plum's being purple causes him to be in sensory state $S^\star$. Since S and $S^\star$ result from different causes and themselves have different effects, we may suppose that they are tokens of different physical types, the types themselves qualifying as sensory by way of sharing whatever general feature science may one day determine to be characteristic of sensation. As a first approximation, we may say that, given their respective causes, S represents the apple as red, $S^\star$ the plum as purple. Since S is caused by the apple's being red and since, other things being equal, similar causes result in similar effects, other things of the same shade of red as the apple will cause in Abelard tokens of the same physical type as S. Hence whatever physical features of S serve to make it a token of its physical type also serve as the Mentalese predicate realized in S. Thus, by being a token of its physical type, S instantiates the Mentalese predicate attributing (still approximately) red.[7] Similarly for $S^\star$ as a Mentalese token predicating purple. Generally, then, specific properties of objects cause occurrences of sensory tokens of corresponding specific physical types. Those features of the sensory tokens that render them members of their physical types constitute the Mentalese predicates they embody, and these predicates ascribe the properties that cause the sensory tokens to occur.

Within a cognitive species, then, sensory Mentalese types are physical types.[8] Across different cognitive species, however, there

6 Assuming, of course, that the Mentalese tokens realized in sensory states are simple declarative sentences.
7 It is being red, rather than, say, being an apple, that the predicate attributes by virtue of the undefended assumption that the state constituting the predicate is caused to occur by some object's being red rather than its being an apple. For our purposes it is inessential that the predicate here attributes red. What is important, however, is that there be some property of the apple that causes the state constituting the predicate to occur. It is that property, whatever it turns out to be, that the predicate is (still approximately) to attribute.
8 This depends on sensory Mentalese type being gauged simply in terms of what is predicated as opposed to what is the object of reference. That is, if one sensory token predicates red of an apple and another sensory token predicates the same

is no reason to suppose that similar causes will have similar effects, and for this reason, spanning species, sameness of sensuous Mentalese type is, at best, fixed by sameness in causal history. Yet this is not, as we have already seen, to admit to the idea that whatever reacts to a cause of a designated type thereby mentally represents that cause. It remains necessary that, even across cognitive species, sensory states, regardless of mental type, must exhibit a certain general type of physical feature in order to qualify as sensory and, thereby, mental types.

Returning to Abelard, S and $S^\star$ not only differently predicate but also differently refer, S to the apple, $S^\star$ to the plum. Why? S refers to the apple since the apple is the object whose property causes S to occur. Even so, we need to know what in S constitutes its referential element. As a distinct sensory token of a specific physical type, S possesses physical features that differentiate it from other tokens of the same physical type. These features individuate S as the unique state it is and also constitute S's referential element. Those of S's properties that differentiate it from other states of the same kind serve as its referential marker; they collectively function as a referential term in S designating that very apple involved in causing S to occur. Analogously for $S^\star$ and its reference to the plum.

So much for approximation. What, exactly, is the content of S? We know that it somehow refers to a particular apple and somehow predicates red of that apple. But how exactly does it refer and predicate? Does it refer to the apple *as* an apple; does it describe the apple *as* red? What, from Abelard's perspective, does S represent? By way of comparison, suppose that Abelard were assertively to utter:

(6.2.1) The man in the chair is pale.

As a sentence, (6.2.1) refers to a specific man, who, we may suppose, happens to be Héloïse's youngest brother. It also predicates a color, which, we may assume, is a specific reflectance gradient. Nonetheless, (6.2.1) neither refers to the brother *as* the brother nor ascribes that specific reflectance gradient *as* such. So, looking back to sensuous reference and predication, although we scribes may know what Abelard's sensuous token refers to and what property

of a ball, the tokens are taken to be of the same Mentalese type despite referring to different objects.

it predicates, we do not, for all that, know, in at least one important sense, how the referent or attributed property is represented by Abelard's token. We do not yet know how Abelard *conceives* of what he represents (Dretske, 1981; Churchland and Churchland, 1983). His occurrent sensuous token does indeed attribute to the apple a property that we scribes know to be red. We also know, though Abelard may not, that the property his sensuous token attributes is a specific reflectance gradient. But this still leaves us ignorant as to whether Abelard's sensuous Mentalese predicate is synonymous with 'red' or some specific mathematical expression specifying the relevant reflectance gradient. That is, although we know what property is designated by Abelard's sensuous Mentalese predicate, we still do not know the content of that predicate within his system of mental terms. Alternatively, we do not yet know whether Abelard's present concept is the concept of red or the concept of some specific reflectance gradient.

Our problem, then, is to begin to explain how meaning accrues to the terms of a sensuous Mentalese representation. We have repudiated nativism. So, in attempting to indicate why a sensuous Mentalese term means what it does, we cannot advert to any stock of antecedently meaningful Mentalese terms. It would be wrong to suppose that sensuous representations mean what they do by virtue of being defined through other Mentalese terms whose meaning is simply given.[9] Since we need to know how an agent's sensory state could, *ab initio*, have content for the agent, we are pressed to determine exactly how sensory predicates capture specific concepts and how sensory terms refer, both solely by virtue of being reactions to the agent's environment.

A sensory Mentalese token consists of a subject and predicate.[10] These Mentalese terms must represent in a way that does not depend on other representations of which the agent is capable. Minimally, then, sensuous representations must feature Mentalese terms of the most semantically impoverished sort, terms whose deployment

9 See Lewis (1969) for an explanation of how spoken language might be acquired independent of understanding any spoken language.
10 We suppress consideration of direct and indirect object constructions and more complicated syntactic structures generally. So nothing will be said about the meaning of such Mentalese terms – if indeed there are such – as logical constants, adverbs, and sentential operators. This is partly because it is plausible to assume – perhaps by way of idealization – that sensuous representations are of simple subject-predicate form.

does not presuppose anything like the possession of definitions of the deployed terms, definition itself involving prior representation. In order to explain this, we take a hint from a familiar feature of spoken language. Demonstrative pronouns, unlike definite and indefinite descriptions, refer without describing, categorizing, or classifying. They refer in the most pristine way without assistance from other lexical items. Sensuous reference, we hypothesize, must be similar. It must involve a type of Mentalese term akin to a spoken demonstrative pronoun, a term that refers by *selecting without describing*. We postulate, then, that the referential elements in sensory states function as Mentalese demonstrative pronouns. They refer simply by virtue of being caused to occur, and they select as their referents the objects that cause them to occur without regard for any other characteristics these objects might possess.

When Abelard senses a red apple, his sensory state, as a Mentalese inscription, includes a Mentalese demonstrative pronoun that refers to the apple without thereby representing it as an apple. Sensuous reference to an apple does not, then, require the possession of a representation whose content is that something is an apple. It does not presuppose the Mentalese term for 'apple' and, accordingly, does not presuppose knowledge of what apples are. So, when we attribute to Abelard a sensation of a red apple, it is misleading to say, "Abelard senses that the apple is red" if, by this expression, we want to convey the content of Abelard's sensuous representation.[11] Rather, we ought to say something like, "Abelard senses of the apple that it is red." In so circumscribing what we say, we do not attribute to Abelard knowledge of the type of the thing to which he sensuously refers. But not even this exhibits how Abelard in fact sensuously refers to the apple. To do that, we can (ignoring considerations pertaining to Abelard's sensuous predicate) at best try to quote (in translation) the Mentalese terms Abelard actually uses. That would necessitate our saying something like

(6.2.2)   Abelard sensuously represents, "This is red."

The assertion (6.2.2) nicely captures exactly how Abelard's sensuous state of the occasion refers. The quoted Mentalese demonstrative, from Abelard's point of view, refers without describing.

---

11 Certainly Abelard might believe, on the basis of what he senses, that the apple is red. Nevertheless, if this is so, then the content of his belief is not the same as the content of the sensation from which it arises.

Of course when we quote Abelard's Mentalese demonstrative, we do not thereby use it to refer, such being the levy for quotation in general. Since the quoted Mentalese term is, as a demonstrative, token reflexive, an unadorned quotation of it, unlike the quotation of either a proper name or a definite description, will typically fail to convey any knowledge of what might be the demonstrative's referent. Simply quoting the sentence containing Abelard's demonstrative does not, then, serve to tell us much about the thing to which Abelard sensuously refers. Even if, alone, it does not reveal to us what Abelard sensuously refers to, it does tell us just what we did want to know, namely, in what manner he sensuously refers. Quoting Abelard's mental sentence does reveal its referential character for him in that it exhibits that the content of his mental referent is exhausted by its isolating an object for his attention. If we want to know more about the object of Abelard's sensuous reference, we must look not to his occurrent mental sentence but to the object itself and its place in our conceptual scheme. Once we do that, however, we run well beyond the content of Abelard's sensuous state. And that is exactly what we should expect. For his sensuous state in itself surely cannot carry the content that we bring to bear in our mental states when we characterize Abelard's present sensory condition.

Sensuous predication is rather more peculiar than sensuous reference, although here too the notion of demonstration, or one like it, is central. We can begin to appreciate this by asking what Abelard has in mind when sensing a red apple. Relative to the normal case, we assume that in order for him to represent the apple *as* red he would need to understand what it is for something to be red. He would thus require the concept of red. That apparently would typically bring in its train his believing, if not knowing, various things about red, perhaps minimally that it is a color.[12] Abelard's

---

12 Actually this overstates the case a bit. Recall the discussion of Mrs. T. in Chapter 4, Section 4.3. There it was argued that an agent could conceivably have a concept without necessarily possessing the cluster of notions normally associated with that concept. Mrs. T.'s conception of assassination is so woefully impoverished that when we attribute such to her, we must take care to explain to our auditors exactly what is being ascribed to her. Similarly, here we could say that Abelard's sensuous state does indeed represent the apple *as* red, so long as we were quick to point out that from this *alone* it does not follow that Abelard knows much about red things. So, to keep the situation as simple as possible, we will avoid attributing to Abelard a sensuous representation that would seem, without ref-

knowing this last would seem to presuppose his having some mental representation for, or concept of, color – a representation or concept whose content would itself require explanation. And yet it is difficult, especially given that nativism is false, to say how this representation of color could have the requisite content independent of how the Mentalese term for 'red' has its content, which is what is to be explained. Thus, since it is evidently possible that Abelard sense the apple and its color before acquiring the concept of color, he must, in sensing the apple and its color, not sense the apple *as* red. What, then, could be the predicate in Abelard's sensory state if not the Mentalese term for 'red'?

In spoken language, demonstrative reference is a species of reference. The point of this unexciting observation is that the notion of demonstration can be teased apart from that of reference, and once they are severed, we can see that demonstration can be predicative as well as referential. To refer demonstratively is simply to isolate *referentially*, but simply to demonstrate is to isolate *representationally*, but not necessarily referentially. This notion of representational isolation can be applied to predication as well as reference. To predicate is to attribute a property, typically by citing an adjective, common noun, or verb form. The term occurring predicatively both selects a property for predication and attributes it. Normally, in using an adjective, common noun, or verb form in predication, we select the property for attribution in a way that locates the property in a conceptual scheme, that – perhaps by the grace of the definition of the term – semantically relates the predicated term to various other understood terms. The suggestion here is that, in predication, we can separate the function of attributing a property from that of locating that property in a scheme of properties. This done, we find that attribution is simply the act of representationally isolating a property for assignment to an object. Although this is standardly done in concert with the act of locating the attributed property in a semantic network of properties, nothing in principle prevents us from attending solely to the attributive aspect of predication and putting it to work in our explication of sensuous representation. Attribution, in its purest form, is the semantic counterpart of simple demonstrative reference. It is the as-

erence to analyses of cases such as Mrs. T.'s, to require detailed knowledge about the redness of things.

signment of a property to an object without thereby also conveying how that property is related to other properties. This pristine attribution is the sheer predicative segregation of a property and does not depend on knowing the semantic connections that bind predicates. Put differently, pristine attribution is, as it were, the use of a primitive, undefined predicate, a predicate that designates a property without betraying that property's (real or supposed) logical or nomic connections with other properties. Here is the essence of sensuous predication: It is the representation of a property merely as a distinct property.[13] For sensuous predication is the pristine attribution of some property only as *that* property.[14]

Abelard's sensuous predication with respect to the apple is pristine attribution. The apple's being red causes sensory state S to occur in Abelard.[15] This state is a Mentalese sentence; the subject term of which is a demonstrative pronoun, the predicate of which

13 Possibly no two objects are the same shade of red. If this should be so, then – given that the physical distinctions among the various shades of red cause different types of sensory states – no pristine predicates for the set of red things would agree. But this is exactly what we should expect. For if the various pristine predicates attribute different properties, as by assumption they do, agents deploying those predicates will thereby differently represent what are in fact different shades of red. This is, then, just a way of saying that the sensory system may produce representations that mirror differences among the things to which the system is sensitive. The sensory system would thus be incapable of producing a mental predicate comprehending the set of disparately red things. And that too is what we should expect if, as seems correct, abstraction is a cognitive function distinct from pure sensation.

14 Pristinely attributed properties are, yes, *given* in sensation. This will probably distress those who have labored to dispel the myth of the given (Sellars, 1963; Goodman, 1973; Paul Churchland, 1979). But pristine attributives are so bereft of semantic force that it is hard to see how they could be subject to the influence of believed theories and spoken, entrenched languages. Anyway, we urgently need a theory of mental representation that comprehends cognitive agents, such as animals, that lack spoken languages as well as those that are linguistically empowered (and perhaps thereby subject to confusing green and blue for grue and bleen). Pristine attributives, as unspoken, mental predicates, seem simple enough for sea slugs and not too simple for humans. Also, Fodor (1984b) has recently discussed some familiar psychological evidence suggesting that some of our sensuous representations are thoroughly nontheoretical cognitive reactions to what is, in a sense, given. Compare Paul Churchland (1988) and Fodor (1988).

15 Nothing fundamental here rests on the status of red as a real property (Campbell, 1966; Hooker, 1978). So, although we have spoken of colors as reflectance gradients, that they might not be so is a matter of indifference here even if, for other reasons, whether they are so is important both to physics and philosophy. Reference to red throughout is simply to be taken as reference to whatever sort of property science settles on as causally efficacious in the production of sensory states.

is a pristinely attributive predicate. This predicate pristinely attributes red to the apple because it is this property that presumably causes S to occur. Yet, in so attributing red to the apple, S fails to convey any information about the color of the apple beyond the fact that it is the property sensuously detected or represented. It is as if Abelard's occurrent Mentalese sentence were 'This thing has that very property' or better (taking 'that' to be a pristine attributive), 'This is that'.[16]

Obviously, pristine attribution could not serve the purposes of communication and, for that reason, is not found in overt language. Still that is no obstacle to its presence in Mentalese, especially that fragment of Mentalese fit for sensuous representation. Mentalese is a vehicle not of communication but, rather, of diaphanous representation. Pristine attributives in Mentalese are capable, as are all predicates, of representing recurrent properties. As sensuous predicates, pristine attributives are tokens of physical types, all tokens of the same type being tokens caused by the same recurrent environmental property and therefore agreeing in representation. Thus, sensuous predicates, even if only attributive, can certainly capture real – if any – commonality.

Still one might reasonably wonder how pristine attributives could function in ratiocination. Mentalese is postulated, in part, as the representational system carrying the computational processes presumed necessary for deliberation (Fodor, 1975). But how might pristine attributives fit in a computational system? What consequences could be drawn from predicates as semantically impoverished as pristine attributives? If this question is taken to ask what, exactly, is the computational structure of the mind, then it is like asking for a specification of the system of inference the mind happens to use. As such, this question could be answered only by empirical work within cognitive science. If we have learned any-

---

16 It is important to realize that to say that red is pristinely attributed is not to say that 'red' is the deployed predicate. For to say that red is pristinely attributed is to assert that some property – which happens to be redness – is that property selected by the occurrent predicate. That redness is the selected property is not conveyed by the pristine predicate. This predicate simply quarantines a property without thereby placing that property in a conceptual scheme. To say that 'red' is the predicate is to say much more. This is because whoever predicates 'red' typically will know that the thing is colored, different from green objects, similar to pink objects, etc. Standard predication, but not pristine predication, marshals clusters of concepts.

thing from Artificial Intelligence and cognitive psychology, and we certainly should have by now, it is that a priori attempts to expose the details of cognitive processes are missions to failure. Nevertheless, we might venture a very general response to the question, a response that transcends details of realization.

Imagine a book in which all pristine attributives are listed, each on its own line. Recall that pristine attributives are, as sensory states, distinguished by those physical properties that differentiate sensory states according to kind. This ensures that different types of pristine attributives differ syntactically – differ, as it were, in their Mentalese spelling. In the imagined book is recorded a parallel list of the scientifically correct descriptions of the properties attributed by the pristine attributives, each description recorded on the same line as its associated attributive. Thus, for example, next to the pristine demonstrative Mentalese predicate for red is the scientific term designating the specific reflectance gradient that constitutes red. Supplement these two lists with a program that includes an (incomplete) axiomatization of laws of nature, reads pristine attributives as input, matches them with their occurrences on the first list and thereby locates their scientific mates on the second list. This done, the program is in a position to apply its axiom set to deduce conclusions that ultimately drive a mobile device whose movements alter its environment. Combine book, program, and device and you have an artificially intelligent cognitive agent, actually a rather bright one who somehow has managed to grasp the true laws of nature.

The interesting thing about this excursion into the imagination is that the reference to the second list is irrelevant. The reason is that pristine attributives that predicate different properties are themselves guaranteed to be different physical types. The program could easily be altered to apply its axioms directly to the pristine attributives. As a program it manipulates terms solely with regard to their shapes, their physically distinctive features. Now that we have dispensed with the second list, let us readjust the connections among the first list, program, and mobile device. Put the book, now containing only the first list, inside the device. Modify the device so as to produce a slot into which inscribed attributive tokens can be fed. Install the program in an external computer equipped to monitor the device. When an attributive token falls through the slot, the program notices this, matches it to its mirror image on the list of attributives inside the device, and applies its own axiom set to produce conclusions, which it then inscribes in the device. These conclusions, in turn and by virtue of their physical features, cause the device to maneuver. Call the program Mother Nature and the device yourself. You internally store pristine attributives, and that is just to say that you sensuously represent by using pristine attributives as predicates. Moreover you also internally represent the consequences of those attributives although you do not contain representations of the axioms yielding those consequences. Mother Nature does that for you and ensures that some of your representations are both the computational results of your sensuous representations and also the causes of your spoken behavior.

Nobody would pretend that this story is in fact true. The reason for the exercise was merely to discern how pristine attributives *might* function in a computational cognitive economy. That now seems assured by virtue of the fact that distinct pristine Mentalese attributives enjoy distinct syntactic properties serving to determine the computational relations into which the attributives enter.

Sensuous Mentalese predicates are pristinely attributive. So what semantic difference is there between different sensuous mental predicates? An agent visually represents of a ripe orange, "This is that way." The same agent, however, visually represents of a withered prune, "This is that way." These representations, however, are the same; so what accounts for their difference in content?

Strictly, when using our spoken languages to quote an agent's sensuous representation, we fail to quote precisely what the agent literally has in mind. This is an artifact of spoken demonstratives. In any given spoken language the number of demonstrative types is far fewer than the number in Mentalese. Context reduces or eliminates ambiguity of reference in overt demonstrative reference, thus enabling different spoken or written tokens of 'this' and 'that' to refer unambiguously. In Mentalese, however, there is, we may conjecture, a unique demonstrative referential type for each object of sensuous reference. This is due to the referential component of a sensuous state being, as previously explained, that physical feature of the state differentiating it from other states of the same physical type. These features, these mental demonstrative pronouns, are as numerous as the objects they designate. It is this that precludes ambiguous reference in the sensuous fragment of Mentalese.

Pristine ascription in Mentalese avoids ambiguity in the same way. As already noted, for each property pristinely ascribed, there is a distinct Mentalese predicate type. This is because pristine mental predicates are those physical features of sensory states that differentiate these states according to physical kind. Only states of the same kind coincide in those properties assigning them to their kind. Thus, there is no ambiguity in sensuous mental predication. So, were English the same as Mentalese, we might suppose that 'thatness' could be pristinely used to predicate a specific color to an apple. The apple's shape might also be sensed, and that too will require a pristine Mentalese predicate. Since the shape is a different property from the color, it will cause to occur within the sensory system of an agent sensing both the color and shape of the apple a sensory state distinct in type from the state resulting from the apple's color. Thus the pristine predicate encoding the apple's shape will differ from the pristine predicate capturing the apple's color. We need to mint a new demonstrative, 'thot', and allow that 'thotness' is the pristine common noun in Mentalese for the apple's shape, whereas 'thatness' pristinely selects its color. Different pristinely predicated properties, therefore, coincide with different pristine predicates.

6.3. OBJECTIONS AND REPLIES

We have taken, at this point, the first few tentative steps toward a causal theory of sensuous representation. Causal theories of representation face a tribunal of, now classical, objections. So we had best begin to address those that are relevant to our unfolding account of the content of sensuous mental states.

If sensory states are the effects of what they represent, then they must be infallibly true representations. After all, everything has a cause, and, according to the present account, sensory states represent their causes, whatever they might be. Thus sensory states, given what has been said so far, are guaranteed to be correct. Still, one might be led to object, this is surely false (Lehrer, 1974), as abundant examples testify. Although, in Abelard, sensory states of S's type typically result from the influence of red things, such as apples, these tokens apparently can be induced independent of the presence of anything red. If Abelard is presented with a white ball bathed in red light, he may mistakenly believe that something red is at hand. Or if his central nervous system is artificially stimulated, he may, again erroneously, *report* the presence of something red. How do these facts jibe with the current version of causal representationalism?

Like so many examples styled to make philosophical points, the present ones suffer from underdescription. Let us, then, fatten the first. Abelard looks at a white ball under red light and reports the presence of something red. Certainly his report is mistaken. That, however, is not at issue. What is relevant but undetermined is whether Abelard is, by virtue of the situation, actually in a sensory state of S's type. For all the example tells us, Abelard might be in a sensory state of some different sort, a state that in fact sensuously, and *correctly*, represents the presence of a white object bathed in red light. Dullard that he is, Abelard might have erroneously *inferred* from this representation that a red object is there before him. If so, his error would have arisen not from a false sensory misrepresentation but rather, as Berkeley suspected, from an unreliable computational process involving a true sensory representation. It should be evident that this example trades on a thoroughly empirical assumption about exactly in which type of sensory state Abelard happens to be. Only a honed neurology can determine whether this assumption is true, and, pending science's verdict, the current example does not obviously vitiate the causal account.

Exactly the same holds for the second example. It mines the assumption that artificial stimulation of Abelard's nervous system will produce a state of exactly S's type. Who knows whether that is true? For all we know, by being artificially stimulated, Abelard's sensory apparatus enters a state quite distinct from S but one that nevertheless *feels* to Abelard much like states of S's type feel. That is, the quale of the bogus sensory state might resemble that occurrent in S-type sensory states. And this may be why Abelard, confused by his quale, incorrectly describes himself as sensing something red. He could not be so sensing since he is not in a state induced by something red. So, if sensory qualia play no direct role in representation (and nothing said so far requires that they do), Abelard's artificially induced state need not coincide in representation with states of S's type.

Still, what if the empirical assumption on which the objection perches should prove true? Either of two explanations would suffice to preserve causal representationalism. First, let us retreat from sensation to mere (nonintentional) information processing. Consider a simple gauge for measuring air pressure in a tire. The gauge contains a register marked with numerals in ascending order and apparently is designed to be caused by air pressure of any given amount to display the numeral correctly designating that amount. When the gauge functions according to design, it accurately measures air pressure. As we all know, the register can be made to display its numerals by forces other than air pressure. Depending on how the gauge is constructed, one might be able to move the register manually so as to display any of its numerals. Or its register may be obstructed so as to register numerals inconsistent with the air pressure in the tire to which the gauge is connected.[17] In either of these latter two situations, we naturally say that the gauge incorrectly indicates air pressure. But is this finally correct? Whenever the register of the gauge moves so as to display a numeral, some cause drives the movement. Is it possible that a single kind of physical force commonly exerts itself whenever the gauge's register moves? Might it be that the same force that causes the gauge to register '32' when attached to a tire containing thirty-two pounds of pressure also causes the register to show '32' when pulled by a determined mechanic? Of course, were this true, we would, in a sense, err when we say that a properly functioning air gauge directly measures air pressure. Rather, it would directly measure this unspecified force and thereby, in normal circumstances, serve as a reliable indicator to us of the pressure of the air in our tires. This may sound ad hoc and far-fetched, but resistance should diminish if one reflects on the impressive fact that *apparently* different kinds of things, air pressure and hands, seem on occasion to have the same effect on the gauge. How could that be? How could two so very different sorts of things produce exactly the same effect? When questions of this sort arise, for example, in medical research, it is natural to look for an underlying common cause.[18] Why not do

17 When, by the way, is an obstructed air gauge no longer an air gauge? Were it encased in solid cement so that its register could not move, would it still be an air gauge? Analogously, when is an impaired sensory system no longer a sensory system? I do not (and suspect that only a mature neurology will) know the answer, but whatever the answer may be, it certainly bears upon the force of the objection to causal accounts of representation.

18 Where would we be in our search for a cure for Acquired Immune Deficiency Syndrome if we accepted that being homosexual and being Haitian were distinct causes of the same disease? Nowhere. That is why we are now spending lots of money to reveal the underlying common cause of this illness.

the same here? The idea is ancient, appealing, and often accurate: If the effects are the same, look for a common cause.

We need not insist on this radical analysis of the air gauge, but we can use it merely to illustrate what may in fact be true of our sensory systems. If our systems actually do go into states of type S in the presence of red apples under white light and white balls under red light and also when artificially stimulated in some specific way, then it may very well be naive to suppose that S-type sensory states are caused by things of such diverse kinds. We should not discount the idea that S tokens are the sensory system's characteristic way of reacting to a physical property that, unknown to us, actually manifests itself in what we take to be totally different, unrelated phenomena.[19]

But this is only the first of two ways of reacting to the objection pertaining to sensory infallibility. The second agrees with the first in denying that sensory states of the same physical type occasionally are, as the example requires, obviously the results of different types of causes. The second strategy, however, is more direct. The objection would have it that some tokens of sensory state S are the effects of some property, F, whereas other S tokens are caused by some different property, G. But why, the reply asks, accept this? Why not say that S tokens are caused by neither F nor G but rather that all such tokens result from the property F-or-G, a property necessarily present whenever either F or G is (Fodor, 1984a)? Were this the case, the objection would fail for want of finding a sensory state type whose tokens can be caused by different environmental factors.

On behalf of this line I offer two comments. First, there is a choice here. Either one can accept this gambit of a disjunctively described property or one can forgo a promising naturalistic explanation of sensuous content. Put that way, the choice, at least for those who appreciate the importance of launching a workable naturalistic account of mental representation, is easy. Second, keep in

19 Never mind, of course, what agents *say* their sensory systems represent. Abelard may believe in witches and say, on looking at a miserable old woman, that he senses her as witch. He does not, and we know better (Paul Churchland, 1979; Maloney, 1986a). And perhaps we too should hesitate to *say* what we sense. Only good science reliably determines what properties, of all those surrounding us, actually cause our sensory states. Sensation is evolution's way of allowing us to negotiate in our environment, and, as such, sensation may more astutely report our world than we verbally represent our sensory representations.

mind that although the F-or-G is disjunctively described here, that does not entail that the property so described is somehow onto-logically disjunctive. If F-or-G should actually be the cause of S-type sensory states, there is a law of nature that comprehends this relationship, and an articulated science may someday hope to pro-vide a label for F-or-G under which it instantiates this law.[20] More-over, should S tokens be caused by and therefore represent F-or-G, they would not sensuously represent F-or-G as F-or-G but rather in a pristinely attributive way, a way that demonstratively attributes F-or-G without describing this property or in any way exposing its structure. That is, even if we had a translation manual taking us from sensory Mentalese predicates into English predicates, we would not find among the sensory predicates the finished lexicon of natural science. All we would have is a listing of pure attributives, something considerably less than a complete enumeration of the predicates of mature science.

There are other objections to the present account of sensuous representation. In sensation, the mind represents particular objects. An agent senses now this thing, now that thing. The world of sense is a world of particular individuals, individuals to which sensory states refer. Sensory states, the theory would have it, refer to those individual objects whose properties cause the states to occur. But this – the objection claims – does not explain how sensation actually selectively refers to, or otherwise representationally distinguishes, objects. For standardly, in any causal chain culminating in a sensory state there simply is no single object that can be designated as *the* cause of the state. An effect is typically the result of collaborating objects, no one of which can lay proprietary claim to being the effect's cause. Accordingly, but contrary to what the current causal account of the content of mental representations proposes, a sensory state does not refer to its cause since, apart from conventional stipulation, no single object constitutes *the* cause of a sensory state (Dretske, 1981).

This objection can also be put as a question. Sensation involves, in the terminology of psychology, distal and proximal stimuli, distal stimuli being the representational foci of sensation. Never-

20 This label need not, and probably would not, be 'F-or-G', which is a temporary philosophical, not a well-established scientific, designation. This is just as 'water' designates H_2O, although 'water' is not a label for H_2O under which water instantiates physical laws. Compare Fodor (1981b) and Davidson (1970).

theless, distal stimuli are always accompanied by proximal stimuli. So how does sensation manage to be of the distal rather than the proximal?

To respond to both objection and question we dissect an example. The moon is new, the stars occluded. Abelard stands below Héloïse's window in the completely darkened courtyard. Nothing is visible. The curtains on the window in Héloïse's room are drawn so as to conceal a solitary candle burning within. At the prearranged time, Héloïse draws the curtains to display to Abelard the luminous signal for their rendezvous. With the curtains parted, the candlelight strikes Abelard's eyes and there creates a pair of retinal images of itself. Abelard senses the light; he does not sense either Héloïse or his retinal images. His occurrent sensory token refers only to the light. How is this consistent with the causal account of sensory reference? For are not Héloïse and the retinal images as instrumental in the production of Abelard's sensory state as is the light?

Abelard senses the light rather than Héloïse because the light, but not Héloïse, is presumably necessary for his occurrent sensory state. Abelard's sensory system is in a type of state that it could not have been in had the candle not been lit. But his sensory system could have been in the state it is even if Héloïse had not thrown open the curtains, so long, of course, as the light of the candle had been otherwise exposed. In calling the light the cause of Abelard's sensory state, we are simply saying that although various things may happen to have joined in producing the state, only the light was, among those things, necessary for generating that type of state. Had the light been removed, Abelard's sensory system could not have been in the kind of state it was.[21] Had the relevant property of the lighted candle not obtained, Abelard's sensory system would not have been in the type of state it was. Had the particular candle that, in fact, was in Héloïse's room been replaced by a similar candle, one with the same property as the original, then (other things being equal) Abelard would have been in the same type of sensory state. Still, that state would refer to the new, rather than

21 Yes, various other kinds of things, e.g., a hologram of a candle, could have caused Abelard's state to occur. But to these sorts of examples the replies to the objection that launches Section 6.3 apply. Here we use the candlelight as an example of whatever (possibly disjunctive) property is had both by candles and by holograms of candles by virtue of which sensory states such as Abelard's are caused to occur.

the old, light, the new light being the one with the property necessary for the occurrence of sensory states of the relevant type.

What of the retinal images? They too are necessary for the production of Abelard's sensory state. Necessary, yes, but, unlike the lighted candle, universal as well. Although the light must be cast if Abelard's sensory system is to be in the type of state it is, the candlelight need not be thrown in order for his sensory system to be in any arbitrarily selected state it might happen to be in. This distinguishes the candlelight from the retinal images. They are properties of Abelard's sensory system itself, properties, then, of an object that must be present in order for Abelard to be in *any and every* sensory state. This object, Abelard's sensory system, being involved in the realization of each of his sensory states, is not peculiar to any particular sensory state. This is why it, as that which instantiates the retinal images, is not referentially represented by Abelard's sensory state. So, when we say that the referent of a sensory state is the object causing that state, we mean that the referent of a sensory state is that object *with the properties* necessary *only* for the occurrence of that type of sensory state.[22] In other words, the referent of a given token of a particular type of sensory state is that object that instantiates the property necessary for occurrences of that token's sensory state type but which property is not necessary for occurrences of tokens of other types of sensory states.

Suppose that Abelard's sensory state is caused by exposure to the candlelight in Héloïse's window but that, somehow, she manages to replace the original candle with another without altering Abelard's sensory state. To which bit of candlelight would Abelard's sensory state refer? We can take our answer from what we would say of a parallel case involving natural language. Imagine that Abelard points to a loaf of bread and says, "This is a fine loaf of bread." He is a slow speaker, and even as he speaks, but unbeknown to him, Héloïse replaces the first loaf with another of the very same quality. To what loaf does Abelard refer? Both, but successively. While the first loaf is present, Abelard refers to it

---

22 It is not to the point to object that candles cause indefinitely many sensory states at different distances or relative speeds of approach. This is true. Still, for each such sensory state it will be the candle that has the property or properties necessary for the occurrence of *that* state. That is why each of the changing states would refer to the candle.

alone, and when the second loaf arrives, he refers only to it. The referents of his spoken token of 'this' change, even though the token remains and he himself is unaware of the change in referent. Exactly the same holds for Abelard's sensory state if it does in fact remain constant while the candlelight that first caused it is replaced with another that maintains it. *If* the sensory state *persists* unchanged while the objects that cause it vary, then the referent of the state changes, regardless of what the sensing agent may believe about the sensed objects.

What if several objects have properties that are jointly necessary only for producing a type of sensory state? Wildly, but to illustrate the point, suppose that, as a matter of nomic necessity, not only the candle's being lit but also Héloïse's opening the curtains should be requisite for bringing about any token of the type of sensory state Abelard enjoys. To which would his state sensuously refer, the candle or Héloïse? Although this may be a contrived way of putting the question, the problem is real enough. It is altogether likely that, relative to the production of any given type of sensory state, there are various properties of distinct objects that are collectively and uniquely necessary for generating that type of state. In looking at a drop of water, do you sense and sensuously refer to a single thing, a drop, or rather a horde of molecules (Churchland and Churchland, 1983)? If you glance at a hexagram, do you sense just that, one geometric figure, or do you really sense six equilateral triangles and a hexagon? Returning to and granting the assumptions relevant to the whimsical case of Héloïse's essential participation in producing Abelard's sensory state, we may concede that Abelard's sensory state would indeed refer to, without distinguishing between, both the light and Héloïse. That is, were both the light and Héloïse necessary for the occurrence of Abelard's specific sensory state but no others, then Abelard's state would fail referentially to differentiate the light and Héloïse. From the perspective of Abelard's sensory system, these two totally distinct objects would be (represented as) one.[23]

Although this countenances the possibility that our sensory states blur reference, it does not mandate it. Yes, Abelard's sensing the

23 Abelard may – somehow – know that Héloïse and the light are different objects. But if so, then this is something Abelard has inferred from his sensory state and his store of background information. It would not be something sensuously given to him.

candlelight does depend on the clarity of the intervening air, but from this it does not follow that his sensory token referentially conflates the candle and the air. For it is only the candle that has the property or properties necessary only for the occurrence of the type of sensory state Abelard now suffers. The clarity of the air is necessary not only for Abelard's having a token of his current kind of sensory state but also for his having a token of the kind of sensory state he would have were he now to sense not a glowing candle but a shooting star. Thus, although Abelard's sensory token refers to the candle, it need not refer to the air.

Remember that sensory states refer by containing an element that functions, semantically, as a demonstrative pronoun. What the specious situation of Héloïse and the light shows us is that Mentalese demonstrative pronouns are not, as it were, declined in both the singular and plural. They are indifferent to number. That is, Mentalese demonstrative pronouns are not syntactically distinguished according to the number, singular or plural, of their referents. But Mentalese is not linguistically unique in this. In various spoken languages some nouns and pronouns are identical in form, within the same case, in singular and plural.[24] Such overt terms alone do not display the number of things to which they refer. Mentalese demonstrative pronouns in sensation are similar. They refer to whatever objects are jointly necessary only for causing states of the types realizing the demonstratives. This is just to say that sensation simply does not distinguish distinct objects whose occurrence must always coincide with types of sensory states. This seems to be exactly the right thing for any theory of sensation to say. Sensation is simply not a sufficiently powerful instrument of observation to discern distinction in nomically united collections. That is a task for science, not sensation.

Let us summarize what we have here. Abelard's sensory state refers to the teardrop of candlelight burning in Héloïse's window because that very bit of light happens to be the object whose property is necessary for the occurrence of Abelard's current sensory state but not similarly necessary for the occurrence of other types of sensory states. The type of sensory state Abelard's sensory system is in is a type caused by exposure to the property that, on that

---

24 For example, *diese* in German and *dies* in Latin are the forms for both the singular and plural nominative.

occasion, is instantiated in that very bit of candlelight. Had that property been realized in the light of a similar candle, similarly placed, then Abelard's sensory token would have been of the same type but would have referred to the new candlelight. This falls to the fact that an agent's sensory state refers to whatever object happens currently to possess the property causally necessary for the occurrence of that token's sensory type but not for tokens of other sensory types. Thus, if a sensory state is induced by a property in one object and maintained by another object with the same property, the referent of the sensory state literally changes with the change in the objects. And when sets of properties in various objects are jointly necessary for only sensory states of the prevailing type, then a token of that sensory type refers at once, but indifferently and indiscriminately, to all the objects that happen to instantiate those properties.

6.4. SENSORY DOPPELGÄNGERS

So much, then, for some of the more pressing classical objections to a causal account of the content of sensory states. Other problems abound, of course, but of particular interest is how such an explanation of sensuous content responds to a problem of representation raised originally by Putnam (1975b) and more recently by Owens (1983).

Consider a world like Putnam's Twin Earth, a world identical in almost all ways with Earth. On both Earth and Twin Earth there are insect-eating frogs. The frogs of Earth and Twin Earth are biologically the same and favor a diet of flies. On Earth, flies are drosophila, but the same is not so on Twin Earth. There are found insects that look exactly like, but nevertheless biologically differ from, earthly drosophila. Call them pseudodrosophila. Frogs, be they on Earth or on Twin Earth, are indifferently affected by drosophila and pseudodrosophila. Thus, frogs affected by either drosophila or pseudodrosophila are in sensory states of the same type. According to the present account of mental representation, on Earth a frog sensing a drosophila represents a drosophila. On Twin Earth a frog sensing a pseudodrosophila represents a pseudodrosophila. How can this be? How can the representations differ, since the frogs are in the same type of sensory state?

From all the foregoing the answer should be evident. If frogs,

200

regardless of being affected by real or false drosophila, are caused to be in exactly the same type of sensory state, then, by being in that type of state, the frogs in fact agree in representational content, despite the fact that they represent different kinds of insects. If drosophila and pseudodrosophila look alike, it seems quite plausible to suppose that they share properties causally responsible for producing the relevant type of sensory state in frogs. Tokens of this type of state represent those properties, despite the fact that those properties are the defining properties of neither drosophila nor pseudodrosophila. For if they were, the species would not, contrary to assumption, be different. Yes, then, frogs on Earth do represent drosophila; frogs on Twin Earth do represent pseudodrosophila. Nonetheless, no frogs represent these insects *as* drosophila or *as* pseudodrosophila. Rather all frogs demonstratively represent these insects *as* possessed of the same causally relevant properties. It is not that an insect is a drosophila or pseudodrosophila that enables it to cause in a frog a sensory state. It is, rather, that black and darting are what presumably cause in frogs sensory states of the specified type. Nothing in the situation entails that anywhere in frogs a representation must be stored whose content is *that* something is a drosophila or *that* something is a pseudodrosophila. Indeed, given the account of pristine attributives, frogs sensuously represent flies, both real and bogus, not *as* "black and darting" but, rather, *as* "being that way." In order to quote (in English translation) a frog's sensuous representation of a drosophila or pseudodrosophila, we say, "This is that way" (again, where 'that way' is used adjectivally as a pristine attributive). This, then, is how frogs may manage the same sensory representation when affected by things of different natural kinds. The frogs are blind to the difference and sense only what is actually common across the different species. And that is why, in the present case, their behavior is the same regardless of whether they sense drosophila or pseudodrosophila.

Of course, a local frog senses some particular fly distinct from the false fly sensed by the frog's distant doppelgänger. This is due to the simple fact that the frogs each possess a distinct sensory token of the same type caused by the same property instantiated in different things, a fly and false fly, respectively. Recall that on the account of sensuous reference under consideration, the referent of a token of a type of a sensory state is whatever object happens to

201

instantiate the property that causes the token to occur. That the frogs have sensory tokens of the same type ensures that their states attribute the same property. This is attributable to the fact that sensory states of the relevant type are caused by instantiations of the same property. But although the frogs' sensory states are of the same type and therefore ascribe the same property, they can still refer differently, so long as their different sensory tokens are caused by instantiations of the same property in different objects.

6.5. UP FROM SENSATION

We have thus far only a sketch of how the sensory fragment of the mental language might come to have content. It cannot pass without comment that the type of content we have managed to smuggle into Mentalese is woefully impoverished when compared to the content we suppose nonsensuous mental states can record. Even if what has been broached up to this point is correct, we have, at best, explained only how a certain type of mental state could represent in the fashion of pristine demonstrative reference and attribution. So, although we may now possess a rudimentary explanation of how the mind might focus on objects and their sensible properties, we certainly await a down payment on an account of how mental states might climb beyond simple demonstration in representing the world. It is not enough to explain how the mind might represent of a sparrow that it has a particular property pristinely demonstrated. The mind is capable of representing a sparrow *as* a sparrow. And, in the standard case, that requires an explanation of how the mind could deploy predicates whose expressive power runs far beyond pristine attributives.

Although no one now is in a position to explain in full detail how any given term, mental or not, comes to mean exactly what it does, something general and, it is to be hoped, not impossibly vague can be said. According to Sententialism, Abelard mentally represents of a sparrow that it is a sparrow by issuing a mental sentence meaning, with respect to some sparrow, that it is a sparrow. This mental sentence will refer to the sparrow and predicate of it the property of being a sparrow. Thus, we stand in need of an explanation of how some Mentalese predicate comes to mean the same as 'sparrow'.

We have already eschewed nativism and, therefore, cannot solve our problem by appealing to any stock of innately endowed mental expressions in terms of which all other mental terms might be defined or otherwise propagated. But we do have available all the mental predicates resulting from sensation. True, these are one and all pristine attributives, but they may yet contribute to an agent's semantic ascent. Sensory predicates, pristine attributives, are encoded in the form of sensory states. These states, as physical elements within a cognitive system, can causally interact with one another to produce nonsensory states. When Abelard sees a sparrow from a certain perspective, some property of the sparrow will cause to occur in him a sensory state of a certain sort. Viewed from another angle, some (other) property of the sparrow will induce in Abelard a sensory state of a different sort. These sensory tokens of different types stand as different attributives; they will, as pristine attributives, predicate different properties of the sparrow. They each also will have various causal consequences *within* Abelard's cognitive system. Indeed, we can hypothesize both that they are collectively implicated in causing various effects and that they individually suffice for causing some common effects. In the event that the sensory states resulting from the causal commerce between an external object and a sensory system do themselves produce various effects within the cognitive system containing the sensory system, we may suppose that such effects constitute Mentalese predicates whose meanings are determined by – although they are not to be equated with – both their causes and their effects.

To clarify this proposal, again suppose for the moment that English and Mentalese are orthographically identical. Exposure to a sparrow will typically cause the human sensory system to enter specified sensory states serving as Mentalese sentences demonstratively referring to and pristinely predicating properties of the sparrow. These sensory states, in turn, will have typical effects within the human cognitive system that themselves serve as Mentalese expressions. Given the assumption of the orthographic coincidence of English and Mentalese, we may suppose that 'is a sparrow' is a characteristic effect of those of a person's sensory states caused by the presentation of a sparrow. As a Mentalese expression, 'is a sparrow' will itself have various effects within an agent, including behavioral effects. If these effects are themselves the type of behavioral episodes predictable and best explained under the assumption that the agent in question is thinking of a sparrow as a sparrow, then it is reasonable to hypothesize that occurrences of 'is a sparrow' function as Mentalese representations of something *as* a sparrow.

The idea is familiar enough. The content of a nonsensuous Mentalese predicate is determined by its typical causes and effects within a cognitive system (Loar, 1981). Of course, the properties of a Mentalese predicate by virtue of which it has the etiological properties it does within its cognitive system determine its syntactic properties so that the causal and inferential properties of the predicate coincide. Thus, behavioral effects of a Mentalese predicate arise as the inferential or rational consequences of the predicate. Obviously bits of behavior normally result from the causal cooperation of great groups of cognitive states. Accordingly, the content of a nonsensuous Mentalese predicate cannot be read off its causal connections in isolation from those of all other Mentalese predicates with which it normally interacts. Fixing the content, then, of a nonsensuous Mentalese predicate is a holistic matter, and hypotheses as to the content of any particular Mentalese predicate are subject to all the difficulties characteristic of radical translation (Quine, 1960) and are constrained by the necessity of preserving the rationality of the agent in whom the predicate occurs.

Although the foregoing maintains that the content of a nonsensuous Mentalese predicate is determined by its causal connections to other Mentalese terms and behavior, we should also remind ourselves that Quine has shown that our *judgments* regarding the contents of tokens of public language cannot be completely settled by appeal to public criteria.[25] The same evidently holds for Mentalese. This should not deter us from saying that Mentalese has content, however. Rather, it should make us keen to the fact that our ascriptions of content are only hypotheses as to the best explanation of an agent's behavior. We simply are not epistemically positioned to know *absolutely* what the content of a mental representation might be.

But this is much the position we are in with respect to other judgments we make about the natural world. Suppose that it is important for us, as historians, to discover exactly how many times

---

25 Also see Stich (1982) for an important discussion of various problems for ascriptions of content.

204

Abelard walked along a certain street. No amount of evidence we *could* garner could settle with certainty this question for us. We cannot travel to the past to observe Abelard during his time in Paris. And even if we could, it is always possible that we would miscount as we watch. No judgment we make about any subject has its truth assured by the evidence possibly available.[26] The best we can do is to judge relative to our best sciences and available information.

This is much the position we are in with respect to our ascriptions of content. The content we attribute to an agent's Mentalese inscriptions should be tempered by what we antecedently know. Over time, we may find that by modifying our ascriptions of content, we can better explain an agent's behavior. If the agent protests that our ascriptions of content do not jibe with what the agent takes himself or herself mentally to represent, we should simply add that bit of information to that which we consult in assessing the correctness of our content ascription. The agent's protests need not alone serve to overturn content ascriptions if we possess compelling evidence to the contrary (Nisbett and Wilson, 1977).

If the content of nonsensuous Mentalese terms is a function of their causal connections to various other Mentalese terms (including both sensuous and nonsensuous Mentalese terms) and behavioral episodes, then nonsensuous mental content is set much in the same manner as is the content of theoretical terms in public language. The causal connections among mental terms do duty as syntactic and thus inferential relations. The inferential relations among Mentalese terms, therefore, contribute to their content just as do the inferential relations among theoretical terms. Theoretical terms are introduced within implicational networks so that the meaning of any given term is set by the manner of its interaction with other terms. Within the physical sciences, theoretical terms normally exhibit some inferential-confirmational relations with certain observation terms. This is much the situation with nonsensuous Mentalese terms. For they too are caught up in inferential relations with great groups of various mental terms, some of which are drawn directly from sensation. Thus, insofar as it is plausible that

---

26 If this is too strong, let's not worry about the analytic-synthetic distinction here and relativize all this to synthetic judgments (Quine, 1951).

public theoretical discourse is meaningful by way of the inferential relations that bind its terms, so too for the meaningfulness of the nonsensuous fragment of Mentalese.

Like English predicates, nonsynonymous Mentalese predicates can be coextensive. In Mentalese, 'water' need not mean the same as 'H_2O' even if all and only the things satisfying the first Mentalese predicate also satisfy the second. This is simply due to the fact that the different causal properties of these coextensive Mentalese predicates ensure their semantic differences (Fodor, 1980a). Difference in the meanings of Mentalese terms thus corresponds to a difference in their syntax since semantic difference falls to causal difference and causal difference ensures syntactic difference.[27]

And so, once again recall Putnam's Twin Earth populated with agents that are pairwise perfect physical replicas of agents on Earth. H_2O exists on Earth but not Twin Earth. On Twin Earth there is a substance, XYZ, that appears the same as water despite not consisting of hydrogen and oxygen. Assume that XYZ produces in agents on Twin Earth the same types of sensory states as water causes in agents on Earth. We already know from Section 6.4 what to say of the contents of these sensory states. They demonstratively represent whatever (possibly disjunctive) property that is in fact both common to H_2O and XYZ and also causes sensory states of the specified type. What of the nonsensory cognitive states that result from these sensory states? These cognitive states presumably are of the same physical and syntactic type regardless of whether they occur in agents on Earth or Twin Earth. How could a type of cognitive state in an agent on Earth represent something as water or as H_2O if the very same type of state in an agent on Twin Earth would represent something as XYZ?

27 This amounts to saying that in Mentalese there cannot be synonymy between syntactically distinct terms. In English 'tire' and 'tyre' may mean the same, but no such synonymous expressions can occur in Mentalese. Otherwise it would be difficult to see how it is that the meaning of a mental representation could have the characteristic behavioral effects that it does. For the behavior that ensues on a mental representation is supposed to be a function of its meaning, which itself supervenes on its (causally efficacious) syntax. Thus, syntactic difference between Mentalese representations should correspond to behavioral difference. Consequently, there cannot be syntactically distinct synonymous Mentalese representations. They would, *per impossibile*, need to be mental representations that have the same behavioral effects although their causal structures are designed to produce different bits of behavior. See Chapter 1, Section 1.6.

Well, suppose that on Earth Abelard senses some H_2O and thus enters a token of sensory state type S. This, in turn, causes his cognitive system to take on a token of a state of type C. Assume that among the characteristic effects of tokens of C's type are those we explain by attributing to Abelard a belief about H_2O *as* water. Accordingly, tokens of C's type would appear to have as their content *that* something is water. Now on Twin Earth, Abelard's doppelgänger, because a perfect physical replica of Abelard, also takes on a token of C's type whose causes and effects within himself are exactly the same as those of Abelard's C token. Hence, the present proposal would seem to dictate that, since the causes and effects of the doppelgänger's C token coincide with those of Abelard's C token, the content of the doppelgänger's C token should be the same as that of Abelard's C token. But it is silly to suppose that the doppelgänger's C token could, like Abelard's C token, represent that something is water. On the doppelgänger's planet there is no H_2O. It makes no more sense to attribute to the doppelgänger's C token the content that something is water than it does to attribute to Abelard's C token the content that something is XYZ. And if this is so, it cannot be, as the current suggestion would have it, that the content of a nonsensuous mental state is determined by its characteristic causes and effects within an agent.

There are several comments to make here. First, we assume that the cognitive states in question have exactly the same causal properties. That is, we suppose that on Earth when Abelard is exposed to H_2O, the sensory states that result in him typically produce a cognitive state of physical type C. And on Twin Earth when Abelard's doppelgänger is exposed to XYZ, the sensory states in him typically cause a cognitive state of the same physical type, C, as found in Abelard. Admittedly, if, while ignoring the situation of Abelard, we ask what might be the content of tokens of C as found in Abelard's doppelgänger, we might be inclined to say that C represents something as XYZ. And, failing to consider the case of Abelard's doppelgänger, we might take the content of tokens of C in Abelard to represent something as water. Once we commit ourselves to ascribing content in this way to C-type tokens, we must be puzzled as to whether it could be correct to take the causal connections of a cognitive state to determine the state's content. For it looks as though the causal properties of C tokens are the same regardless of whether they are found in agents on Earth or Twin Earth although the contents of C tokens vary depending on their locations.

Nevertheless, the case against the content of a cognitive state being determined by its causal connections is not so clear. An error may well be concealed in the assumption that the content of C tokens must differ depending on whether they occur in agents on Earth or Twin Earth. True, we are inclined to attribute to Abelard's C token the content that something is water and to the doppel-gänger's C token the content that something is XYZ. But that intuition is fed by the fact that we ourselves, as the theorists who attribute content to the states of Abelard and his doppelgänger, use a language to attribute mental content that does not contain an entrenched term that comprehends whatever is H_2O or XYZ.

In order to see just how our spoken language fosters a misguided intuition, consider what we should say of agents who regularly travel between Earth and Twin Earth and in whom C tokens are caused by sensory states themselves indifferently induced by H_2O and XYZ. By assumption, the location of the agent and whether H_2O or XYZ causes the relevant sensory states make no difference to the agents' internal cognitive economy and behavior. Once we appreciate this, it begins to wax plausible that C tokens may have the same meaning regardless of their occurring on Earth or Twin Earth. If so, it would be provincial to assign to the commuting agent's C tokens either the content that something is water or the content that something is XYZ. Rather, it seems much more likely that the content of an agent's C state is constrained by the fact that its sensory progenitors are indifferently caused by H_2O and XYZ.

This suggests that the extension of a C token is set by the union of the extensions of 'H_2O' and 'XYZ'. That is, the extension of C tokens is the set of things that are either H_2O or XYZ. If such is the extension of the Mentalese term C tokens realize, then the content of this term is itself restricted by the fact that any term synonymous with it must have the same extension. The fact is that in English we simply do not have an entrenched term whose extension is the set of things made of either H_2O or XYZ.[28] We do not, therefore, have a familiar term whose meaning is constrained

---

28 That is, the union of the nonempty set of things that are H_2O and the supposed nonempty set of things that are XYZ.

by this extension. Consequently, we lack an available English term that naturally and neatly carries the content of, or is otherwise synonymous with, the Mentalese term constituted by C tokens.

Since we lack an English term adequate for translating the Mentalese term encoded in C tokens, it is not at all surprising that we find it very difficult to say what, precisely, is the content of the Mentalese term instantiated in C tokens. We cannot, for example, confidently translate this Mentalese term so as to make it synonymous with the concocted English disjunction 'H$_2$O-or-XYZ'. Although this English hybrid is evidently equivalent to the Mentalese predicate realized in C tokens, that is no guarantee of the synonymy of the English and Mentalese terms. Certainly the sheer fact that the Mentalese term in question is coextensive with 'H$_2$O-or-XYZ' shows nothing whatsoever regarding whether the Mentalese term is disjunctive.[29] Rather, wisdom dictates that if we suppose that the Mentalese term constituted by C tokens is invariant in meaning across residents of Earth and their Twin Earth doppelgängers and that the extension of this term is the set of things that are either H$_2$O or XYZ, then we ought to demur from the challenge to specify in current, standard English the Mentalese term's content and chalk this up to the theoretically unimportant fact that English and Mentalese are not necessarily perfectly translatable term for term.

Although, because of the present poverty of English, we do not venture a translation of what the Mentalese term formed by C tokens may mean, we had better conclude neither that Mentalese terms do not have meaning nor that their standard causal interconnections do not contribute to their meanings. For on the one hand, that a particular Mentalese term defies quick and elegant translation into English no more shows that Mentalese is without content than does the fact that an idiom from one spoken language resists translation into another language illustrate the semantic vacuity of the idiom or its encompassing language. And on the other hand, the whole point of supposing that C tokens realize a Mentalese term whose meaning is constant across Earth and Twin Earth is to respect the causal relations in which C tokens are involved. After all, the example lays it down that C tokens on Earth and Twin Earth ultimately originate in things of the same kind, namely,

---

29 'Green' is not conjunctive even if it means the same as 'grue before A.D. 2000 and bleen thereafter' (Goodman, 1973).

things that are H_2O-or-XYZ, and eventuate in the same sort of behavioral episodes.[30] And it is difficult to see how it could be reasonable to attribute different content to mental states whose behavioral consequences are assured to be the same.[31]

It is important to appreciate that the separation of Earth and Twin Earth and the consequent segregation of H_2O and XYZ is an irrelevant and misleading artifact of the example. What is crucial is the imagined fact that H_2O and XYZ have exactly the same effects on cognitive agents. The significance of this can be illuminated by considering another emended version of the example. Just suppose that Earth itself contains lots of H_2O and XYZ. Half of Earth's lakes, puddles, and oceans are made of H_2O; half are of XYZ. Again, each person on Earth has a doppelgänger, but now both people and their doppelgängers live here on Earth. Imagine further that it accidentally happens that half of the people on Earth have sensed H_2O but not XYZ. As you must by now expect, their doppelgängers have sensed XYZ but not H_2O. The other half of the people have sensed XYZ but not H_2O. And, of course, their

30 Notice that it is no use to complain that it is ad hoc to maintain that the ultimate cause of C tokens is H_2O-or-XYZ on the grounds that no natural kind corresponds to 'H_2O-or-XYZ'. Such a complaint is predicated on the prejudice that 'H_2O-or-XYZ' is not a term fit for the expression of causal laws. But this intuition must evaporate once the example of Twin Earth is taken seriously, since the example hangs on the assumption that C tokens are indeed indifferently caused by H_2O and XYZ. When tokens of the same type of state are caused by apparently different types of things, it is, as previously noted, not implausible to conjecture that some common cause underlies the phenomenon. That hypothesis here amounts to supposing that even if 'H_2O-or-XYZ' is not fit for the expression of a causal law, it does nevertheless take a natural kind as its extension.

31 Perhaps one might object that this has explosive consequences for mental reference. If C tokens mean H_2O or XYZ, then the referent of any given C token would, but contrary to reason, be all possible instances of H_2O or XYZ rather than any particular instance of H_2O or XYZ. Now, according to the objection, a C token is supposed to refer to some particular instance of H_2O or XYZ. So the structure of a C token is presumably akin to 'This is F'. Otherwise, it would not be to the point to worry that the present account suffers an explosion of referents for C tokens. In English the sentence type 'This is F' has no referent. Rather, its tokens have referents, and these are fixed by the context of the tokens' occurrences. Similarly, as a Mentalese type, C does not refer; its tokens do. So how is the referent of a C token established? We borrow the answer from Section 6.2. Normally, a C token will have among its causes a token of some sensuous Mentalese inscription that demonstratively refers to some instance of H_2O or XYZ. The referent of a given C token will then be just the referent of the sensuous Mentalese token that is itself causally responsible for the C token's occurrence. Since the sensuous mental token has a singular referent, so too for the C token.

doppelgängers have sensed H_2O but not XYZ. Finally assume that for each person it is equally probable that he or she be exposed to H_2O or XYZ. That is, where and how one lives has no bearing on whether one is exposed to H_2O rather than XYZ. Such is luck. We assume that C tokens are as before. They arise upon exposure to either H_2O or XYZ and have indistinguishable effects across people and their doppelgängers. Let us assume that we can attribute to the C tokens of people who have been exposed to H_2O the content that something is water. Evidently we can say the same of the C contents of those doppelgängers who have sensed only H_2O. Given all this, it seems quite clear that we should attribute the same to those people and doppelgängers who have witnessed only XYZ. For once XYZ has entered the picture, so long as we use 'water' to characterize the content of C tokens that result from exposure to H_2O, we should use the *same word* to characterize the content of C states emerging upon exposure to XYZ. This is because it is an accident that any given C state arises from either H_2O or XYZ. C states do not distinguish between H_2O and XYZ, and hence their content is the same. If so, should we not use the same English word in attributing content to these states? If we want to reserve 'water' to mean H_2O, then we had better not use it to ascribe content to C states. If we do want to speak of the content of C states, however, we must settle on a terminology that we can comfortably use regardless of whether the C token arises from exposure to H_2O or XYZ.

Much the same can be said in reply to Burge's (1979) argument that the content of an agent's mental state is not established simply by the causal-inferential connections it shares with all other mental states comprising the agent's system of mental representation. Burge urges that considerations of the agent's social circumstances, which can vary independently of variation within the agent's internal system of representation, partially determine the very content of his or her mental state.

We are to imagine that Héloïse has long suffered from arthritis. She knows how arthritis feels and is as conversant about it as one might expect of someone who has not studied the etiology of the disease. As her condition spreads throughout her joints, Héloïse comes to experience a pain in her thigh that she incorrectly describes as arthritic. Certainly we can say that Héloïse believes that arthritis has spread to her thigh. Nonetheless, her belief is false, since, by definition, 'arthritic' applies to joints, not muscles. But now suppose, contrary to fact, that Héloïse's situation is exactly as described except that her community happens to use 'arthritic' to describe a certain sort of pain in either joints or muscles. Nothing internal to Héloïse differs across the actual and counterfactual situations. Thus, her internal mental states of the actual and counterfactual cases are physically and hence causally the same. Still, Burge insists, the belief that Héloïse has about the pain in her thigh in the counterfactual case must be true. Consequently, this belief could not have the same content as its analogue in the actual situation, despite the fact that the relevant beliefs have exactly the same physical-causal properties. Hence, the content of a mental state cannot, contrary to Sentientialism, be fixed simply by its causal-inferential role within an agent's internal system of mental representation. Rather, the social practices, including linguistic policies, of an agent's community contribute to the determination of the content of his or her mental states.

Burge's argument is contingent on his claim that Héloïse's belief about the pain in her thigh could not be the same belief across the actual and counterfactual situations. This rests on the actual belief's being false while the counterfactual belief is true. Nevertheless, it is not so clear that we should accept this reading of the case. We can elicit conflicting intuitions if we slightly but irrelevantly alter the description of the counterfactual situation. Let us imagine two linguistic communities, respectively corresponding to the linguistic communities of Héloïse's actual and counterfactual situations. Additionally assume that Héloïse regularly passes between these two communities. She will not notice that the communities are linguistically different. Although she is a member of the first community whose use of 'arthritis' corresponds to the actual situation, she unwittingly happens to use this term in a slightly deviant way so as accidentally to make her verbal practice coincide with that of the second community, the community in which 'arthritis' corresponds to the counterfactual situation. If Burge were right in holding that the content of Héloïse's belief is a function of the community in which she is located, then her belief should change as she herself travels back and forth between the two communities. Yet the clear fact is that Héloïse's belief does not so change. That part of her behavioral repertoire that depends on the belief in question evidently does not vary depending simply on the fact that Héloïse happens now to be in the one community, now the other. And yet if there is no conceivable variation in behavior, it is wild to suppose that the belief could vary in content. If anything is clear about attributions of content to mental states, it is that ascriptions of different content are not warranted when they correspond to no conceivable differences in behavior.

Héloïse's belief in the actual situation is the same in content as her belief in the counterfactual situation. Our inclination to specify the content of her belief by using 'Héloïse believes that her thigh is arthritic' may indeed atrophy when we place Héloïse in the counterfactual situation. This, however, is simply because when we use English to attribute content to mental states, the conditions for successful communication normally transcend considerations of differences in linguistic practice between ourselves and the subject of the belief ascription. When we are apprised of Héloïse's counterfactual situation and are pressed to use our edition of English to specify the content of her state, we naturally find it a bit difficult because we realize that the language Héloïse speaks is somewhat different from ours. In particular, it happens that the languages are perfectly homophonic and also synonymous across nearly all homonyms. So if we want to convey the content of Héloïse's belief in the counterfactual situation, we need to advise our audience of the differences between Héloïse's use of 'arthritis' and our own. But, and centrally, this does not commit us to the conclusion that the belief Héloïse has in the counterfactual situation is different in content from her belief in the actual situation.

But how is this possible if the one is false and the other true? Well, the beliefs could not strictly coincide in content if they diverged in truth-value. Nevertheless it is a mistake to suppose that their truth-values differ. What does differ in truth-value, depending on the situation, is the expression 'Her thigh is arthritic'. In the actual, but not the counterfactual, case, this expression is false. This is for the uninteresting reason that orthographically identical expressions in different languages need not have the same truth-values. Yet, from none of this does it follow that Héloïse's belief varies in truth-value across the situations. Now, Héloïse's belief does, we may assume, have a specific truth-value; it is either true or false but not both. So which is it? Asking this amounts to wondering whether the Mentalese sentence that encodes Héloïse's belief is true or false. Let this sentence be A. Whether A is true or false

213

depends on what terms it contains, what those terms mean, and whether the world is as described by those terms. If A is true, then we cannot, in the actual case, use 'Her thigh is arthritic' to convey the content of Héloïse's belief. For the mentioned expression is false, whereas – by hypothesis – Héloïse's belief is true. And if A is false, then we cannot, in the counterfactual case, use 'Her thigh is arthritic' to convey the content of Héloïse's belief. For now the mentioned expression is true, whereas – again by hypothesis – Héloïse's belief is false.

Just which English sentence we should use in specifying the content of an agent's belief depends on which English sentence best translates the Mentalese sentence encoding the belief. Obviously we do not now have a way of discerning just which Mentalese sentence encodes any given belief, and even if we did we would still need a reliable translation scheme between English and Mentalese before we could say with perfect confidence what, exactly, the content of a particular belief might be. Moreover, there is every possibility that Mentalese resists facile translation into any spoken language. After all, even among spoken languages, translation is a messy affair, and we should expect no less from Mentalese. The best we can do at present is look to the causes and effects of a belief and note which of our spoken sentences would, if translatable with the Mentalese sentence encoding the belief, convey the content that must accrue to the Mentalese sentence so as to render that sentence the rational consequence of its causes and a premise from which its effects rationally follow.

Well, perhaps the objection to all this can be put as follows: Let Héloïse tell us what she believes. In both the actual and counterfactual cases she says, "My thigh is arthritic." What she says in the actual case is false, but what she says in the counterfactual case is true. Still, in each case she adequately expresses her belief. So her beliefs differ in truth-value and must accordingly differ in content.

This is much too fast. When Héloïse expresses her belief, she is in the same boat as is anyone attempting to gauge the content of her mental state. That is, Héloïse, in expressing her belief, is proposing a hypothesis as to which sentence in her spoken language is the best translation of her current Mentalese target sentence. Normally we can take Héloïse's word for it. We can typically accept her candidate for translation and rely on her to specify the content of her belief. Nonetheless, one plausible reaction to Burge's description of the counterfactual case is to suspect that in at least one of the two situations Héloïse has failed to pin down the content of her own belief. We should appreciate that in various circumstances we are warranted in rejecting an agent's report of the content of his or her current mental state because of what we may know of the agent's situation. I certainly know the difference between elks and moose, but recently, while hiking with a friend, I referred to some grazing elks as moose only quickly to be corrected by my companion. I proposed a rendition of the content of my current belief state, but given all that my friend knew of me and my situation, he was better able to state the content of my belief than I. I did not mistake the elks for moose. Rather, I mistakenly reported the content of my belief. Héloïse's situation may be similar. She too may err in reporting the content of her belief in either the actual or counterfactual situation. And when we ourselves know that, regardless of the situation, both Héloïse's behavior and its supporting mental mechanisms are invariant, we may be advised seriously to consider the possibility that her own testimony as to the content of her belief may be mistaken.

6.6. MEANING AND DEFINITION

Let us come up for air for a moment. We take it that for a Mentalese term to be meaningful, it must be made of some as yet unspecified physical stuff. Such, at least, was the thesis of the preceding chapter. This leaves it open, however, as to how mental terms come to mean what they specifically do. So we distinguish between mental terms constituted by sensory states and those that are not. The former demonstratively refer to the objects that cause them and predicate, in a demonstrative way, the properties of the objects that cause the sensory states. Mental terms not realized in sensory states take their meanings from the causal connections they enjoy with sensory states, one another, and behavior.

Notice that this is *not* to say that nonsensuous states represent either what they are caused by or what they cause. The hypothesis is, rather, that nonsensuous mental states are mental terms functioning within a coordinated network of terms. Each term in such a network is causally related to various other terms, sensory states, and behavior. These causal relations are typically long, involved causal chains. An agent's Mentalese term 'sparrow', when predicated, means that something is a sparrow just in case 'sparrow' standardly occupies a certain role in the agent's cognitive economy. That is, 'sparrow' would play a designated causal role in prompting the agent, say, to identify sparrows as such, to feed sparrows when the agent so desires, to flee from sparrows when the agent fears them, and so on.

Cognitive psychology begins with the assumption that, for the most part, an agent's activity is the rational result of computationally related states. The rationality of an agent's activity requires that the activity be caused by rational inferences defined over the agent's internal representational states. The rationality of these inferences presupposes that the terms they feature so represent as generally to ensure the truth, probability, or appropriateness of the inferences' conclusions relative to the same in the inferences' premises. This, in turn, amounts to saying that meaning must accrue to Mentalese terms so as to render their causal relations tantamount to rational inferential relations. Thus, the meaning of a nonsensuous Mentalese term is what it must be in order that the causal relations in which the term is implicated qualify as rational relations.[32]

If this should prove not utterly implausible, then all meaningful mental terms will finally trace unique causal routes back to sensory origins. Nonetheless, this certainly and most emphatically is not to say that all meaningful mental terms are *definable* by way of combinations of sensory mental predicates. It is not difficult to see why. Assume, consistent with the preceding, that we have a mental term that means the same as 'sparrow'. Additionally, suppose that this term means what it does because, on the one hand, it is the causal distillation of those sensory mental predicates that result from

32 We all know that semantics is very difficult since for any language it is possible to devise different interpretations or translation schemes all of which preserve rationality in the speakers of the language. Similarly for Mentalese. But just as English terms do not, in fact, mean whatever they could mean while preserving the rationality of users of English, so too for Mentalese. Thus, while rationality constrains the interpretations that Mentalese might have, it does not alone determine which interpretation Mentalese in fact has. Still, and this is important, sensuous Mentalese predicates realized in sensuous states both have their meanings fixed by the properties that cause these states to occur and also contribute to the determination of the meanings of the nonsensuous mental representations to which they are in any way connected. Given this, we might hopefully hypothesize that the role of sensuous Mentalese terms in contributing to the content of their nonsensuous descendants constrains the range of interpretations for the whole of Mentalese.

216

an agent's being exposed to sparrows and, on the other hand, it is the mental term whose effects ramify in a certain way throughout the agent's cognitive system. Nowhere in this account is it claimed that the mental predicate for 'sparrow' is defined in terms of any of its causally associated mental predicates, sensuous or not. All that is maintained is that there is a causal connection from a certain class of semantic structures, namely, sensuous mental predicates, to a certain semantic structure, that is, the mental predicate for 'sparrow', and on to other semantic structures, to wit certain other mental predicates and behavioral episodes. It is by virtue of this causal web that the mental term for 'sparrow' is said to mean what it does. Period. Of course, we suppose that inferential relations supervene on these causal relations. That, however, is consistent with none of these relations being definitional. The thesis is not that the mental term for 'sparrow' means what it does because it is causally connected to other mental terms through which it also happens to be defined. So the idea is not that mental terms are definable by means of one another. That may be so, but it is not what is proposed here. All that is required for the meaningfulness of mental terms is that, in *normal* situations, they stand in certain causal relations to stimuli, other mental terms, and behavior.[33] The meaning of one mental term differs from that of another just in case the terms are causally related to some different mental terms. Of course, this presupposes some primitive meaningful mental terms from which others might derive their own peculiar semantic features. And so long as we can depend on sensory mental predicates to take their content directly from the properties of the objects that cause the sensory states to occur, we can rely on sensory mental predicates to function as semantic primitives in Mentalese.

The picture to hold fast to, then, is this: Sensory states constitute primitive terms in Mentalese. Each distinct type of sensory state functions semantically to ostend a distinct property, the property that causes that sensory state to occur. A token of any given type of sensory state refers to whatever object happens to instantiate the occurrence of the property that causes sensory states of that token's

---

33 Things are a bit different in abnormal agents, such as Mrs. T. (Chapter 4, Section 4.3). But even here, the Mentalese expression 'McKinley was assassinated' means, in Mrs. T., that McKinley was assassinated because in normal agents Mentalese expressions of the same syntactic type result from and in incidents best explained by reference to representations that McKinley was assassinated.

type. A sensory state token, like all tokens of its type, predicates the property of which it is the effect. So sensory-state types serve as Mentalese predicates, predicates that simply label properties without thereby indicating how those properties may be related to one another. But sensory states do give rise to other states within an agent's cognitive system, states that, in turn, interact at length finally to produce behavior. These latter states take their content from their causal relations, the content of any given state depending on its relations to other states much in the way that theoretical terms within a spoken language may take their meaning from the roles they play within the theories they populate.

From this it follows that sensory states are incorrigible. Since they necessarily represent their causes, what they represent must obtain. A sensory state says, roughly, "This is just that way," where 'this' refers to the object that instantiates the property that causes the sensory state and 'is just that way' predicates of that object the property it instantiates that causes the sensory state to occur. The truth of a Mentalese sentence recording a sensation is thus guaranteed by the fact that the sentence expresses, albeit demonstratively, the conditions necessary for its own inscription.

Still, room remains for *so-called* sensory illusion and hallucination. These are actually nonsensuous judgments that arise as the consequences of unsound inferences from true sensuous representations as premises. Abelard suffers the illusion of something red there before him. This is because his sensory system has been affected in some way so as to produce a true pristine sensuous representation. This representation does correctly represent what may have caused it, but – circumstances being as they are – it, in turn, causes to occur in Abelard some nonsensuous representation to the effect that something there is red. Here is Abelard's illusion: Nothing there is red, but something there did cause his sensuous representation to occur. So his sensuous representation remains correct, even if not very informative, while his nonsensuous representation falsely posits something red.

Although an agent's sensory states may be perfectly reliable indicators of their causes, they certainly do not carry much, if any, information about how the environment is assembled, how it will affect the agent's future, or how it might react to the agent's attempts to manipulate it. Such representations run beyond the reach of sensory states and naturally fall to the complexly interrelated

218

cognitive states that emerge within an agent consequent upon his or her sensory states. It is here that the possibility of error arises. Nothing in the account of the content of nonsensuous representational states implies that what such states represent must be true. That an agent's particular cognitive state is caused by a certain class of sensory states, interacts with other cognitive states, and finally causes the agent to act may well settle what the state represents, but it certainly does not ensure that the world is as represented. So, if the possibility of mental misrepresentation resides in the causal commerce of nonsensuous mental terms and if the inferential relations among mental representations ride on their causal connections, then error is attributable to inference's transcending sensation.

7

The quality of consciousness

7.1. FUNCTIONAL ACCOUNTS OF CONSCIOUSNESS

This, in order, is how it was with Abelard: lust, love, pain, then sorrow. During its time, each feeling varied in intensity, and each was distinct from the others. Certainly you yourself have felt the same, or nearly so. And for that reason you understand how it was with Abelard. But, had you never experienced as did Abelard, could you appreciate, simply from his telling alone, what – to modify Nagel's (1974) apt expression – it must have been like to be Abelard? Indeed, if you had not felt and never were to feel precisely the same sort and intensity of lust, love, pain, and sorrow as did Abelard, could you ever hope to understand precisely how he felt throughout his affair with Héloïse?

When we wonder about what it was like to be Abelard, we find ourselves asking about the nature of consciousness, that irrepressible, phenomenologically elusive quality that unquestionably pervades mentation. It is not easy to say what consciousness is or includes. Surely, however, it is all that we try to describe when we speak of the character of our sensations, feelings, and moods. Yet, because it is so very difficult to capture descriptively the nature of consciousness, some conclude that it is psychological chaff, a by-product of cognition safely and best ignored by the cognitive sciences.[1] Others insist that consciousness distinguishes us from imagined mindless robots or zombies that perfectly mimic our behavior. If so, consciousness would be an absolutely essential feature of human and, apparently, all other types of cognition.[2] Others still

1 Almost all efforts in cognitive science, including Artificial Intelligence, are silent regarding the nature of consciousness. Whereas Rorty (1979) would scuttle the "raw feeling" of consciousness, Dennett (1969, 1978a, 1982b) has persistently attempted to indicate the manner in which consciousness might best be studied within the confines of cognitive science.
2 Compare Block and Fodor (1972), Block (1980a,b), Davis (1982), and Graham

take something of each of the first two positions, contending that consciousness is fundamental to mentation but that, because of its subjective character, it never can be properly comprehended by an objective science of the mind.

The last of these positions is the one that will exercise us. Its spokesmen, Nagel (1974) and Jackson (1982, 1986), insist that consciousness represents an intractable problem for the philosophy of mind. For while they suppose that consciousness is basic to the mental life, they argue that it defies analysis of the sort characteristic of any physicalistic or scientific approach to mentation. This is a remarkably strong claim, one that almost forces comparison with what we may imagine once were among the more popular criticisms of the scientific method in its early days. No doubt, many in the seventeenth century doubted that a satisfying and thoroughly scientific account of the fury of lightning would be forthcoming. They were wrong, of course, and this feeds the suspicion that it may be premature to consign consciousness to a zone beyond the reach of cognitive science. So we will assume with Nagel and Jackson that consciousness is one of the more important mental phenomena and proceed to consider what, consistent with the version of Sententialism already set forth, can be said about what it is like to be a thing of a certain conscious kind.

One point on which there is something approaching general agreement is this: Consciousness presupposes cognition. That is, if a creature is conscious, it must be capable of thinking. Rocks do not think; that is why we all suppose that they are not conscious. Yet, if consciousness requires cognition, then, according to the version of Sententialism outlined in the previous chapters, consciousness can occur only in creatures that have the kind of matter necessary for mental representation. This is because the theory would have it that cognition involves mental representations in the form of a mental language, the symbols of which, in order to be contentful, must be encoded in the kind of material that supports intentionality. So much is entailed by the hypothesis of the Material Basis of Cognition. Consequently, it would be inconsistent with the version of Sententialism promoted here for consciousness to be

and Stephens (1985) with Shoemaker (1975, 1982), Patricia Smith Churchland (1983), Paul Churchland (1985a), and Churchland and Churchland (1981).

explicated in terms of a purely functional account of cognition, an account according to which mentation can occur in any device, *regardless of its composition,* whose internal states are related in certain functional ways. Sententialism, as here conceived, does indeed maintain that the specific content of a nonsensuous mental state is determined by its relations to stimuli, other mental states, and behavior. But it also requires, as a condition of a mental state's having content at all, that the state be composed of the kind of matter that admits of intentionality.

Nevertheless, it must be granted that Sententialism may err in hypothesizing that mentation requires a certain kind of material basis. If so, cognition might occur in devices without regard for their matter, so long as transformations of their internal states were orchestrated to the proper functional tune. Let us, then, for the moment allow that this is so. We suppose for the moment that cognition does not demand instantiation in any specific sort of matter. And so we may temporarily allow that insofar as cognition secures consciousness, consciousness does not require realization in any particular material kind. This sanctions our asking whether we might hope to unravel the mysteries of consciousness by way of mapping the functional relations among the mental states of a con-scious creature. Could we, for example, come to understand what it is like to be Abelard simply by learning how Abelard's mental states are interrelated when he lusts after and then loves Héloïse and when he first suffers the pain of emasculation and then the sorrow of separation?

Davis (1982) and Block (1980a) have drawn attention to a class of arguments that seem to undermine the plausibility of any purely functional explanation of the phenomenology of consciousness. They ask us to imagine that careful study has at last yielded a satisfying map of the functional relations among Abelard's mental states. We are to pretend that when Abelard is driven by his relation with Héloïse, we can say with certainty exactly how all of his cognitive states bearing on his relevant behavior are organized. At the most general level of understanding, we could construct a flow chart to indicate how Abelard's mental states are mutually related and how they arise from sensation and result in behavior. At a deeper level, we could write a program, which if realized in any device, would ensure that the device possesses the same cognitive states as Abelard and therefore also experiences the lust, love, pain, and sorrow that rack Abelard.

Although there may be some reason to concede that such a device does indeed share Abelard's cognitive states, intuition rebels at the idea that the device would or could coincide with Abelard in his affective states. Of course, the voice of intuition may well be the call of false but entrenched presuppositions. So we ought to consider what reasons might support the hunch that the device that duplicates Abelard's cognitive states need not thereby experience the same, if any, qualia characteristic of Abelard's consciousness.

First, there is this: Many are impressed with the assumption that it is conceivable, and therefore possible, that the qualia associated with the sensation of color are inverted across pairs of cognitively similar agents (Shoemaker, 1975). Abelard and Héloïse both might have all the same beliefs about colors although the qualia of Abelard's sensations of color are inverted relative to Héloïse's sensations of the same. Just as colors are organized on a spectrum, so too – the assumption goes – are their corresponding sensory qualia within an agent. Still, there is no apparent necessity in the color qualia space of different agents' agreeing. If so, then Abelard and Héloïse might experience in remarkably different ways when they sense the same colors and form the same beliefs about colors. Should this be possible, then the sheer fact that Héloïse emulates Abelard's cognitive states does not entail that her states have for her the same affective nature as Abelard's states have for him. Thus it would seem that a purely functional or cognitive account of an agent's mental life need not suffice to expose the character of the agent's consciousness. Knowing how Abelard's states are functionally related, then, appears to be short of knowing what it is like to be Abelard.

The preceding rests on the assumption that color qualia, in particular, and qualia, in general, can be differently structured within agents with the same cognitive, representational states. That, evidently, is an empirical assumption, an assumption some may be unprepared to make. But there are other reasons that march against the hypothesis that the nature of an agent's consciousness is to be explained within the confines of a functional account of the agent's mental states. After all, it is by now almost universally accepted that it is possible for the functional relations exhibited in an agent's mental processes to be exemplified in systems that would appear to have no claim whatsoever to consciousness. A large cooperative group of people might so function as to simulate the functionally characterized processes occurrent in Abelard. But it strains the imagination to suppose that this system of people, not the people themselves, could itself in any way feel, suffer, or enjoy. This suggests, as does the inverted qualia argument, that functional replication of the cognitive states of a conscious agent does not, after all, suffice for the replication of the agent's consciousness.

Even this reaction some will think wrong. For, as Dennett (1978a, pp. 171–2) says, were the conjectured system of people that duplicates the functional organization of Abelard's relevant mental states to continue to replicate the functional relations of Abelard's mental states over a very long period of time, the idea that it would share both Abelard's cognitive and affective states must begin to look more likely. This would be especially so if we were to recognize the possibility of there being genuinely conscious creatures quite unlike ourselves that operate on time frames much faster or slower than our own. Recognizing this should alert us to the possibility that, because of our lack of familiarity with alien conscious creatures, we could well be blind to the consciousness of nonlocal or artificial cognitive systems, both actual and imagined.

Be this as it may, there is another reason why one might hesitate generally to attribute consciousness to information processors of certain functional complexity. Consider two powerful computers, distant from one another but connected through a telecommunications system. Their distinct software allows them to exchange information and permits each to monitor and, to some extent, direct the other's operations. Suppose that each computer, when running its specified program, functionally replicates the mental states of some naturally intelligent, conscious agent and therefore itself qualifies as an intelligent, conscious agent. What should we say of the system they together constitute? Whether or not we should take the summation of their cooperation to constitute a third intelligent, conscious system appears to be a conventional matter. We could just as neatly and reasonably take them to be a team of individual players as we could construe them to be a pair of players whose interactions produce a third. But what ought we to make of Abelard and Héloïse if they take it upon themselves to simulate the two computers? Each person honestly answers the questions of the other and does what the other reasonably requests. What is the product of their joint venture? Although convention may reasonably deem the result of the two cooperating computers a third intelligent, conscious system, it seems most implausible that convention could establish either that cooperating Abelard and Héloïse merge into a single conscious system or that their joint venture brings about the existence of a third conscious agent. Abelard and Héloïse, despite their cooperation, remain, in rerum natura, distinct, conscious agents; and the result of their cooperation may be harmony, but it certainly is not a conscious agent. Nature is more circumspect in its determination of the loci of consciousness than convention is inclined to be. And this indicates, though it certainly does not indisputably prove, that it simply cannot be correct to maintain that consciousness is only a matter of functionally characterized relations among the states of information processors.

7.2. COULD QUALIA BE NONPSYCHOLOGICAL?

We shall take it not as an established fact but, rather, as a working hypothesis, then, that consciousness is not reducible simply to the functional relations exhibited in a cognitive agent.

Graham and Stephens (1985 and 1987) agree and contend that this is because the qualia characteristic of types of conscious episodes are themselves thoroughly nonpsychological.[3] This is not a thesis for the timid, and Graham and Stephens ably argue for their view by showing how it applies to pain, which the literature takes to be the paradigmatic quale. The model they urge treats the occurrence of an instance of pain as an essentially complex affair. To be in pain, if they are right, is much like seeing a tree. When seeing a tree, an agent occupies a certain sort of psychological state. But that is not enough. There must also exist that very tree that stands as the object of the agent's psychological state. The tree, quite evidently, is no element of the psychological state. The state is internal to the agent; the tree is not. Similarly, an agent suffering pain is in a certain kind of psychological state that is directed toward something not itself a part of that state. The type of psychological

---

3 Graham and Stephens recognize that Armstrong (1962) once considered but finally rejected a similar view. Various other philosophers have entertained the idea that consciousness involves states of a complex sort including psychological and non-psychological aspects. See, for example, Block (1980a) and Conee (1984).

state involved in pain is one that typically will cause an agent to behave in the manner characteristic of agents in pain. Still, what the psychological state focuses on is a sensible quality of a certain sort within the agent's body. This sensible quality is not part of the psychological state; it is rather a property of some part of the agent's body. Like the tree the agent may see, the sensible quality occurrent in pain does not in any way depend for its existence on being sensed or otherwise acknowledged by the agent. The sensible quality occurrent in pain is certainly sensible: It can be mentally detected or represented. When it is detected, it is that to which some mental state refers. Consider now the compound consisting of the sensible quality and the psychological state referring to it. One part of the compound structure is a nonpsychological but sensible property of the suffering agent's body. The other part is the psychological state of the agent that represents the sensible property. It is just such a compound configuration that Graham and Stephens take to constitute an episode of pain. The psychological element in this compound is exhausted by the psychological state. The sensible quality within the compound is, for Graham and Stephens, the qualitative aspect of the compound state. The sensible quality is, then, the quale of the pain. So, pain qualia, according to Graham and Stephens, are not at all psychological.

There is much to recommend the position that Graham and Stephens take. It allows them to explain, for example, why and how they think both nonaversive and unfelt pains are possible. Nonaversive pain is, like unfelt pain, only incorrectly called 'pain'. That is, given the hypothesis of Graham and Stephens, pain is the complex of a psychological state and a sensible quality. So-called nonaversive pain is just the occurrence of the sensible quality as the object of some type of psychological state different from that type of psychological state that forms part of the compound properly called 'pain'. So-called unfelt pains are much the same. They too are not really pains; they are not compound in the requisite sense. Rather, what is dubbed 'unfelt pain' is actually just the occurrence of a sensible quality that could but – as a matter of happenstance – does not occur as the referent of any psychological state.

Nevertheless, there are two reasons that may lead one away from the direction in which Graham and Stephens point. First, Graham and Stephens offer as evidence that qualia are nonpsychological the apparent fact that there are familiar, nonscientific terms that refer to

226

qualia while not also in any way referring to those qualia as the objects of psychological states. The idea goes back to Berkeley: If quale are nonpsychological, then there should be ready ways of referring to them that show that they can occur in the absence of psychological states. Graham and Stephens maintain that there are just such expressions. They cite, for example, 'throbbing' and 'burning'.

It is not finally clear, however, that such terms do not implicitly refer to psychological states. Abelard stumbles and gashes his knee. Héloïse cleans the wound with a harsh solution, and Abelard complains of a burning sensation in his knee. This story is intelligible in part because we take Abelard's description of a burning sensation to amount to his testifying to the experience of a certain pain quale. Now, if we could use 'burning' to pick out a quale in such a way as not to betray an agent's apprehension of the quale, then it would seem as if Graham and Stephens would be right in saying that qualia, since not in themselves psychological, can be designated in ways that do not presuppose that any agent suffers the qualia. But to say that "Abelard's knee is burning but he does not sense it" looks, on the face of it, to be inconsistent. Yes, we could expand and say that while Abelard sleeps under the influence of a powerful narcotic, someone maliciously places a lit match to his knee and scorches his skin. If we add this background information, then it does make perfect sense to say, "Abelard's knee is burning, but he does not sense it." But now we have apparently altered the meaning of 'burning'. In the first instance it was to designate a quale, and that it did so seemed to render the sentence in which it occurred inconsistent. But once we do away with the inconsistency by explaining that Abelard is drugged and his knee scorched, it is not at all evident that 'burning' still refers to a quale. In other words, when 'burning' refers to a quale, it seems to be used metaphorically and to mean that an agent experiences a quale of a certain sort. When 'burning' is not used metaphorically, it can refer to something of which the agent in question is unaware. But this shows just that 'burning' is ambiguous, not that it can be used to designate an undetected quale. Failing that, we must wonder whether Graham and Stephens are right when they say both that qualia are nonpsychological because familiar but nonpsychologically laden terms designate them.[4]

4 There may be a way for Graham and Stephens to sidestep this criticism. Even if terms like 'burning' are psychologically significant whenever they refer to qualia, Graham and Stephens could yet be right in maintaining that qualia are nonpsy-

Be this as it may, there is another and more important reason to worry that the view advanced by Graham and Stephens might not be right. What they say of the experience of pain is to hold with minor modification for other qualia as well. Color vision certainly carries qualia. So, in their view, when Abelard sees the color of a particular red flower, he is in a complex state consisting of a psychological state directed toward a certain sensible quality, apparently the color in the flower. A passing bee sees the same flower. Bees have a visual system that differs in important physical details from the human visual system. Both Abelard and the bee see the color of the flower. They have, we may suppose, the same simple psychological attitude toward the same sensible quality in the flower. Thus, for Graham and Stephens, both Abelard and the bee are in the same complex state consisting of the same psychological state and the same sensible quality. It would seem, then, that Graham and Stephens are committed to maintaining that the qualitative character of Abelard's experience is the same as that of the bee's. But this seems most unlikely, given the difference in the hardware comprising the visual systems of human and bee. So, marking our difference with Graham and Stephens, we may conclude, tentatively at least, that qualia are psychological and that we had better look to psychological states in attempting to find a place for qualia.[5]

7.3. SENTENTIALISM AND CONSCIOUSNESS

Sententialism is primarily a theory of how the mind aspires to the cognitive. But it also yields some understanding of the nature of consciousness. Indeed, within certain limitations, it can serve to determine what it is like to be a thing of a conscious kind.

chological. It could be that our spoken language itself, but wrongly, incorporates the assumption that qualia are essentially psychological (Paul Churchland, 1979). If so, it would be a task for science to frame terms that unambiguously select qualia without reference to their being given in awareness. That is, Graham and Stephens may be correct in supposing that if qualia are nonpsychological, then there should be ways of referring to them that do not also refer to psychological states. Their mistake – if indeed there is a mistake – could innocuously lie in supposing that the relevant referential expression must already be entrenched.

5 A similar argument with equal effect could be run in which reference to the bee is replaced by reference to a color-blind person who cannot distinguish red from some other color.

Consciousness, at least as found in its noncontroversial instances, such as humans and other mammals, requires intelligence. If Sententialism is correct, intelligence amounts to the possession of a language of thought. We have already discussed in Chapter 6 how structures within Mentalese might come to have content. So we have it that consciousness occurs in creatures equipped with a contentful language of mentation. This invites us to conjecture that consciousness might somehow emerge from the very *use* of a system of mental representation. To be conscious, according to this as yet to be developed hypothesis, is to be an intelligent agent, an agent whose intelligence is fixed by the agent's use of a mental language. Different kinds of naturally conscious agents (e.g., humans and – following Nagel [1974] – bats) would differ consciously by way of deploying different mental systems of representation. What it is like to be Abelard would be to use the mental language he uses to think. What it is like to be a bat would be to use the mental language naturally encoded in the bat enabling it to represent its environment and compute the functions necessary for the production of its behavior. Artificially conscious kinds, if such there should finally prove to be, would be intelligent systems that deploy systems of representation sufficient to explain the behavior of the artificially intelligent agents comprehended by the kinds.

Chapter 5 presents the argument that, in order for a language to serve as a system of mental representation, it must be contentful, this in turn requiring that the language be encoded in matter of a certain, even if not yet discerned, type. So much is entailed by the hypothesis of the Material Basis of Cognition. Thus, when Sententialism posits that consciousness amounts to the use of a mental language, it is wedded to the idea that consciousness is restricted to instantiation in systems possessed of the matter necessary for mental representation. Consciousness, if this is right, is necessarily limited to creatures, natural or artificial, with a specified material nature. This, as we shall see, does not imply that the character of consciousness is univocal across all types of intelligent creatures. Nonetheless, it does mandate that only creatures with certain physical properties could realize consciousness of any sort.

Whether, finally, anything is to be gained by saying, as a first approximation, that consciousness comes to the use of mental representations depends on how what we antecedently know of consciousness can be accommodated by Sententialism. Our very concept of consciousness is certainly amorphous and needs to be pruned (Dennett, 1968, 1978h; Patricia Smith Churchland, 1982), but it is clear that it is informed by application primarily to ourselves, secondarily to other kinds of animated conscious forms, known and imagined, and only last of all to envisioned artificially intelligent systems. So our best hope in extending our understanding of consciousness consistent with the constraints of Sententialism lies in formulating an account applicable to ourselves and capable of orderly extension to other conscious kinds.

When we ask what it is like to be Abelard, it helps to focus on a specific and relatively clear episode of consciousness. Since pain is the literature's favored example, we follow suit. Abelard is assaulted and feels a particular and distinctive pain, recognizing it as such. To be in pain is to be aware of pain, at least insofar as being in pain is an instance of consciousness. And doubtless, to feel pain requires being in a sensory state. Pains, after all, are sensuous.[6] To say that Abelard suffers some particular pain is, by Sententialism's lights, to say that he issues a sensuous mental representation of the locus of the pain. We assume without argumentation that the sensuous representation occurrent in an instance of pain is, in the standard case, the representation of the state of some part of the body. Since pain involves sensuous representation, its mental representation is achieved by way of demonstrative reference and predication. Sensuous mental representation in an episode of pain thus amounts to the deployment of a Mentalese sentence to the effect 'This (bodily part) is (affected in just) that (painful manner)'. Of course, Abelard will typically form judgments based on his sensuous representations of pain. These inferential consequences will normally serve to classify the location and type of pain sensed and will themselves occur in the form of nonsensuous Mentalese sentences perhaps to the effect of 'I am in pain' or, more specifically, 'I have an excruciating, burning sensation in my lower abdomen'.[7]

6 Is unconscious pain possible? Perhaps, but we need not worry here about that. Our concern is the nature of conscious experience, and we may thus concern ourselves with conscious pain. See Graham and Stephens (1987) and Melzack (1961) for discussions of situations in which some sense can be given to the notion of unexperienced pain.

7 What of the pains in phantom limbs? These we take to be sensations arising from disturbances in real parts of the body. An agent who reports suffering pain in a phantom limb simply mistakenly judges the location of the cause of the pain. That is, the agent sensuously represents a real pain in a real part of his or her

230

Still, what we need to appreciate here is that Abelard's awareness of his own pain is itself one of his sensuous states. The point may be trivial, but it should not be ignored. Abelard's detection of pain in himself takes the form of a sensuous Mentalese representation. It is here that the awfulness of pain is registered; it is in sensation that the qualia of pain are lodged. With this in mind, it is both hard and ill advised to suppress the suspicion that qualia of all sorts are essentially linked to sensation.

Let us take it as a hypothesis, then, that qualia are somehow located in sensation.[8] What should we say of the quale associated with an occurrence of a particular sort of pain? What is it in Abelard's sensuous representation of pain that infuses it with its inherent awfulness, the phenomenologically distinctive quale that marks his specific pain?

To answer this, recall that the sensuous Mentalese sentence Abelard uses mentally to represent his pain has, as a physical structure internal to Abelard, various properties. Some of these properties are syntactic, some are not. The syntactic properties of the sensuous representation are those of its causal properties that link the state to other mental representations and its behavioral effects. Presumably it is the awfulness of pain that causes an agent to attempt to eliminate what offends. It is the quale of Abelard's current pain that leads him to try to alter his situation. The quale of an instance of pain thus appears to be what, in the sensuous representation of the pain, results in the representation's behavioral effects. But if this is so, then, since the causal properties of a mental representation are its syntactic features, it would seem reasonable to conjecture that the quale of an episode of consciousness may well be the physical properties that constitute the syntactic features of the sensuous Mentalese token encoded in that episode.

The awfulness of Abelard's pain is, as his occurrent quale, identical with the structure of physical properties constituting the syntax of his current sensuous token.[9] That means that the quale that

body and, on that basis, wrongly infers a nonsensuous judgment as to where the pain is located. In this sense, reports of pains in phantom limbs are just a species of mistaken nonsensuous judgment inferred from correct sensuous premises. See Chapter 6, Sections 6.3 and 6.6.

8 This is not news. Others have said something of the same before. See, for example, Descartes (1649) and Spinoza (1671).

9 This distances the present notion of qualia from that open to functionalism. For whereas functionalism abstracts from considerations of physical detail in char-

231

characterizes an episode of pain is identical with those structured physical properties of a token sensory state that place the token in its sensory type. This devolves from the fact that a sensuous Mentalese representation is encoded in the form of a sensory-state token and consists, syntactically, of a predicate and a demonstrative pronoun. The predicate is constituted by the properties of the sensory token that qualify the token as an instance of the type of sensory state it is. So, if, as seems right, the qualia of consciousness, as mental phenomena, do in fact have behavioral results, then it is all but inevitable that Sententialism will identify qualia with the syntactic and hence physical features of sensuous Mentalese tokens. Types of qualia appear, then, to be syntactic types of Mentalese predicates. Thus, to use a sensuous Mentalese token realized as a token of a specified sensory type is to experience the phenomenologically apparent quale characteristic of the kind of experience registered by the sensation embodying the sensuous Mentalese token. How else could qualia, as elements of psychological states, induce the forms of behavior they characteristically do?

If we adopt this way of construing qualia, we can make some sense of both undetected and nonaversive pain. An undetected pain is simply the abnormal occurrence of an injury or condition of the body. Because the conditions of the injury's occurrence are abnormal, it does not affect the sensory system and so is not sensed. Were the conditions normal, the injury would cause a certain kind of sensory state that would represent the injury. This sensory state would also embody the quale characteristic of sensations of injuries of the present sort. Notice that to say that a pain is undetected is not to say that a quale is undetected. In cases of undetected pains injuries are present but quale are not. And this is simply because the normal causal chain from insult to sensation has been broken.

Nonaversive pain is different (Melzack, 1973 and 1961; Hilgard and Hilgard, 1975; Lewis, 1980; Tursky, Jammer, and Friedman 1982). A nonaversive pain takes one of two forms. On the one hand, it is the occurrence of a sensuously detected injury in abnormal conditions. The injury is sensuously detected by virtue of causing a sensory token to occur, but since the conditions are abnormal, the sensory token caused to occur is not of the sensory

acterizing mental phenomena and, hence, qualia, the view before us identifies qualia with physically characterized properties of an agent.

232

type normally caused by injuries of the present kind. Thus the occurrent sensory token does not have the same physical properties as a sensory token of the kind normally caused by injuries of the type at hand. Consequently, the sensory token that detects the injury in the abnormal conditions will not embody the same awful quale as would be found in a sensory token normally induced by injuries of the current kind. The quale involved in the abnormal sensuous representation of the injury, therefore, need not be aversive. On the other hand, a nonaversive pain could amount to a simple case of perceptual misidentification. An agent may sensuously detect a harmless state of his or her body but, because of what the agent knows or anticipates, come wrongly to judge that the detected state is an injury. Since the sensory state implicated in the detection of the harmless bodily condition is the sort of sensory state that it is, the quale it forms need not be in any way disquieting. The subject, mistakenly postulating an injury, notes the absence of any aversive quale and reports the occurrence of a nonaversive pain. Here there is a quale, and the subject is right to call it nonaversive. Nevertheless, there is no injury, and the subject is wrong to call the detected bodily condition a pain.

Plainly the idea here is that qualia are nothing but physical properties that determine the syntactic features of sensuous representations. Differences among the qualia that Abelard experiences are thus attributable to differences among the physical properties of the states encoding his sensuous representations. This implies that different agents can experience the same qualia only if their sensuous representations can be encoded in states with the same relevant physical properties. Some (Lewis, 1980) will object to this, no doubt, arguing that it is possible that there are conscious agents sharing none of our physical properties, at least none that are germane to our mental states, who nonetheless agree with us in our qualia. Might there not be a Martian who is composed of stuff utterly different from that from which Abelard is drawn yet who has the same pain quale as Abelard? But this possibility is inconsistent with Abelard's pain being identified with the physical property defining the syntax of his current mental state. For, by hypothesis, the Martian shares Abelard's quale but none of his physical properties.

The first comment to make is that the example of the Martian appears to violate the hypothesis of the Material Basis of Cognition,

233

which requires that intelligence, in presupposing mental representation, can occur only in agents who contain the kind of matter
necessary for encoding intentional structures. If Martians do not
agree with Abelard in any physical way, they cannot satisfy, as
Abelard does, the material condition on mentation. If Martians
cannot mentally represent, they cannot be genuine subjects of cognition. And that in turn implies that Martians, if utterly different
in physical composition from Abelard, could not be conscious at
all. For consciousness, by hypothesis, occurs only in cognitive
agents.

The second point to raise against the Martian counterexample
involves questioning the assumption on which it is based. Suppose
that we set aside the hypothesis of the Material Basis of Cognition.
Would that make it at all evident that it is possible that creatures
that disagree in their physical properties nevertheless experience the
same qualia? Surely the simple fact that we can conceive of the
Martian's situation does not prove the possibility of such. One who
is ignorant of the identity of water and H_2O can easily conceive of
their divergence even though it remains literally impossible that
water could be other than what it is. The same may be so for qualia.
Given the little we now know of qualia, it may wrongly appear to
us that Abelard's pain could also be found in the Martian. But in
fact it may be nomically necessary that the qualia constitutive of
Abelard's pain occur nowhere else other than in the type of sensory-
physical state Abelard realizes when in such pain. Still, this certainly
does not demonstrate beyond all doubt that Abelard's pain qualia
are essentially limited to states of the physical kind he possesses.
The present view is contingent, then, on what we may come to
discover about the necessity, or lack thereof, of qualia occurring in
agents of divergent physical kinds. So, while we await the crucial
discoveries, we are well advised to scout some accounts of consciousness that do not admit of qualia being constant across fundamentally different physical types of agents.[10]

If it should, after all, turn out that the Martian scenario is possible,
then the line laid down here is false, plain false. But it is worth

10 Thus, whereas Lewis (1980) is prompted to formulate an account of pain, and
   other mental states, based on the assumption that it is indeed possible for there
   to be agents of fundamentally distinct physical kinds that nevertheless exhibit
   the same qualia, we begin with the opposing assumption, recognizing that neither
   assumption is beyond question.

reminding ourselves that should we find Martians who appear to fit the example's bill, we would still need to settle some difficult issues before we certify them as sharing our qualia but not our relevant physical properties. Suppose we were to find a Martian who appears to conform to the conditions of the example. Qualia identical with Abelard's would occur in this Martian, but its mental representations would not be comprehended by any of the same physical kinds as Abelard's. Before leaping to any conclusions, we would need to entertain the hypothesis that, contrary to appearances, the qualia common to Abelard and the Martian are supported by some common but not yet identified physical kind. Indeed, the discovery of such Martians would certainly call into question any physical taxonomy, developed in ignorance of Martians and relative only to our knowledge of how things are on Earth, that purports to distinguish Martians and humans.

A local example may help. Let us suppose ourselves to be linguists completely ignorant of English. We travel to a country where English is written but never spoken. Naturally, we are curious about this strange new language and wonder just what count as English inscriptions. As it turns out, all English inscriptions are prepared by people using, as a matter of the strictest law, a single kind of typewriter, all instances of which produce exactly the same kind of type. Although there is only one kind of typewriter on which English inscriptions are produced, two types of ribbons are available, red and black. Red ink is used for all documents pertaining to the finances of the government; black ink serves otherwise. We begin our linguistic investigations with the evidence at hand. Since we happen to have landed at the seat of government, however, all the many instances of English we find are recorded in red ink. We mistakenly hypothesize that being recorded in red ink is essential to English inscription. It is only after many years of swimming in red ink that we at last float outside of the mainstream of government and climb into the black. Shocked by what we find, we are at first unsure as to whether the black inscriptions count as English. After all, they do look so very different from all the English inscriptions we have previously seen. If we are lucky, it will occur to us that our original hypothesis was all wrong; the color of the inscription is irrelevant to its being English or not. What determines whether an inscription is English is the typeface in which it is recorded, whether, that is, it has just the right shape in abstraction from the

235

color in which it is printed. For that, unbeknown to us, is the civil law.

In our analysis of the Martians' situation we should attend to the moral of the just told tale. Although it may at first seem to us that Martians with qualia the same as our own do not have their qualia installed in physical states of the same sort as ours, we should pause and ask how it is possible that Martians are able to enjoy the same qualia as we do if their mental states differ so completely from ours in their physical composition. Having asked this question, we may proceed to find that our original taxonomy of the properties relevant for fixing local mental states is woefully provincial. We might then see that an alternative conception of the matter relevant to mentation may establish that Martians, in experiencing the same qualia as we experience, do indeed possess mental states comprehended by the same physical properties as those characteristic of our mental states. Such would amount to finding, if Sententialism should be true, that at least some of the syntactic properties of at least some Martian and human mental representations are the same. For that, but unknown to us, may be the natural law.

So, we shall retain the hypothesis that qualia are essentially identical with the physical properties constituting the syntax of sensuous mental representation. This forces us to set to one side the countervailing conjecture that qualia are only contingently identical with the physical properties of mental states. Still, while we recognize that the latter hypothesis may, in the end, prove correct, we take heart in the fact that our hypothesis goes some way toward indicating how qualia could have the behavioral effects they seem destined to have. Pain would not be awful – it would not be the quale it is – if it did not cause agents to attempt to quiet its causes. So, surely we want an account of qualia that exhibits why they must have the behavioral effects they normally have. And the hypothesis that identifies qualia with the syntactic features of sensuous representations does just that if Sententialism rightly takes the syntactic features of a mental representation to supervene on its physical properties.

The objection concerning the Martian involved the assumption that agents whose mental representations were instantiated in quite different types of physical states might nonetheless have qualia of the same sort. This objection has a mirror image, which raises the possibility that there are agents whose mental states are physically

236

the same but whose qualia somehow diverge. This, evidently, is to posit that qualia could be inverted across agents of the same cognitive kind. But it should not be hard to see the flaw in this objection. Qualia certainly are causal. So agents with different qualia should behave differently. If Abelard and Héloïse are both in pain of the same type, then, other things being equal, they will behave the same: Both will attempt to avoid what hurts them. This they do, we say, because their qualia are installed in the same kind of physical states, states with the same causal properties. The current objection insists that Abelard and Héloïse could be in exactly the same physical states, so far as their mental representations are concerned, and yet experience different qualia. Still, if their qualia were to differ, Abelard and Héloïse would behave differently. But how could they, since, by hypothesis, they are in the same physical states, states whose behavioral effects are bound to be the same?

Much the same reply can be differently formulated. The objection allows for different qualia in agents whose mental states have the same physical and causal properties. If the objection allows this, however, there can be no reason to deny that the same agent could, at different times, realize mental states encoded in the same physical way, which mental states nevertheless are associated with different qualia on the different occasions. But if this were so, we would be frustrated in attempting to explain how the agent's various qualia could have the different behavioral consequences they must, as different qualia, have. For, holding all else the same, since the physical states instantiating the agent's qualia are, by hypothesis, the same, their effects could not differ. Thus, were we to yield to the objection, we would abdicate all hope for any sort of scientific psychology that allows for efficacious qualia. Prudence cannot counsel that.

7.4. SENSATION AND QUALIA

I have ventured that all qualia are instantiated in sensory states, that all qualia are identical with the physical properties forming the syntactic character of Mentalese representations occurrent in sensation. The leap to this hypothesis may seem rash. On the basis of the relatively clear case of pain qualia being essentially sensory, we supposed the same for all qualia. What other, hopefully better, reasons might prompt this thesis?

237

It would be handy if we had a complete list of qualia, for we could scan it for nonsensuous candidates. Of course, one reason why there is no ready list of qualia is that we do not have a regimented taxonomy for qualia. Plainly, there are lots of sensuous qualia. Relative to each sensory modality, we can think of various characteristic experiences, each recognizing for oneself what it is like so to experience. But we generally lack terms that select and discriminate among, for example, the many kinds of olfactory qualia we have. Still, once we reflect on the range of qualia with which we are acquainted, we cannot fail to appreciate that the inductive hypothesis that all qualia are delivered in sensation rests on no unrepresentative sample.

Nevertheless, there is this to consider: Abelard fears that Héloïse's brothers will assault him. He is thus in a mental state of a certain sort, evidently not a sensory state. But apparently associated with this state is a quale of a certain sort. Fear, like pain, is unpleasant and distressing; it too can be awful. But it makes little sense to say that the quale characteristic of the sort of fear felt by Abelard is realized in the syntax of the Mentalese sentence encoding his representation that Héloïse's brothers will assault him. Tokens of the same Mentalese sentence could well be encoded in Abelard without his feeling the unpleasantness of fear. Prior to coming to fear that Héloïse's brothers will assault him, Abelard might have merely considered the possibility, wondering, that is, whether Héloïse's brothers will assault him. When Abelard wonders this, he issues a Mentalese sentence of the same type as when he fears the same. When wondering rather than fearing, however, Abelard does not experience the quale associated with the fear. Hence, Abelard's encoding of the Mentalese sentence representing that Héloïse's brothers will assault him itself cannot serve to realize the quale he experiences when fearful. What does account for the quale of fear that tortures Abelard?

When Abelard fears that Héloïse's brothers will assault him, he encodes some Mentalese sentence. Were English and Mentalese the same, this sentence might be 'Héloïse's brothers will assault me'. But Abelard also desires not to be assaulted, and this he does by means of encoding, say, 'It would be dreadful for Héloïse's brother's to assault me'. Together, these two Mentalese inscriptions will have various consequences. They may cause Abelard to attempt to flee Paris, and they may cause his stomach to flutter. It is awful for

Abelard when his stomach flutters. That is, he senses the fluttering of his stomach, and that sensing takes the form of a sensuous mental representation whose syntactic properties possibly constitute the quale that Abelard experiences when fearing the assault of Héloïse's brothers.

If Abelard should happen to believe, but not fear, that Héloïse's brothers will assault him, he still will encode 'Héloïse's brothers will assault me'. But because he is not afraid, he will differ with respect to his encoding of some other Mentalese token. Perhaps he will not now encode 'It would be awful for Héloïse's brothers to assault me'. And by virtue of the absence of this inscription, his stomach will not be caused to flutter. His sensory system will therefore not detect any fluttering of his stomach, and hence there will not occur in Abelard a sensuous representation carrying the quale of fear. The idea, then, is that the qualia we associate with certain types of propositional attitudes in an agent – fear, hope, intense desire, and others – are always features of sensory states that the Mentalese sentences encoding the propositional attitudes induce within the agent.

Some will want no more of this, arguing that it depends on lots of empirical assumptions about Abelard's cognitive system and how it works, assumptions that must find their way to verification if they are finally to be accepted.

Certainly the proposal before us does depend on a clutch of empirical assumptions. Nonetheless, at this stage of our understanding of qualia, it is the very best we can do. Yes, we are hypothesizing; no, we do not have conclusive proof. But we should be cheered that we do have hypotheses that admit of disconfirmation, even if we do hope for their survival. Still, there are some comments to make on behalf of the idea that the qualia of fear and other nonsensuous mental states may devolve onto sensory states.

First, there is the obvious fact that fear, to retain the example, does produce changes in the body. Mental states certainly can have bodily effects. Those engendered by fear may be for better or worse and may or may not be detectable by the sensory system. Those that are detectable can be expected to be detected by sensory states whose syntax constitutes qualia. Such qualia are available to mark the phenomenology of fear. Why should we not suppose, then, that they account for what it is like to fear?

Second, the notion that qualia are always realized in sensory states

239

does not in any way imply that agents will understand the etiology of their qualia. One lesson to be learned from cognitive psychology is that cognitive processes are normally mysterious to those in whom they occur (Lackner and Garrett, 1973; Nisbett and Wilson, 1977). Our account of sensuous representation respects this. We suppose that sensuous predication is demonstrative. It is sheer detection and thus always less than classification. Even if it is the fluttering of Abelard's stomach that is caused by his attitudes and is represented by the sensation that constitutes his fear quale, Abelard's sensuous representation of the fluttering does not represent it as such. Rather, his sensuous representation consists of a pristinely attributive predicate applied to a purely referential demonstrative pronoun. The predicate isolates the fluttering of the stomach without categorizing it as such; the pronoun isolates the subject of the fluttering without determining what kind of thing it is that flutters. So Abelard, in sensing the condition of his stomach, need not know that it is his stomach or its fluttering he senses. Indeed, it seems most likely that the changes in Abelard's body brought about by his fear are due to chemical variations of complicated sorts. But even if Abelard has no conception of these chemical changes, much less of chemistry, he may nevertheless sense their occurrences and thereby suffer the qualia installed in his corresponding sensuous representations.

If we think of the qualia of consciousness in this way, we can count among the benefits an explanation of why *seeing* something is so phenomenologically different from *remembering* it. When Abelard spies Héloïse, he may see (i.e., infer on the basis of what he senses and what he may independently know) that Héloïse is in the window. This he does by encoding a Mentalese token to that effect. The token is itself caused by a particular sensory state induced in Abelard by Héloïse's appearance in the window. The physical character of this sensory state is the very quale Abelard takes his perceptual experience to have. Later he remembers Héloïse as in the window. Now he encodes another token of the same type as that he issued when judging, on the basis of his sensation, Héloïse to be in the window. That is why he can be said to remember what he saw. But although he remembers what he saw, the quale associated with the perceptual case is absent from the mnemonic. And this is simply because the latter occurs independent of the activation of Abelard's sensory system. Accordingly, there is no sensory state associated with the Mentalese token that instantiates Abelard's mnemonic state. Hence, there is no quale corresponding to the memory, or at least no quale of the sort characteristic of the perception from which the memory is derived.

More generally, then, whether a cognitive state carries with it anything that consciousness would recognize as a quale – whether, that is, being in a certain type of cognitive state has a characteristic "feel" to it – is a straightforward function of its link to sensation. If a cognitive state's relation to sensation is remote, then that state will not be phenomenologically distinguished from other such states. Perhaps wishing and believing, despite all their great cognitive differences, are not phenomenologically different. Does believing that Abelard was a great philosopher feel different from wishing the same? Apparently not, but if these different attitudes in fact do feel different, it is because of their different connections to sensation.

When we think about what it is like to be conscious, we naturally find ourselves wondering about what to say about paradigmatic qualia such as those characteristic of sensations of pain and color. Nevertheless, we should not let this obscure the fact that consciousness is a matter of moods as well. Perhaps we can indicate what it is like for Abelard to feel pain, but what should we say of the sorrow that overcomes him upon his final separation from Héloïse? If we want to understand what it is like to be Abelard, we must appreciate not only what it is like for him to feel pain but also what it is like for him to be sorrowful in particular, and moody in general.[11]

Moods persist over time and fluctuate in intensity, but while they last, they tend to affect the flow of thought. Abelard, in his sorrow, is more inclined to think of Héloïse than he is to ponder logic, and

---

11 Haugeland (1981b, pp. 270–2) remarks that cognitive models of mentation are hard pressed to explain moods. These models make much of the linguistic structure of mental processes, but moods, he claims, defy analysis in terms of what we know of linguistic information processing: "Moods permeate and affect all kinds of cognitive states and processes, and yet, on the face of it, they don't seem at all cognitive themselves. That suggests, at least until someone shows otherwise, that moods can neither be segregated from the explanation of cognition, nor incorporated in a Cognitivist explanation" (pp. 271–2).

when he does consider problems in logic, he finds them more difficult to solve than he normally would. He is generally disinterested in what previously fascinated him. His appetite atrophies, and sleep comes grudgingly. And beyond all this, he just feels a certain way. What to make of this?

We can take a hint from the discussion in the previous section. There we recognized that some qualia, fear in the example, are properties of sensory states caused by propositional attitudes within an agent. Moods may be much the same, as the etiology of Abelard's sorrow suggests. It is only after he learns that he will not soon, if ever again, see Héloïse that Abelard succumbs to sorrow. This suggests that this mood is the result of some of Abelard's beliefs. These, we know, are propositional attitudes realized as Mentalese inscriptions encoded within Abelard. As such they have various effects, some of which are purely cognitive, some of which may be sensory. His belief that he may never again see Héloïse causes Abelard to find it difficult to solve logic problems. This may be because the inscription of this belief, *like the inscription of any belief*, tends to have characteristic cognitive results that effectively preclude certain other types of cognitive events. Abelard's belief that he may never again see Héloïse causes him to believe that his life will be empty and meaningless, and, by way of causing this belief and others, it effectively prevents Abelard from thinking about logic. This is a straightforward cognitive phenomenon. When Abelard is not sad, his interest in logic, as exhibited by various of his beliefs, may, by virtue of their causal properties, prevent him from thinking of Héloïse. Thus, that Abelard's sorrow controls the direction of his thoughts is to be attributed to the fact that his sorrow involves his having certain beliefs that have, as beliefs will, certain cognitive consequences. To say that Abelard is in the *grip* of sorrow, then, is, in part, to say both that, as always, Abelard's cognitive processing system is generating conclusions from certain selected beliefs and that the beliefs currently selected for processing are such that their processing precludes the processing of others.

Of course, there is more to sorrow and its grip than this. Abelard, if sad, also feels a certain way for a certain period of time. This we may suppose is because the beliefs that consume Abelard's cognitive mechanisms also have effects within other parts of his body that, in turn, affect his sensory system. The resulting sensory states, as sensory states, carry qualia identical with physical properties of the

242

sensory states. Most likely there are various types of sensory states activated by the effects of Abelard's cognitive processing. If so, the feeling of sorrow may amount to the summation of the various qualia determined by all the activated sensory states. Indeed, this seems almost assured if the sorrow Abelard feels varies in quality and intensity over time. That the feeling of sorrow persists for as long as it does falls to the simple fact that the relevant sensory states endure for as long as they collectively do, this being jointly determined by the temporal spread of their own bodily causes and the nature of the sensory states themselves.

Generally, then, moods are best understood as exhibiting a dual character. They consist, in the first part, of certain propositional attitudes together with the cognitive effects of these attitudes. So much for the fact that moods influence or dictate an agent's train of thought, blocking some avenues and opening others. For the second part, moods involve qualia. They are realized in the form of the physical properties of sensory states whose causal history runs back through bodily events themselves caused by the propositional attitudes forming the cognitive aspect of the moods.

This account of moods evidently roots occurrences of moods in specific propositional attitudes. Abelard's sorrow specifically pertains to his believing that he may never again see Héloïse. But what of "free-floating" moods that do not appear connected with any particular cognitive episode? Héloïse says that she feels depressed; she does not know why. She is just depressed.

So-called free-floating depression might not be free at all. That is, some precise cognitive event, some specific belief, may be central to Héloïse's depression. She might be depressed today because of what she heard last week, even though she herself has no idea whatsoever that her hearing what she did is the cause of her depression. Certainly the whole point of particular types of counseling is to expose those of an agent's cognitive states that may, but unbeknown to the agent, contribute to his or her mood. And nothing in the present account of moods implies that an agent must be appraised of those of his or her cognitive states that may make for the mood of the moment.

Nevertheless, perhaps there are moods that do float free of any cognitive moorings. Perhaps Héloïse might, when all is said and done, feel depressed regardless of what she might happen to believe. Some drugs may affect an agent's mood without altering his or her beliefs. But this too fits with the current account of moods. For moods are, at least typically, compound, with cognitive and sensory components. If so, genuinely free-floating depression might simply amount to the occurrence of the types of sensory states normally brought on by depressing beliefs but now induced by something else. In such an event, the qualia characteristic of depression would be realized in the relevant sensory states in isolation from the cognitive states that would, in normal circumstances, bring about the sensory states. Should Héloïse suffer a genuinely free-floating depression, she would suffer the types of sensory states usually caused by depressing beliefs, but which, as a matter of abnormal fact, happen to be caused by some chemical aberration. In this case, she would suffer the qualia characteristic of depression without having any depressing beliefs. All this would be essentially consistent with the current account of moods, so long as the bodily events registered by sensory states characteristic of moods can be caused by noncognitive episodes.

7.6. THE SUBJECTIVITY OF CONSCIOUSNESS

The quale characteristic of a type of episode of consciousness is, according to the evolving proposal, identical with the syntactic properties of the sensuous Mentalese representation occurrent in that episode. These properties are themselves just the physical properties of the sensory state encoding the sensuous representation that fix the physical kind of the state and account for its causal connections to its source, other mental states, and behavior. So, one way to know what it is like to be Abelard is to understand the physical nature of his sensuous representation. What better way is there to comprehend the physical nature of Abelard's sensuous representations than to learn the objectively scientific analysis of the physical properties constituting the essential features of those representations? Surely there is none. Thus, in order best to understand the nature of consciousness, we must discover all we can about the physical composition of systems of mental representation. Find out what Abelard is made of, and you will thereby understand what it is like to be Abelard.

Some philosophers are convinced that this must be wrong. Nagel (1974) and Jackson (1982, 1986) worry that even an exhaustive understanding of the physical would leave us thoroughly ignorant of the phenomenal.[12] The objection to any physicalistic analysis of qualia seems to be that such an analysis would necessarily fail to convey what it is like, *really* like, to be conscious. No matter what we might know of the physical character of sensory states, we would not thereby fully appreciate what, for example, it is like to sense color – this, that is, if the objection is sound.

To make his point, Jackson asks us to imagine a situation in which Héloïse is transformed into a future brilliant neuroscientist who, for reasons that are irrelevant to the description of her case, has never seen colors besides black and white. Perhaps she has lived only in a contrived, enclosed, monochromatic environment. She monitors events beyond her immediate vicinity through a black-and-white television monitor. Jackson's claim is that, because of her deep understanding of neurology, Héloïse might understand all there is to know of the physical properties involved in color sensation. But, Jackson asks, who could be so blind as not to see that Héloïse must, because of her sensory deprivation, fail to appreciate fully what it is like to see colors? Is it not plain that if Héloïse is released from her drab prison and at last granted direct vision of colors, she herself would testify that she previously did not understand and, so long as she was prevented from sensing colors, never could have understood what it was like to see them? Thus one cannot understand what, in particular, it is like to be conscious of colors or what, in general, it is like to be conscious of anything simply by knowing all there is to know of the physical nature of a conscious system. Consciousness is finally subjective; a full appreciation of what it is to be conscious cannot amount only to objective knowledge of the physical. The only way to know what it is like to be a thing of a conscious kind is to experience what and as things of that kind do. No amount of objective description of any sort will suffice. You just have to be there to know what it is like.

This thought experiment does bite deeply. But upon reflection, its proper interpretation would seem not to favor the idea that consciousness is ultimately accessible only subjectively. Remember that the account of Héloïse's situation attributes to her an understanding of *all* there is to know regarding the physical nature of

12 Jackson's views will occupy us here. For related discussions, see Lewis (1983), Horgan (1984), and Conee (1985). Regarding Nagel, see Nimerow (1980). On both Jackson and Nagel, see Paul Churchland (1985a) and Maloney (1985a).

color vision. So, she must after all know exactly what, for example, it is like to see red. It is to be in some determinate physical state, S, and Héloïse knows all about this state. She knows how it is constituted and how it affects and is affected by all other types of states to which it is related within the sensory system. The causes and effects of tokens of S-type states are evident to her, and she can describe them ad nauseam. This is crucial. For should Héloïse at last be exposed to colors, she would describe her experience in just the sort of language that she has always used to describe color vision. When she sees her first burst of red, she will report her sensory system as being in state S. And although she admits to never having been in this state before, Héloïse will insist that it is just as she had expected. After all, she had always expected that this state would be caused as it actually was, would have the effects in her that it now does, and would have – just as it now does – the characteristic physical features of S-type states. What else could there be to it, she will ask?

Perhaps the suspicion is that Héloïse remains, even when released from her enclosure, still a prisoner of sorts. Her language, by virtue of her history, is so limited as to prevent her from describing fully what she is now experiencing. Had she only been raised and educated like the rest of us, she would describe her sensation of color quite differently, and that would show that, prior to actually sensing colors, she had no idea what it is like to see them.

This retort just will not do. It begs the question. Precisely how, we may inquire, is it to be established that Héloïse's scientific language is inadequately expressive, that it somehow hampers her enjoyment of color? True, she does not describe her experiences as we do, but this may be attributed to our ignorance of what it is *really* like to be conscious of color. If we had a deep understanding of what it is like to be conscious of color, perhaps we too would describe it as Héloïse does. Certainly she, as opposed to us, has the better claim to understanding the character of color vision. After all, she knows the science of color vision, finally sees colors, and recounts her experiences in a language that relates her experience to the science she knows. We are ignorant of much of what Héloïse knows and so are locked into different descriptions of our color states. Sadly for us, our descriptions convey much less information than do hers. Whereas Héloïse's enable her to predict and explain color sensations, ours stand as obstacles to our understanding. The proof of this is that if we were to become as fluent in Héloïse's method of description, prediction, and explanation of color vision as she is, we too would describe our color sensations as she does. Should we come to understand what Héloïse does, we would appreciate the quantum leap in understanding of the phenomenology of color vision that her knowledge, couched as it is in the vocabulary of science, offers. We would be sobered to see exposed the dogmatism that drove us to deny Héloïse the understanding she had long had. Consciousness is a physical phenomenon, and the only way to understand it fully is to get busy in the laboratory. It is only there that we have any chance of assaying the properties that constitute sensory states. Those states are bound to be physical, and the sooner we learn to talk about them, the sooner we will confidently speak of the true character of the qualia that invigorate consciousness (Paul Churchland, 1979).

7.7. WHAT IT IS LIKE TO BE DIFFERENT

It is the height of chauvinism to suppose oneself alone to be conscious. One step removed from this is to postulate that consciousness is peculiar to our species. Surely those intelligent species way out on our limb of the phylogenetic tree are conscious, even if it is difficult to estimate where else in the boughs and how far down along the trunk consciousness might have managed to evolve. Nonetheless, although we may be quick to concede consciousness to other types of intelligent animals, we must suspect that whatever it is like to be an individual of one of these conscious kinds, it must be very different from what it is like to be one of ourselves. With Nagel (1974), then, we might fret that bats, for example, are conscious but in a way strikingly different from the way in which we are. If the mental reach of bats is as distinct from ours as it seems, what can we know about what it is like to be a bat?

There are important cognitive differences that separate us from bats. We can write, understand, and enjoy poetry; they cannot. This, if it serves relevantly to differentiate us from bats, must be due to the great differences in the computational powers between the system of mental representations respectively deployed by humans and bats. Certainly, if bats are conscious, they must have cognitive capacities. And if Sententialism is correct, cognition requires a medium of computation, a mental language. So bats, if

247

conscious, must use, well, Batese – a mental language suited to their own cognitive demands. Part, then, of what distinguishes what it is to be a bat from what it is to be human falls to the differences in the computational and representational resources differentiating Mentalese from Batese.

This is not to say that what it is like to be a bat is simply to use a system of mental representation with the same semantic tricks as Batese. The suspicion will not be quiet that says that even if a person were either to know what a particular bat is thinking or, even better, actually to have thoughts with the same presumably impoverished content as the bat's, that person still would not fully know or experience what it is like to be a bat. If this worry is well founded, it amounts to asking two distinct questions: First, what would a person need to know in order to *know* what it is like to be a bat? Second, what would a person need to *experience* in order to *enjoy* or *suffer* the consciousness of a bat?

We can elicit the difference between these two questions by considering the characterization of Héloïse in the preceding section. There, reconstructing Jackson's example, we supposed Héloïse to be a knowledgeable neuroscientist informed about all the physical properties of sensory states implicated in color vision. We argued that, by virtue of understanding all there is to understand about the physiology of color vision, Héloïse would *know* exactly what it is like to sense color. But this was not to attribute to her the qualia occurrent in one who does sense color. For Héloïse actually to have or experience such qualia, she would, of course, need to be in the sort of sensory states she understands so well.

Returning to the difference between the two questions lately asked, we can see that the first takes as its answer an account of the physical nature of the representational system of bats. Héloïse was able to know what it is like to sense color by way of knowing all about the physical properties of the visual system. This is because the states of the visual system count as sensuous representations of color, and, by hypothesis, the qualia of color vision are nothing but the physical properties of sensory states that place those states in their physical and, therefore, syntactic types. One can answer the second question by attending to what was required of Héloïse in order that she experience color vision. She had to leave her monochromatic environment so that her own sensory system could be stimulated by colors. Once her sensory system was thus acti-

248

vated, it took on the states characteristic of color vision, and Héloïse immediately experienced what it is to enjoy consciousness of color.

We can now apply all this to bats. If we want to know what it is like to be a bat, it suffices to determine what goes on in a bat's sensory system. In particular, we will need to know what, from a physical point of view, counts as sensuous Batese tokens. We will need to understand the physical properties of these tokens determining the tokens' physical kinds. These properties we will take to determine the syntactic properties of sensuous Batese representations. And knowing this, we will know everything there is to know about the qualia in which bats are awash. We will understand what their qualia are made of and both how and why they interact. When we are informed of this, nothing will prevent us from adopting the roles of linguists engaged in devising a translation scheme for an alien language. We might, that is, do our best to note the correlations between variations in occurrences of Batese expressions and variations in the activity of bats. If we are very fortunate and have lots of patience and just as much funding, we might confirm, within the tolerance allowed in the practice of translation, some of the hypotheses taking Batese into English. Most likely, perhaps even inevitably, it will turn out that bats just have a different way of looking at things, that many of the expressions in their system of mental representation simply do not align in any natural way with English. Should this be so, we would still know, by virtue of knowing the physiology of sensation in bats, whatever one could want to know about bat qualia. Still, we would not have any idea as to how, recalling one of the notions of rationality discussed in Chapter 3, the behavior of bats is rational relative to the contents of the computational states that cause behavior. But even if we should fail finally to comprehend how the behavior of bats is rational relative to what their cognitive states represent, that would be no bar whatsoever to our knowing what, with respect to qualia, it is like to be a bat. Knowing that requires only knowing the syntax of Batese as realized in the physical states of the sensory system of bats.

With respect to the second question, that of what a person would need to experience in order to enjoy or suffer the consciousness of a bat, the answer should now be plain. One would need to undergo sensory states the same in physical kind as those found in bats. Because bats and humans are both mammals with sensory systems that share some of the same evolutionary history, it is not manifestly impossible that humans and bats do, in fact, share some sensory states of the same type. Thus, for all we know, even if we do not now *know* what it is like to be a bat, we naturally do experience some of the qualia that bats do. There is nothing particularly surprising in this possibility. Certainly, however, great differences remain. Among the sensory systems of bats, the auditory system – if not the others – differs greatly from ours. Bats are sensitive to sounds we cannot hear; their auditory systems operate on frequencies distant from those perceptible to us. Surely, then, bats do undergo sensory states different in physical character from those we suffer; Batese, in large part, thus must conform to a different syntax than does Mentalese. And thus, since qualia correspond to the syntactic features of sensory states, the qualia bats experience must, for the most part, differ from those experienced by humans.

This may inspire an objection to the thesis that qualia are to be identified with the physical properties of sensory states. Let us suppose that bats and humans are both sensitive to a certain common sort of stimulus. Both suffer burns when too closely exposed to fire. When Abelard is burned, he feels pain. The quale of his pain is identical to that property of his sensory state that certifies the state as the physical kind of sensory state it is. When a bat is burned, it too, we say, feels pain. Indeed, judging from the stimuli to which Abelard and the bat react and how they react, we might suppose that the quale of the bat's pain is exactly the same as Abelard's. What should we say, however, in the event that we also discover that the kind of sensory state that registers pain in the bat is, since the sensory systems of bats and humans differ in some physical detail, different in physical kind from the sensory state that serves to encode Abelard's pain? If qualia are identical with properties of sensory states, then the quale we call 'pain' in Abelard simply could not be the same as the quale we call 'pain' in the bat. That is, the identification of sensory qualia with properties of sensory states effectively precludes identifying the so-called pain qualia in Abelard with those of the bat. And the objection takes this to be an untoward consequence of identifying qualia and sensory properties. For it falsifies the supposed truth that Abelard and the bat both feel the same type of pain.

Nevertheless, once we are apprised of the physical differences between the sensory systems of humans and bats, this seems to be

250

exactly the right reading of the example. We simply take 'pain', insofar as it designates qualia, to be ambiguous across attributions to humans and bats. Even if this may appear to be the proper reaction to the example of pain in bats and humans, the case is not as plain when we consider qualia of an order other than pain. To be fearful is, recall, to suffer a certain quale. We know what it is like, and there seems to be no reason to suppose that other creatures with intelligence to match our own might not also be capable of suffering fear. Let Martians be so intelligent, but assume that just as the sensory systems of bats and humans differ in physical detail without precluding consciousness among bats, so too do the sensory systems of Martians and humans differ. This is not to say that Martians have the same sensory apparatus as do bats but, rather, that Martians, like bats, do not have all and only the same kinds of sensory states as do humans. Abelard fears that the sun will fall from the sky. That is, he has a certain propositional attitude encoded in a nonsensuous Mentalese representation whose content is that the sun will fall from the sky. This representation causes Abelard's heart to palpitate, which in turn affects his sensory system so as to produce a sensuous representation of the palpitation. Physical properties of the sensuous representation constitute the fear quale suffered by Abelard. Some Martian, however, also fears that the sun will fall from the sky, and the result of this is that something in the Martian wiggles. The Martian's sensory system reacts, and physical properties of the resulting sensory state form the Martian's fear quale. But, and here is the rub, the sensory states of Abelard and his Martian partner in fear might very well be of different physical kinds. And that would imply that the qualia in Abelard and the Martian differ. This entails, counterintuitively, that Abelard and the Martian would not, after all, both be fearful. Surely, the objection urges, this is wrong. Certainly, it must be that both are fearful, especially if, as we might additionally assume, their behavior is effectively the same.

Yes, both Abelard and the Martian are fearful in the sense that they both have the same propositional attitude and both behave much the same. And no, they are not both fearful in the sense that what it is like to experience Abelard's quale simply is not at all like what it is to experience the Martian's. 'Fear' and its inflections ambiguously refer to propositional attitudes and qualia. We can, then, endorse attributions of fear to both Abelard and the Martian

251

while conceding that they suffer different types of sensory states. This so long as we deny that common attributions of fear to these two agents do not, if true, serve to attribute common qualia. Thus, when 'fear' refers to an agent's nonsensuous propositional attitude, we can know what it is like for a Martian so to fear. For in the same sense of the term, we need only know what it is like for ourselves to fear that the sun will fall from the sky. Indeed, in this sense of 'fear', we can ourselves experience what it is to fear à la Martian. It suffices that we entertain the same propositional attitude. Moreover, when we take 'fear' to refer to the Martian's quale caused by his, her, or its propositional attitude, we can know what it is like for a Martian so to fear so long as we understand the physical nature of the properties of the Martian's sensory state that constitute the quale embodied in the state. That is all there is to know about what it is like to be a fearful Martian. Of course, to know any or all of this is not to experience a Martian's fear quale. That evidently requires instantiating in one's sensory system the physical properties constitutive of the Martian's quale. And by hypothesis, our sensory systems cannot tolerate such properties. So, although we can know all there is to know about what it is like to be a fearful Martian, we cannot in every sense of 'fear' feel the fear that may plague a Martian.

7.8. ARTIFICIAL CONSCIOUSNESS

Chapter 5 presented an argument that conformity to a formal program of a certain sort does not suffice for genuine intelligence. Such conformity alone does not establish that the states of the device transformed in accordance with the program have, as mental states must, content. To mend this, we hypothesized that mentation must be based in matter of a specified kind. But even if this should prove correct, it remains quite possible that real intelligence can be artificially created. All that should be necessary is that the proper type of program be artificially installed in the proper type of matter in the proper way. There seems to be no principled reason why artifice, as opposed to nature, could not effect the right combination of the right elements so as to ensure the instantiation, perhaps even in an improved form, of intelligence.

Once we recognize that, at bottom, all intelligence possibly shares a common material substrate, we should not flinch at the idea that artificially intelligent devices could have rich conscious lives. All that is necessary for artificially intelligent devices to be conscious is that they contain sensory systems that conform to the physical dictates nature imposes on sensation. If artificially intelligent devices include such sensory systems, the physical properties of their sensory states will qualify as qualia just as surely as ours do.

This is not to say that an artificially conscious device has to feel as we do. After all, naturally conscious kinds – humans, bats, and perhaps Martians – can, by virtue of having sensory systems of different detail, experience different kinds of qualia. Thus, should an artificially conscious device have a sensory apparatus whose states are different in kind from those occurrent in our own sensory system, what it is like to be that device will differ from what it is like to be one of us. Of course, we can know exactly what it is like to be that device, just as we can know what it is like to be a bat or a Martian. Nonetheless, we will not be able to experience as the device does – we will not have its qualia. This is because, by assumption, its sensory system relies on physical states that differ from ours as do different species of a common genus.

So much, then, for the problem of other minds: Who is conscious, and what is it like to be conscious? We philosophers can talk about it forever in the classroom, over coffee, and at our annual meetings. Still, *we* shall never discern the final answer. What matters to having a mind is, first of all, the matter, and only our colleagues across campus with the large, expensive laboratories are in a position to find what is the matter with being consciously intelligent. Someday, it is to be hoped, some bright graduate student over there will be awarded a Nobel prize for writing a dissertation explaining to all of us what makes an idea substantial. Perhaps, when that happens, we might even have begun to learn how to treat other conscious creatures. But to understand that completely, we will need to march back across campus to the philosophy department. For once we have a completed science of the cognitive and conscious, we shall more than ever before need a science of the conscience.

References

Abelard, Peter. 1964. *The Story of Abelard's Adversities*. Trans. J. T. Muckle. Toronto: Pontifical Institute of Mediaeval Studies.

Anderson, J., and G. Bower. 1973. *Human Associative Memory*. Washington, D.C.: Winston.

Anderson, John. 1980. *Cognitive Psychology and Its Implications*. San Francisco: Freeman.

 1983. *The Architecture of Cognition*. Cambridge, Mass.: Harvard University Press.

Armstrong, David. 1962. *Bodily Sensations*. London: Routledge & Kegan Paul.

 1968. *A Materialist Theory of the Mind*. London: Routledge & Kegan Paul.

 1973. *Belief, Truth, and Knowledge*. Cambridge: Cambridge University Press.

Augustine. 1953. "De Magistro." In J. H. S. Burleigh (trans.), *Augustine's Earlier Writings*, Vol. VI, LCC. Philadelphia: Westminster Press.

Baker, Lynne Rudder. 1985. "A Farewell to Functionalism." *Philosophical Studies*, 48: 1–14.

 1987. *Saving Belief*. Princeton, N.J.: Princeton University Press.

Bennett, Jonathon. 1964. *Rationality*. London: Routledge & Kegan Paul.

 1976. *Linguistic Behavior*. Cambridge: Cambridge University Press.

Block, Ned. 1980a. "Troubles with Functionalism." In C. W. Savage (ed.), *Perception and Cognition: Issues in the Foundations of Psychology. Minnesota Studies in the Philosophy of Science*. Vol. 9. Minneapolis: University of Minnesota Press, pp. 261–325.

 1980b. "Are Absent Qualia Possible?" *Philosophical Review*, 89: 257–74.

 1980c. *Readings in Philosophy of Psychology*, Vol. 1. Cambridge, Mass.: Harvard University Press.

 1980d. "What Is Functionalism?" In Block, 1980c, pp. 171–84.

 1981a. *Readings in Philosophy of Psychology*, Vol. 2. Cambridge, Mass.: Harvard University Press.

 1981b. *Imagery*. Cambridge, Mass.: MIT Press/Bradford Books.

 1983a. "Mental Pictures and Cognitive Science." *Philosophical Review*, 92: 499–542.

 1983b. "The Photographic Fallacy in the Debate about Mental Imagery." *Noûs*, 17: 651–61.

Block, Ned, and Jerry Fodor. 1972. "What Psychological States Are Not." *Philosophical Review*, 81: 159–81.

Bobrow, D., and A. Collins. 1975. *Representation and Understanding*. New York: Academic Press.

Bobrow, D., and T. Winograd. 1977. "An Overview of KRL, a Knowledge Representation Language." *Cognitive Science*, 1: 3–46.

Boden, Margaret. 1977. *Artificial Intelligence and Natural Man*. New York: Basic Books.

Brand, Myles. 1984. *Intending and Acting*. Cambridge, Mass.: MIT Press/ Bradford Books.

Brentano, Franz. 1874. "The Distinction Between Mental and Physical Phenomena." Translated by D. B. Terrell in R. M. Chisholm (ed.), *Realism and the Background of Phenomenology*. Glencoe, Ill.: The Free Press, 1960, pp. 39–61.

Brown, J. 1958. "Some Tests of Decay Theory of Immediate Memory." *Quarterly Journal of Experimental Psychology*, 10: 12–21.

Burdick, Howard. 1982. "A Logical Form for the Propositional Attitudes." *Synthese*, 52: 185–230.

Burge, Tyler. 1977. "Belief *De Re*." *Journal of Philosophy*, 74: 338–62.

1978. "Belief and Synonymy." *Journal of Philosophy*, 75: 119–38.

1979. "Individualism and the Mental." In P. A. French, T. E. Uehling, and H. K. Wettstein (eds.), *Midwest Studies in Philosophy: Studies in Metaphysics*. Vol. 4. Minneapolis: University of Minnesota Press, pp. 73–122.

1982. "Other Bodies." In Andrew Woodfield (ed.), *Thought and Object*. Oxford: Clarendon Press, pp. 97–119.

Cam, Philip. 1985. "Dennett on Intelligent Storage." *Philosophy and Phenomenological Research*, 45: 263–72.

Campbell, Keith. 1966. "Colours." In R. Brown and C. D. Rollins (eds.), *Contemporary Philosophy in Australia*. New York: Humanities Press, pp. 132–57.

Castañeda, Hector-Neri. 1972. "Thinking and the Structure of the World." *Philosophia*, 4: 3–40.

1975. *Thinking and Doing*. Dordrecht: Reidel.

Chisholm, Roderick. 1966. "Freedom and Action." In K. Lehrer (ed.), *Freedom and Determinism*. New York: Random House, pp. 28–44.

Chomsky, Noam. 1959. "Review of Skinner's *Verbal Behavior*." *Language*, 35: 26–58.

1968. *Language and Mind*. New York: Harcourt, Brace & World.

1980. *Rules and Representations*. New York: Columbia University Press.

Churchland, Patricia Smith. 1978. "Fodor on Language Learning." *Synthese*, 38: 149–59.

1980a. "Language, Thought and Information Processing." *Noûs*, 14: 147–70.

1980b. "A Perspective on Mind-Brain Research." *Journal of Philosophy*, 87: 185–207.

1983. "Consciousness: The Transmutation of a Concept." *Pacific Philosophical Quarterly*, 64: 80–95.

Churchland, Patricia Smith, and Paul Churchland. 1981. "Functionalism, Qualia, and Intentionality." *Philosophical Topics*, 12: 121–45.

1983. "Stalking the Wild Epistemic Engine." *Noûs*, 17: 5–18.

Churchland, Paul. 1970. "The Logical Character of Action Explanations." *Philosophical Review*, 79: 214–36.

1975. "Popper's Philosophy of Science." *Canadian Journal of Philosophy*, 5: 145–56.

1979. *Scientific Realism and the Plasticity of Mind*. Cambridge: Cambridge University Press.

1981. "Eliminative Materialism and the Propositional Attitudes." *Journal of Philosophy*, 78: 67–90.

1982. "Is *Thinker* a Natural Kind?" *Dialogue*, 21: 223–38.

1985a. "Reduction, Qualia and the Direct Introspection of Brain States." *Journal of Philosophy*, 82: 8–28.

1985b. "Conceptual Progress and Word/World Relations: In Search of the Essence of Natural Kinds." *Canadian Journal of Philosophy*, 15: 1–17.

1986a. "Cognitive Neurobiology: A Computational Hypothesis for Laminar Cortex." *Biology and Philosophy*, 1: 25–51.

1986b. "Some Reductive Strategies in Cognitive Neurobiology." *Mind*, 95: 279–309.

1988. "Perceptual Plasticity and Theoretical Neutrality: A Reply to Jerry Fodor." *Philosophy of Science*, 55: 167–87.

Clark, Romane. 1970. "The Sensuous Content of Experience." *Noûs*, 4: 311–35.

1978. "Not Every Object of Thought Has Being: A Paradox in Naive Predication Theory." *Noûs*, 12: 181–8.

Cole, David. 1984. "Thought and Thought Experiments." *Philosophical Studies*, 45: 431–44.

Conee, Earl. 1984. "A Defense of Pain." *Philosophical Studies*, 46: 239–48.

1985. "Physicalism and Phenomenal Properties." *Philosophical Quarterly*, 35: 296–302.

Cummins, Robert. 1983. *The Nature of Psychological Explanation*. Cambridge, Mass.: MIT Press/Bradford Books.

Davidson, Donald. 1963. "Actions, Reasons and Causes." *Journal of Philosophy*, 60: 685–700.

1970. "Mental Events." In L. Foster and J. W. Swanson (eds.), *Experience and Theory*. Amherst: University of Massachusetts Press, pp. 79–101.

1974. "On the Very Idea of a Conceptual Scheme." *Addresses and Proceedings of the American Philosophical Association*, 47: 5–20.

1975. "Thought and Talk." In S. Guttenplan (ed.), *Mind and Language*. Oxford: Oxford University Press, pp. 7–22. Reprinted in Davidson's *Inquiries into Truth and Meaning*. Oxford: Clarendon Press, pp. 155–70.

1979. "Quotation." *Theory and Decision*, 11: 27–40.

1982. "Rational Animals." *Dialectica*, 36: 317–28.

Davis, Lawrence, 1982. "Functionalism and Absent Qualia." *Philosophical Studies*, 41: 231–50.

Dennett, Daniel C. 1969. *Content and Consciousness*. London: Routledge & Kegan Paul.
1978a. "Toward a Cognitive Theory of Consciousness." In Dennett, *Brainstorms*. Montgomery, Vt.: Bradford Books, pp. 149–73.
1978b. "A Cure for the Common Code." In Dennett, *Brainstorms*, pp. 90–108.
1978c. "Intentional Systems." In Dennett, *Brainstorms*, pp. 3–22.
1978d. "Brain Writing and Mind Reading." In Dennett, *Brainstorms*, pp. 39–50.
1978e. "Artificial Intelligence as Philosophy and Psychology." In Dennett, *Brainstorms*, pp. 109–26.
1978f. "How to Change Your Mind." In Dennett, *Brainstorms*, pp. 300–9.
1978g. "Mechanism and Responsibility." In Dennett, *Brainstorms*, pp. 233–255.
1978h. "Why You Can't Make a Computer That Feels Pain." In Dennett, *Brainstorms*, pp. 190–229.
1980. "The Milk of Human Intentionality." *Behavioral and Brain Sciences*, 3: 428.
1982a. "Beyond Belief." In A. Woodfield (ed.), *Thought and Object*. Oxford: Clarendon Press, pp. 1–95.
1982b. "How to Study Consciousness Empirically or Nothing Comes to Mind." *Synthese*, 53: 159–80.
1984. *Elbow Room*. Cambridge, Mass.: MIT Press/Bradford Books.
Dennett, Daniel, and John Searle. 1982. "The Myth of the Computer: An Exchange." *New York Review of Books*, June 24: 56–7.
Descartes, René. 1649. *Passions of the Soul*. In J. Cottingham, R. Stoothoff, and D. Murdoch (trans.), *The Philosophical Writings of Descartes*. Cambridge: Cambridge University Press, 1985, pp. 325–404.
Dretske, Fred I. 1981. *Knowledge and the Flow of Information*. Cambridge, Mass.: MIT Press/Bradford Books.
1985. "Machines and the Mental." *Proceedings and Addresses of the American Philosophical Association*, 59: 23–33.
1988. *Explaining Behavior*. Cambridge, Mass.: MIT Press/Bradford Books.
Dreyfus, Hurbert. 1979. *What Computers Can't Do*. New York: Harper & Row.
1981. "From Micro-Worlds to Knowledge: AI at an Impasse." In J. Haugeland (ed.), *Mind Design*. Cambridge, Mass.: MIT Press/Bradford Books, pp. 161–204.
Eckardt, Barbara. 1984. "Cognitive Psychology and Principled Skepticism." *Journal of Philosophy*, 81: 67–88.
Eells, E. 1982. *Rational Decision and Causality*. Cambridge: Cambridge University Press.
Evans, Gareth. 1973. "The Causal Theory of Names." *Proceedings of the Aristotelian Society*, n.s., supp. vol. 47: 187–208.
Feyerabend, Paul. 1962. "Explanation, Reduction, and Empiricism." In

257

H. Feigl and G. Maxwell (eds.), *Minnesota Studies in the Philosophy of Science*. Vol. 3. Minneapolis: University of Minnesota Press, pp. 28–97.

1963. "Materialism and the Mind-Body Problem." *Review of Metaphysics*, 17: 49–66.

1970. "Against Method: Outline of an Anarchistic Theory of Knowledge." In M. Radner and S. Winokur (eds.), *Minnesota Studies in the Philosophy of Science*. Vol. 4. Minneapolis: University of Minnesota Press, pp. 17–130.

Field, Hartry. 1977. "Mental Representations." *Erkenntnis*, 13: 9–18.

Finke, R. A. 1980. "Levels of Equivalence in Imagery and Perception." *Psychological Review*, 87: 113–32.

Flanagan, Owen J. 1984. *The Science of the Mind*. Cambridge, Mass.: MIT Press/Bradford Books.

Fodor, Jerry. 1968. *Psychological Explanation*. New York: Random House.

1975. *The Language of Thought*. New York: Thomas Crowell.

1980a. "Methodological Solipsism Considered as a Research Strategy in Cognitive Psychology." *Behavioral and Brain Sciences*, 3: 63–109 (including peer review).

1980b. "Searle on What Only Brains Can Do." *Behavioral and Brain Sciences*, 3: 431.

1981a. "The Present Status of the Innateness Controversy." In Fodor, *Representations*. Cambridge, Mass.: MIT Press/Bradford Books, pp. 257–316.

1981b. "Computation and Reduction." In Fodor, *Representations*, pp. 146–74.

1981c. "Tom Swift and His Procedural Grandmother." In Fodor, *Representations*, pp. 204–24.

1981d. "Three Cheers for Propositional Attitudes." In Fodor, *Representations*, pp. 100–23.

1983. *Modularity of Mind*. Cambridge, Mass.: MIT Press/Bradford Books.

1984a. "Semantics, Wisconsin Style." *Synthese*, 59: 231–50.

1984b. "Observation Reconsidered." *Philosophy of Science*, 51: 23–43.

1985. "Fodor's Guide to Mental Representation: The Intelligent Auntie's Vade-Mecum." *Mind*, 94: 76–100.

1987. *Psychosemantics*. Cambridge, Mass.: MIT Press/Bradford Books.

1988. "A Reply to Churchland's Perceptual Plasticity and Theoretical Neutrality." *Philosophy of Science*, 55: 188–98.

Follesdal, D. 1982. "The Status of Rationality Assumptions in Interpretation and Explanation of Action." *Dialectica*, 36: 301–16.

Frege, Gottlob. 1892. "On Sense and Reference." In P. Geach and M. Black (eds.), *Translations from the Philosophical Writings of Gottlob Frege*. Oxford: Blackwell, 1960, pp. 56–78.

1918–19. "The Thought: A Logical Inquiry." Trans. A. M. and M. Quinton in E. D. Klempke (ed.), *Essays on Frege*. Urbana: University of Illinois Press, 1968, pp. 507–36.

Garcia, J., B. K. McGowan, and K. F. Green. 1972. "Biological Con-

258

straints on Conditioning." In A. H. Black and W. F. Prokasy (eds.), *Classical Conditioning II: Current Research and Theory*. New York: Appleton-Century-Crofts.

Gibson, James J. 1966. *The Senses Considered as Perceptual Systems*. Boston: Houghton Mifflin.

Goldman, Alvin. 1970. *A Theory of Human Action*. Englewood Cliffs, N.J.: Prentice-Hall.

1986. *Epistemology and Cognition*. Cambridge, Mass.: Harvard University Press.

Goodman, Nelson. 1949. "On Likeness of Meaning." *Analysis*, 10: 1–7.

1972. *Problems and Projects*. Indianapolis: Bobbs-Merrill.

1973. *Fact, Fiction and Forecast*. Indianapolis: Hackett.

1978. *Ways of World Making*. Indianapolis: Hackett.

Graham, G., and Richard Garrett. 1986. "In Defense of Naturalistic Psychology." *New Ideas in Phychology*, 4: 323–32.

Graham, G., and G. L. Stephens. 1985. "Are Qualia a Pain in the Neck for Functionalists?" *American Philosophical Quarterly*, 22: 73–80.

1987. "Minding Your P's and Q's: Pain and Sensible Qualities." *Noûs*, 21: 395–405.

Gregory, R. 1970. *The Intelligent Eye*. New York: McGraw-Hill.

Harman, Gilbert. 1968. "Three Levels of Meaning." *Journal of Philosophy*, 65: 590–602.

1970. "Language and Learning." *Noûs*, 4: 33–43.

1973. *Thought*. Princeton: Princeton University Press.

Haugeland, John. 1981a. *Mind Design*. Cambridge, Mass.: MIT Press/ Bradford Books.

1981b. "On the Nature and Plausibility of Cognitivism." In Haugeland, *Mind Design*, pp. 243–81.

1985. *Artificial Intelligence: The Very Idea*. Cambridge, Mass.: MIT Press/ Bradford Books.

Heil, John. 1981. "Does Cognitive Psychology Rest on a Mistake?" *Mind*, 90: 321–42.

1984. "Doxastic Incontinence." *Mind*, 93: 56–70.

1985. "Rationality and Psychological Explanation." *Inquiry*, 28: 359–71.

Hilgard, E. R., and J. R. Hilgard. 1975. *Hypnosis in the Relief of Pain*. Los Altos, Calif.: Kaufman.

Hooker, C. A. 1976. "The Information-Processing Approach and Its Philosophical Ramifications." *Philosophy and Phenomenological Research*, 36: 1–15.

1978. "An Evolutionary Naturalist Doctrine of Perception and Secondary Qualities." *Minnesota Studies in the Philosophy of Science*, 9: 405–40.

Horgan, Terrence. 1984. "Jackson on Physical Information and Qualia." *Philosophical Quarterly*, 34: 147–83.

Horgan, T[erence], and M. Tye. 1985. "Against the Token Identity Theory." In E. LePore (ed.), *Actions and Events*. Oxford: Blackwell, pp. 427–43.

Horgan, T[erence], and J. Woodward. 1985. "Folk Psychology Is Here to Stay." *Philosophical Review*, 94: 197–225.

Hornsby, Jennifer. 1980. *Actions*. London: Routledge & Kegan Paul.

259

Horwich, Paul. 1985. "Decision Theory in Light of Newcomb's Problem." *Philosophy of Science*, 52: 431–50.

Irwin, Terence. 1977. *Plato's Moral Theory*. Oxford: Oxford University Press.

Jackson, Frank. 1982. "Epiphenomenal Qualia." *Philosophical Quarterly*, 32: 127–36.

1986. "What Mary Didn't Know." *Journal of Philosophy*, 83: 291–5.

Jeffrey, R. 1983. *The Logic of Decision*. 2nd ed. Chicago: University of Chicago Press.

Johnson-Laird, Philip. 1977. "Procedural Semantics." *Cognition*, 5: 189–214.

Kitcher, Patricia. 1984. "In Defense of Intentional Psychology." *Journal of Philosophy*, 81: 89–106.

1985. "Narrow Taxonomy and Wide Functionalism." *Philosophy of Science*, 52: 78–97.

Kosslyn, S. 1980. *Imagery and Mind*. Cambridge, Mass.: Harvard University Press.

1981. "The Medium and the Message in Mental Imagery." In Ned Block (ed.), *Imagery*. Cambridge, Mass.: MIT Press/Bradford Books, pp. 207–46.

1983. *Ghosts in the Mind's Machine: Creating and Using Images in the Brain*. New York: Norton.

Kosslyn, S., T. Ball, and B. Reiser. 1978. "Visual Image Scanning." *Journal of Experimental Psychology: Human Perception and Performance*, 4: 47–60.

Kripke, Saul. 1982. *Wittgenstein on Rules and Private Language*. Oxford: Basil Blackwell.

Kuhn, Thomas. 1972. *The Structure of Scientific Revolutions*. Chicago: University of Chicago Press.

Lackner, J., and M. Garrett. 1973. "Resolving Ambiguity: Effects of Biasing Context in the Unattended Ear." *Cognition*, 1: 359–72.

Lehrer, Keith. 1974. *Knowledge*. Oxford: Clarendon Press.

Lettvin, J., R. R. Maturana, W. S. McCulloch, and W. H. Pitts. 1959. "What the Frog's Eye Tells the Frog's Brain." *Proceedings of the Institute for Radio Engineers*, 47: 1940–59. Reprinted in W. S. McCulloch, *Embodiments of Mind*. Cambridge, Mass.: MIT Press, pp. 230–55.

Lewis, David. 1969. *Convention: A Philosophical Study*. Cambridge, Mass.: Harvard University Press.

1973. *Counterfactuals*. Cambridge, Mass.: Harvard University Press.

1980. "Mad Pain and Martian Pain." In Block, *Readings in Philosophy of Psychology* I, pp. 216–22.

1981. "Causal Decision Theory." *Australasian Journal of Philosophy*, 59: 5–30.

1983. "Postscript to 'Mad Pain and Martian Pain.' " In Lewis, *Philosophical Papers*. Vol. 1. Oxford: Oxford University Press, pp. 130–2.

Loar, Brian. 1981. *Mind and Meaning*. Cambridge: Cambridge University Press.

Lycan, William. 1979. "A New Lilliputian Argument Against Machine Functionalism." *Philosophical Studies*, 35: 379–87.

1980. "The Functionalist Reply (Ohio State)." *Behavioral and Brain Sciences*, 3: 434–5.

1987. *Consciousness*. Cambridge, Mass.: MIT Press/Bradford Books.

McCarthy, J., and P. Hayes. 1969. "Some Philosophical Problems from the Standpoint of Artificial Intelligence." In B. Meltzer and D. Michie (eds.), *Machine Intelligence*. Vol. 4. Edinburgh: Edinburgh University Press, pp. 463–502.

McDermott, Drew. 1976. "Artificial Intelligence Meets Natural Stupidity." *SIGART Newsletter*, no. 57 (April): 4–9. Reprinted in Haugeland, *Mind Design*, pp. 143–60.

McGinn, Colin. 1982. "The Structure of Content." In Andrew Woodfield (ed.), *Thought and Object*. Oxford: Clarendon Press, pp. 207–58.

Maloney, J. Christopher. 1984. "Mental Images and Cognitive Theory." *American Philosophical Quarterly*, 21: 237–47.

1985a. "About Being a Bat." *Australasian Journal of Philosophy*, 63: 26–49.

1985b. "Methodological Solipsism Reconsidered as a Research Strategy in Cognitive Psychology." *Philosophy of Science*, 52: 451–69.

1986a. "Sensation and Scientific Realism." *Philosophy and Phenomenological Research*, 46: 471–82.

1986b. "Sensuous Content." *Philosophical Papers*, 15: 131–54.

1987. "The Right Stuff: The Mundane Matter of the Mind." *Synthese*, 70: 349–72.

1988. "In Praise of Narrow Minds: The Frame Problem." In J. Fetzer (ed.), *Aspects of Artificial Intelligence*. Dordrecht: Reidel, pp. 55–80.

Maras, Ausonio. 1985. "The Churchlands on Methodological Solipsism and Computational Psychology." *Philosophy of Science*, 52: 295–309.

Margolis, Joseph. 1978. *Persons and Minds*. Boston: Reidel.

Marr, D. 1982. *Vision*. San Francisco: Freeman.

Mayr, Ernst. 1960. "The Emergence of Evolutionary Novelty." In S. Tax (ed.), *Evolution After Darwin*, Vol. 1. *The Evolution of Life: Its Origin, History, and Future*. Chicago: University of Chicago Press.

Mele, A. 1983. "Self Deception." *Philosophical Quarterly*, 33: 365–77.

1986. "Incontinent Believing." *Philosophical Quarterly*, 36: 212–22.

Melzack, Ronald. 1961. "The Perception of Pain." *Scientific American*, 204 (February): 41–9.

1973. "How Acupuncture Can Block Pain." *Impact of Science on Society*, 23: 65–75.

Miller, G. A. 1956. "The Magical Number Seven Plus or Minus Two: Some Limits on Our Capacity for Processing Information." *Psychological Review*, 63: 81–97.

Minsky, Marvin. 1975. "A Framework for Representing Knowledge." In P. Winston (ed.), *The Psychology of Computer Vision*. New York: McGraw-Hill. Reprinted in Haugeland, *Mind Design*, pp. 95–128.

Nagel, Thomas. 1974. "What Is It Like to Be a Bat?" *Philosophical Review*, 83: 435–50.

Neisser, Ulric. 1966. *Cognitive Psychology*. New York: Appleton-Century-Crofts.

Newell, Alan, and Herbert A. Simon. 1981. "Computer Science as Empirical Inquiry." Reprinted in Haugeland, *Mind Design*, pp. 35–66.
Nimerow, Laurence. 1980. "Review of Thomas Nagel's *Mortal Questions*." *Philosophical Review*, 89: 473–77.
Nisbett, R. E., and T. D. Wilson. 1977. "Telling More Than We Can Know: Verbal Reports on Mental Processes." *Psychological Review*, 84: 321–59.
Nozick, Robert. 1969. "Newcomb's Problem and Two Principles of Choice." In N. Rescher et al. (eds.), *Essays in Honor of Carl G. Hempel*. Dordrecht: Reidel, pp. 114–46.
Nute, Donald. 1980. *Topics in Conditional Logic*. Dordrecht: Reidel.
Owens, Joseph. 1983. "Functionalism and Propositional Attitudes." *Noûs*, 17: 529–49.
Peterson, S. B., and M. Peterson. 1959. "Short-Term Retention of Individual Items." *Journal of Experimental Psychology*, 58: 193–8.
Putnam, Hilary. 1969. "Is Logic Empirical?" *Boston Studies in the Philosophy of Science*, 5, ed. Cohen and Wartofsky, pp. 216–41.
    1975a. "The Nature of Mental States." In Putnam, *Mind, Language and Reality, Philosophical Papers*. Vol. 2. Cambridge: Cambridge University Press, pp. 429–40.
    1975b. "The Meaning of 'Meaning.' " In Putnam, *Mind, Language and Reality, Philosophical Papers*, Vol. 2, pp. 215–71.
    1975c. "Minds and Machines." In Putnam, *Mind, Language and Reality, Philosophical Papers*, Vol. 2, pp. 362–85.
    1975d. "Robots: Machines or Artificially Created Life?" In Putnam, *Mind, Language and Reality, Philosophical Papers*, Vol. 2, pp. 386–407.
    1981. *Reason, Truth and History*. Cambridge: Cambridge University Press.
    1983. "Computational Psychology and Interpretation Theory." In Putnam, *Realism and Reason, Philosophical Papers*. Vol. 3. Cambridge: Cambridge University Press, pp. 139–54.
Pylyshyn, Zenon. 1973. "What the Mind's Eye Tells the Mind's Brain." *Psychological Bulletin*, 80: 1–24.
    1980. "Computation and Cognition: Issues in the Foundations of Cognitive Science." *Behavioral and Brain Sciences*, 3: 111–32.
    1981a. "Imagery and Artificial Intelligence." In Ned Block (ed.), *Readings in the Philosophy of Psychology*. Vol. 2, Cambridge, Mass.: Harvard University Press, pp. 170–94.
    1981b. "The Imagery Debate: Analogue Media Versus Tacit Knowledge." *Psychological Review*, 88: 16–45.
    1984. *Computation and Cognition: Toward a Foundation for Cognitive Science*. Cambridge, Mass.: MIT Press/Bradford Books.
Quine, Willard Van Orman. 1951. "Two Dogmas of Empiricism." Reprinted in Quine, *From a Logical Point of View*. Cambridge, Mass.: Harvard University Press, 1980, pp. 20–46.
    1956. "Quantifiers and Propositional Attitudes." *Journal of Philosophy*, 53: 177–87.
    1960. *Word and Object*. Cambridge, Mass.: MIT Press.

262

1969. "Epistemology Naturalized." In Quine, *Ontological Relativity and Other Essays*. New York: Columbia University Press, pp. 69–90.

Rapaport, William J. 1978. "Meinongian Theories and a Russellian Paradox." *Noûs*, 12: 153–80.

Raphael, B. 1971. "The Frame Problem in Problem-Solving Systems." In N. V. Findler and B. Meltzer (eds.), *Artificial Intelligence and Heuristic Programming*. New York: American Elsevier, pp. 159–69.

Rey, Georges. 1980. "The Formal and Opaque." *Behavioral and Brain Sciences*, 3: 90–2.

Rorty, Richard. 1965. "Mind-Body Identity, Privacy, and Categories." *Review of Metaphysics*, 19: 24–54.

1979. *Philosophy and the Mirror of Nature*. Princeton: Princeton University Press.

Russow, Lilly-Marlene. 1984. "Unlocking the Chinese Room." *Nature and System*, 6: 221–8.

1985. "Dennett, Mental Images, and Images in Context." *Philosophy and Phenomenological Research*, 45: 581–94.

Ryle, Gilbert. 1949. *The Concept of Mind*. London: Hutcheson.

Samet, Jerry. 1982. "Understanding and Integration." *Behavioral and Brain Sciences*, 5: 341–2.

Schank, R. C. 1982. *Dynamic Memory*. Cambridge: Cambridge University Press.

Schank, R. C., and R. P. Abelson. 1977. *Scripts, Plans, Goals and Understanding*. Hillsdale, N.J.: Erlbaum.

Schiffer, Stephen. 1987. *Remnants of Meaning*. Cambridge, Mass.: MIT Press/Bradford Books.

Searle, John. 1980. "Minds, Brains and Computers." *Behavioral and Brain Sciences*, 3: 417–57 (including peer review).

1982a. "The Chinese Room Revised." *Behavioral and Brain Sciences*, 5: 345–8.

1982b. "The Myth of the Computer." *New York Review of Books*, April 29: 3–6.

1983. *Intentionality: An Essay in the Philosophy of Mind*. Cambridge: Cambridge University Press.

1984. "Intentionality and Its Place in Nature." *Dialectica*, 38: 87–99.

Sellars, Wilfrid. 1963. "Empiricism and the Philosophy of Mind." In Sellars, *Science, Perception and Reality*. London: Routledge & Kegan Paul, pp. 127–96.

1973. "Actions and Events." *Noûs*, 7: 179–202.

Shepard, R. N. 1978. "The Mental Image." *American Psychologist*, 133: 125–37.

Shepard, R. N., and Lynn A. Cooper. 1982. *Mental Images and Their Transformations*. Cambridge, Mass.: MIT Press/Bradford Books.

Shepard, R. N., and J. Metzler. 1971. "Mental Rotation of Three-dimensional Objects." *Science*, 171: 701–3.

Shoemaker, Sydney. 1975. "Functionalism and Qualia." *Philosophical Studies*, 27: 291–315.

1982. "The Inverted Spectrum." *Journal of Philosophy*, 79: 357–81.
Simon, Herbert A. 1969. *The Sciences of the Artificial*. Cambridge, Mass.: MIT Press.
Smart, J. J. C. 1969. "Sensations and Brain Processes." Reprinted in John O'Connor (ed.), *Modern Materialism: Readings on Mind-Body Identity*. New York: Harcourt, Brace & World, pp. 32–47.
Smythe, William. 1982. "Rule Following and Rule Reduction." *Behavioral and Brain Sciences*, 5: 343–4.
Sober, Elliott. 1976. "Mental Representations." *Synthese*, 33: 101–48.
Sosa, E. 1970. "Propositional Attitudes *de Dicto* and *de Re*." *Journal of Philosophy*, 67: 883–96.
Sperry, R. W. 1974. "Lateral Specialization in the Surgically Separated Hemispheres." In F. O. Schmitt and R. G. Worden (eds.), *The Neurosciences Third Study Program*. Cambridge, Mass.: MIT Press, pp. 5–20.
Spinoza, B. 1671. *Ethics*, II–IV. Trans. S. Shirley and S. Feldman, *The Ethics and Selected Letters*. Indianapolis: Hackett, 1982.
Stabler, Edward P. 1983. "How Are Grammars Represented?" *Behavioral and Brain Sciences*, 6: 391–402 (peer commentary and replies pp. 402–21).
1985. "Rationality in Naturalized Epistemology." *Philosophy of Science*, 51: 64–78.
Stampe, D. W. 1975. "Show and Tell." In B. Freed et al. (eds.), *Forms of Representation*. New York: North Holland Press.
1977. "Toward a Causal Theory of Linguistic Representation." *Midwest Studies in Philosophy*, 2: 42–63.
Sternberg, S. 1966. "High Speed Scanning in Human Memory." *Science* 153: 652–4.
Stich, Stephen. 1978a. "Autonomous Psychology and the Belief-Desire Thesis." *Monist*, 61: 573–91.
1978b. "Beliefs and Subdoxastic States." *Philosophy of Science*, 45: 499–518.
1979. "Do Animals Have Beliefs?" *Australasian Journal of Philosophy*, 57: 15–28.
1982. "On the Ascription of Content." In A. Woodfield (ed.), *Thought and Object*. Oxford: Clarendon Press, pp. 153–206.
1983. *From Folk Psychology to Cognitive Science*. Cambridge, Mass.: MIT Press/Bradford Books.
1985. "Could Man Be an Irrational Animal?" *Synthese*, 64: 115–35.
Tursky, B., L. Jammer, and R. Friedman. 1982. "The Pain Perception Profile: A Psychological Approach to the Assessment of Pain Reports." *Behavior Therapy*, 13: 376–94.
Tversky, A., and D. Kahneman. 1974. "Judgment Under Uncertainty: Heuristics and Biases." *Science*, 185: 1124–31.
1982. "Judgments of and by Representativeness." In D. Kahneman, P. Slovic, and A. Tversky (eds.), *Judgment under Uncertainty: Heuristics and Biases*. Cambridge: Cambridge University Press, pp. 84–98.

Tweney, Ryan D., and Michael E. Doherty. 1983. "Rationality and the Psychology of Inference." *Synthese*, 57: 129–38.

Tye, Michael. 1984a. "The Debate About Mental Imagery." *Journal of Philosophy*, 81: 678–91.

1984b. "The Adverbial Approach to Visual Experience." *Philosophical Review*, 93: 195–226.

1984c. "Pain and the Adverbial Theory." *American Philosophical Quarterly*, 21: 319–27.

Waltz, David L. 1982. "Artificial Intelligence." *Scientific American*, 247 (October): 118–33.

Wason, P. C., and P. Johnson-Laird. 1972. *The Psychology of Reasoning*. London: Batsford.

1977. *Thinking*. Cambridge: Cambridge University Press.

Wilensky, Robert. 1980. "Computers, Cognition and Philosophy." *Behavioral and Brain Sciences*, 3: 449–50.

William of Ockham. 1349. *Ockham's Theory of Propositions: Part II of the Summa Logicae*. Trans. Alfred J. Freddoso and Henry Schuurman. Notre Dame, Ind.: University of Notre Dame Press, 1980.

Winograd, Terry. 1971. *Procedures as a Representation for Data in a Computer Program for Understanding Natural Languages*. Cambridge: MIT Project MAC.

Wittgenstein, Ludwig. *Philosophical Investigations*. Trans. G. E. M. Anscombe. New York: Macmillan.

Wooldridge, D. 1963. *The Machinery of the Brain*. New York: McGraw-Hill.

Index

267

biology, 14, 52, 177
Block, N., 8, 32–33, 180, 220, 222, 225
Bobrow, D., 22, 54
Boden, M., 1, 22–23, 52, 62
bodily movement, 51, 78, 161
bodily property, xvi
bodily state, xvi
Bower, G., 10
brain, 9, 15, 47–48, 54, 66, 77, 110, 121–122, 140–142, 158, 172, 175
brain state (see also brain), 110, 141–142
Brand, M., 54, 77–78, 94–95
Brentano, F., 3
Brown, J., 48
Burge, T., xv, 4–5, 59, 134, 211–212, 214

calculator, 102–104
Campbell, K., 187
capacity, 3, 27, 29, 122, 146, 149, 162, 170, 247
Castañeda, H., 20, 98
causal theory, 30, 180, 191; of representation, xxvi; of sensuous representation, 179–194, 196–200, 202–203, 215–218
causal waywardness, 94
causation. See belief, and causation
Champeaux, William of, 16
chemistry, 14–15, 31, 128, 171, 175–177, 240
chess, 16, 53, 125–126, 131–133
Chinese, 144–158, 160–162, 167, 173–175
Chisholm, R., 94
Chomsky, N., 9, 19, 41, 54, 71, 121
Churchland, Patricia, viii, xii, xxv–xxvi, 2, 9–11, 14, 19, 22, 25, 41, 109–113, 121–122, 179–180, 183, 198, 221, 230
Churchland, Paul, viii, xii, xxv–xxvi, 1–2, 10–12, 19, 24–25, 41, 51, 109–110, 116–119, 121–123, 171–172, 176, 180, 183, 187, 194, 198, 221, 228, 245
Clark, R., xxv–xxvi, 18, 20, 98
cognition, xvi, xxi, xxiii–xxiv, xxvi–xxvii, 16, 32, 55, 61–62, 68, 72, 109, 111, 159, 167, 178–180, 220–222, 234, 241, 247

cognitive agent, xi–xiv, xxiv, 3, 9, 16–17, 19, 22, 27–28, 33, 36–37, 39–41, 45, 51–55, 61, 64–65, 68, 71–73, 75, 79, 81–82, 104–106, 109, 126, 158–161, 178–180, 187, 189, 210, 223–225
cognitive kind, 36–39, 44, 82, 178, 237
cognitive penetrability, 60
cognitive psychology (see also cognitive science; psychology), 10–11, 52, 92, 94, 143, 162, 189, 216, 240
cognitive science (see also cognitive psychology; psychology), viii, xxiii, xxvi–xxvii, 1–3, 23, 52, 59, 90–91, 104, 106, 117, 143, 164, 178–179, 188, 220–221
cognitive scientist, xxi, xxvii, 52
cognitive system, x, xv–xvi, 29, 32, 53, 68–69, 111, 159, 203–204, 207, 217–218, 224, 239
cognitive theory, xxvi, 163
Cohen, R., 262
Cole, D., 143, 153
Collins, A., 22
combinatorial explosion, 53, 58
commonsense psychology (see also folk psychology), 11, 13
communication, 18, 110–111, 115, 177, 188, 213
computation (see also computing), x, xii, xxi–xxiv, 9, 18–19, 48, 52, 54, 60, 63, 67–68, 70–72, 74, 76, 107, 109, 111, 116, 158, 162, 169, 172, 178, 188, 190, 192, 216, 247, 249
computationalism, xxi, xxiv, 54, 63, 70–71, 76, 109, 111, 216, 247
computer, xxi–xxiv, 16, 22–23, 74, 125–126, 143–144, 166, 189, 224–225
computing, (see also computation), 18, 53, 159
concept, vii, x, xii–xiii, xxii–xxiii, 1–2, 6–7, 11–12, 14–15, 24, 31, 56–58, 78–79, 112–119, 128–129, 131, 156, 183, 185–186, 188, 230
concept learning, (see also learning), 114–116, 129
conception, xxiii, 4, 12, 15, 78–79, 99, 119, 121, 176, 185, 236, 240
conceptual change, xii
conceptual scheme/system, x, 114–115, 185–186, 188
Conee, E., 225, 245

functionalism, xvi, xxvi, 25, 32–33,
51, 142, 170–171, 173, 176, 220,
222–225, 231

Garcia, J., 106
Garrett, M., 19, 52
Garrett, R., 5, 174
Gibson, J., 18
given, 187
Goldman, A., 77
Goodman, N., 18, 42, 187, 209
Graham, G., xvi, xxv–xxvi, 5, 148,
174, 180, 220, 225–228, 230
grammar, viii, xxi, 7–9, 19, 21, 71–72,
157, 161, 163, 166, 173, 177, 179
grammatical mood, 20–21
Green, K., 106, 209
Gregory, R., 18

hallucination, 8, 218
Harman, G., 8–9, 18
Haugeland, J., 22, 34, 52, 59, 241
Hayes, P., 52
Heil, J., 16, 64, 81, 86
heuristics, 54, 65, 100
Hilgard, E., 232
Hilgard, J., 232
holism, xiii, 6–8, 57, 124, 204–205
homomorphism, 165
homonym, 213
homonymous hemianopia, 15
Hooker, C., 109, 187
Horgan, T., 2, 10, 14, 109, 245
Hornsby, J., 77
Horwich, P., 79
human language, xii, 110
hypothesis to best explanation, 64

illocutionary act, 146
illusion, xii, 8, 84, 112, 218
implication, 6, 190, 205
incorrigibility, 19, 218
indexical, 35, 40, 137
infallibility, xv–xvi, 161, 191, 194, 218
infant, xii, 111, 116–122
inference, 16
information, 110, 137–138
information bearing, xxvi, 23, 72, 136
information processing, xxiii, 18, 24,
54, 64, 67, 109, 117–118, 121–122,
192, 224–225, 241
infralinguistic catastrophe, 111
instrumentalism, 46

intelligence, ix–x, xxv, 10, 23–24, 33,
36–37, 55–57, 61, 63, 70–72, 76, 99,
118, 121, 133, 140–143, 145, 147,
151, 155, 167, 169, 172, 175–176,
229, 234, 251–252
intention, 77–78, 97–98, 122
intentionality, vii, ix, xiii–xiv, xxiv, 3,
24–33, 50, 73–76, 93, 140, 143, 152,
157, 167, 169, 170, 172–176, 180,
221–222
interpretation, 24
introspection, viii, 13, 19, 46, 52
inverted qualia (see also qualia), xvi,
223, 237
irrationality, 80, 83–86, 100, 104, 132
Irwin, T., 83
isotropy, x, 63–68

Jackson, F., xvii, xxv–xxvi, 180, 221,
244–245, 248
Jammer, B., 232
Japanese, 157
Jeffrey, R., 79
Johnson–laird, P., 17, 81, 84, 99, 100

Kahneman, D., 16, 55, 64–66, 81, 84,
99–100, 104–105
Kitcher, P., 10, 14, 109, 111
Kosslyn, S., 8
Kripke, S., 19

Lackner, J., 19, 52
language, vii–viii, xiii, xxi–xxii, xxvi–
xxvii, 3, 7–9, 19, 31, 36–37, 40, 42–
43, 45–46, 67, 89, 99, 110–112, 115,
118, 121, 124, 143–157, 160, 162,
167, 172–175, 177–178, 187, 208–
209, 213, 216, 229, 235, 246, 249; of
thought, viii, xxvi–xxvii, 9, 111,
145, 162, 167, 173, 177–178, 229
language acquisition, xiii
language comprehension, xiii, 143–
151, 153–158, 160–162, 173–175
learning (see also concept learning), xii,
xxii, 9, 62, 112–115, 120, 129, 154,
162, 222
Lehrer, K., 191
Lettvin, J., 18
Lewis, D., 30, 79, 154, 183, 232–234, 245
linguistic behavior, 71, 151
linguistic mood, viii
linguistic tokens, 134

Locke, J., xxii, 9, 29–30, 178
Lycan, W., xxvi, 145, 148

McCarthy, J., 52, 157–158
McCulloch, W., 18
McDermott, D., 158
McGowan, B., 106
machine language, 40, 51
Maloney, J. C., 5, 8, 18, 36, 42, 69, 143, 174, 180, 194, 245
Marco, 144–162, 167, 170, 173–175
Material Basis of Cognition, ix, xiv, xvi–xviii, xxiv–xxv, xxvii, 25–26, 28–33, 73–75, 170–177, 215, 221–222, 229, 233–234, 252–253
material composition, 26, 28–29, 142, 172
material structure, xiv, 74
material type, 172
materialism, xxvi, 175
Maturana, R., 18
Mayr, E., 111
meaning, xv–xvi, xxii–xxvi, 40, 74, 125, 130, 156, 175, 178–179, 183–184, 202, 204–209, 211–213, 215–218, 227
Melzack, R., 230, 232
memory, 8, 10–11, 48, 52, 64, 115, 124, 240–241
mental content, ix, xiv, 4, 24, 25, 29, 30, 41, 43–45, 164–165, 168, 177, 205, 208
mental imagery, 8, 18, 19, 109
mental language, xii, xxi–xxii, xxiv–xxvii, 9, 18, 36–42, 44–46, 111–112, 115, 172–173, 177–178, 202, 221, 229, 247–248
mental lexicon, 179
mental representation, viii–x, xii, xiv–xv, xvii, 9, 19, 22–25, 27–30, 33, 38, 51, 53, 58–60, 71, 73, 76, 78, 82–89, 91–94, 98, 122, 141, 169, 178, 186–187, 194–195, 200, 204, 206, 211–212, 219, 221, 229–231, 234–237, 244, 247–249
mental sentence (see also Mentalese sentence), 9, 16–20, 22–23, 38, 41, 43, 49, 109, 115, 128–129, 132, 140–141, 173, 179, 185, 202, 214
mental state, viii–ix, xi, xiii–xiv, xxiv, xxvi, 3–5, 7, 9–10, 15–16, 19–20, 25, 27–30, 32–33, 37, 41, 43–45, 50–51, 58–59, 70–71, 76, 79–80, 83–85,

90–93, 95–99, 141–143, 147, 164–169, 173, 175, 177, 179, 185, 191, 202, 207, 210–215, 222–224, 226, 233–234, 236–239, 244, 252
mental token, 210
mental type, 142–143, 182, 202
Mentalese, viii–ix, xiii–xvi, 9, 18–21, 24–25, 29–31, 33–35, 42–44, 47, 49, 66, 73, 76, 87, 112–116, 118, 121, 141, 162–166, 172, 177–191, 195, 199, 202–206, 208–210, 213–218, 229–232, 237–242, 244, 248, 250–251
Mentalese sentence(s) (see also mental sentence), viii, xvi, 19–21, 24–25, 29, 31, 33–34, 49, 66, 73, 76, 87, 112–116, 118, 122–141, 162–165, 177–178, 187–188, 203, 213–214, 218, 230–231, 238–239; of same type, viii, 20–21
Mentalese token, viii, 20, 33, 125, 127–132, 134–137, 178, 180–181, 183, 210, 231–232, 239–241
Mentalese type, xiv, 20, 139, 166, 181–182, 210
mentalistic construct, vii–viii, 1–3
mentation, ix, xxiii–xxv, 9, 12, 15, 22, 24, 31–32, 36–37, 47, 50, 56, 67, 82, 84, 92, 97, 99, 113, 116, 143, 173, 178, 220–222, 229, 234, 236, 241, 252
Metzler, J., 8, 19
Miller, G., 10
mind, xxi–xxvi, 2, 9, 12, 18–19, 23–24, 33–35, 38, 47, 54–55, 60–61, 65, 86, 92, 107, 111, 124, 129, 133, 138, 143–144, 163, 169, 171–172, 178, 185, 188, 190, 194, 195, 202, 221, 228, 231, 253
Minsky, M., 54, 60
misrepresentation, 192, 219
modal operators, 21
modularity, x, 54, 63–65, 67–69
mood, xvii, 59–60, 220, 241–244
multilingual agent, xiii, 154
multiple realizability, xiv, 142, 175

Nagel, T., xvii, xxv–xxvi, 180, 220–221, 229, 244–245, 247
native language, 144
native speaker, 143, 145, 147, 149–153, 173–175
nativism, xiv, xxii–xxiii, 9, 121, 154, 178–179, 183, 186, 202–203

271

natural kind, 26–27, 31, 39, 73, 170–172, 174, 176–178, 201, 210
natural language, 41–42, 121, 134, 137, 197
Neisser, U., 1, 19, 48
neural state, 14, 74, 163
neurology, 14–15, 31, 126, 180, 192–193, 245
neuroscience, 43, 172, 175–176
Nimerow, L., 245
Nisbett, R., 19, 52, 205, 240
nonsensuous content, 205–206
nonsensuous predication, 204, 217
nonsensuous representation, xvii, 203, 205–209, 216, 218–219, 251
nonverbal agent (see also nonverbal animal), xii, 110
nonverbal animal (see also nonverbal agent), 109, 111
nonverbal behavior, 147, 149, 150
nonverbal creatures (see also nonverbal agent), 110
notation, ix, 33–40, 42–46
Nozick, R., 79
Nute, D., 30

occurrent belief, 72
Ockham, William of, 9
opacity, vii, 3, 4
ostension (see also demonstration), 114
other minds, 253
overt behavior, 15, 18, 45, 148, 151
overt language (see also public language; spoken language), 110, 112, 115, 188
Owens, J., 33, 200

pain, xvi, 211–212, 220, 222–223, 225–228, 230–234, 236–238, 241, 250–251
perception, 15, 18–19, 48–49, 52, 61, 67, 98, 117, 136–137, 180, 233, 240–241
perlocutionary act, 146
Peterson, M., 48
Peterson, S., 48
phenomenology, xxvi, 180, 222, 239, 241, 247
physical composition, 25, 30–31, 234, 236, 244
physical property, xvii, xxiv, 9, 16, 25, 29, 34, 43, 172, 189, 194, 229, 231–237, 242–245, 248–253
physical realization, 14, 43, 91

physical state, 25, 40, 59, 70–71, 73, 76, 141–142, 166, 177, 236–237, 246, 249, 253
physical structure, 16, 30, 37, 39, 41, 49–50, 70, 73, 96, 134, 177, 179–180, 231
physical type, xiv, xvii, 29, 43, 142, 161, 181–182, 188, 190, 194, 207, 234
physicalism, xxvi, 141–142
physics, 13–15, 25, 27, 144, 187
physiological state, 77
physiology, xvii, xxiv, 32, 177, 248–249
Pitts, W., 18
plan (see also intention), 97–98
plasticity, 26–27, 68, 99, 107, 122, 141, 170
Plato, 12, 33–34, 42, 85
pleiotropy, 111
Polo, 157–160
practical reasoning, 13
predicate modifier, viii, 21
predication (see also attribution), viii, xiv–xv, 5–6, 9, 21, 110, 114–115, 179, 182, 185–188, 190–191, 195, 202–203, 206, 216–217, 230, 232, 240
preverbal agent, 111
primitive representation, 111
PRIMUS, 34, 36–40, 42–43, 45–46
principle: of autonomy, 166–167; of charity, 89
pristine demonstration, 185
pristine predication, 187–191, 201–203, 218, 240
pristine reference, 184, 202, 218, 240
pristine representation, 184, 187–191, 195, 201–203, 218, 240
private language, 19, 111
probability, 4
problem solving, 7
productivity of belief, 8
program, 14, 34–36, 40, 43, 125, 141–143, 145–152, 154–155, 157, 159–162, 189, 222, 252
programming, 34, 40, 51, 61, 68, 126, 147
programming language, 51
proper name, 173, 185
propositional attitudes, xii, xvii, xxv–xxvi, 1–3, 10–15, 73–74, 102–104, 109, 117–119, 239–243, 251–252
proximal object/stimulus, 195–196

272

psychological chauvinism, 32, 247
psychological reduction, 13–14
psychological state, xvi, xxvi, 8, 33,
  163, 166–169, 225–228, 232
psychologist, vii, 18, 48, 83, 166
psychology, (see also cognitive psychology; cognitive science), vii–viii,
  xii, xiv, xxv–xxvi, 1–2, 10–15, 19,
  32, 78–79, 81, 92, 99, 104, 110–111,
  122, 153, 162–164, 195
public language (see also overt language; spoken language), xv, 204–
  205
Putnam, H., xv, xxv–xxvi, 5, 56–57,
  64, 79, 113, 122, 134, 142, 174, 176,
  200, 206
Pylyshyn, Z., 1, 9–10, 43, 59–60, 92

qualia, xvi–xvii, xxvi, 179–180, 192,
  220, 223, 225–228, 231–245, 247–
  253; and causation, 237
Quine, W., 4, 41, 81, 99, 122, 204–205
Quinean, x, 63–68
quotation, vii, 4–5, 9, 185, 190

Rapaport, W., 98
Raphael, B., 52
rationality, viii, x–xi, 16–18, 41, 67,
  70, 75, 79–87, 89–91, 93–95, 98–99,
  102, 104–108, 123, 132–133, 204,
  216, 249
reasoning, 100, 102, 104–108
reference (see also demonstrative reference; pristine reference), vii–viii,
  xiv–xv, 5–6, 131, 133–137, 180,
  184–186, 190, 196–199, 202, 210,
  226
regress of embedded/nested agents, 23,
  33, 140–141, 143, 145, 167
Reiser, B., 8
representation of rules, 71–72, 75–76,
  78–79
representational state, vii, xv, 31, 75–
  79, 82, 85, 179, 216, 219, 223
Representational Theory of the Mind,
  vii, viii, 3, 8–9, 22, 37, 163
representationalism, viii, 9–10, 22,
  179, 192
retinal images, 196–197
Rey, G., 161
robot, 151, 166–169, 220
Rorty, R., 2, 220
rule-governed, 71, 123

Russow, L., 143, 145, 148, 154–155, 160

Sanskrit, 157
Schank, R., 22, 54, 60, 91
Schiffer, S., xxvi
scientific psychology (see also cognitive
  psychology), vii, 11, 59, 81, 237
script, ix–x, 47, 54, 56–66
Searle, J., xiii, xxv–xxvi, 3, 23, 140,
  142–145, 148–149, 151, 156, 160,
  162, 167, 173
SECUNDUS, 34, 36–40, 42–43, 45–46
seeing, 240
Sellars, W., 18, 52, 77, 187
semantic content, 130, 153
semantic primitives, 217
semantic property, xxvi, 5, 54, 85–86,
  124–125, 134
semantic type, 124
semantic value, 131
semantics (see also semantic property;
  semantic value), xvi, xxvi, 5–7, 35,
  42, 51, 54, 85, 86, 92, 124–126, 130–
  135, 137, 144, 153, 155–157, 161–
  162, 165, 169, 173, 175, 178, 180,
  183, 186–188, 190, 199, 203, 206,
  209, 216–217, 248
sensation, xiv–xv, xvii, xxii–xxiv,
  xxvi, 8, 25, 122, 148–149, 178–181,
  184, 187, 192, 194–196, 199, 202–
  203, 205, 218–220, 222–223, 226–
  227, 230–233, 237–238, 240–241,
  243–253
sensible property, 8, 202, 226
sensory state, xiv–xvii, 178, 180–184,
  186–187, 189–192, 194–203, 206–
  208, 215, 217–219, 230, 232–233,
  237–245, 247–253
sensory token, 181–182, 196, 199, 200–
  203, 232–233
sensory type, 200, 232
sensuous content, 179, 202
sensuous predication, 181–183, 185,
  187, 201, 217–218, 240
sensuous reference, 181–182, 197–202,
  210, 215, 217
sensuous representation, xv, 178, 180,
  183–188, 190–191, 195, 201, 218,
  230–233, 236, 239–240, 244, 248,
  251
sensuous token, 182–183, 231
sentential modifier (see also sentential
  operator), viii

273